What Happened to History?

Willie Thompson

Pluto Press

LONDON • STERLING, VIRGINIA

First published 2000 by Pluto Press
345 Archway Road, London N6 5AA
and 22883 Quicksilver Drive, Sterling, VA 20166-2012, USA

www.plutobooks.com

British Library Cataloguing in Publication Data
A catalogue record for this book is available from the British Library

Library of Congress Cataloging-in-Publication Data

Thompson, Willie.
What happened to history? / Willie Thompson.
p. cm.
ISBN 0-7453-1268-3
1. Historiography. 2. Historiography—History—20th century. 3. History. I. Title.
D13 .T5123 2001
907'.2—dc21
00-009579

ISBN 07453 1268 3 hardback
ISBN 0 7453 1263 2 paperback

10 09 08 07 06 05 04 03 02 01
10 9 8 7 6 5 4 3 2 1

Designed and produced for Pluto Press by
Chase Publishing Services
Typeset from disk by Gilbert Composing Services, Leighton Buzzard
Printed in the European Union by TJ International, Padstow, England

Contents

Preface: Where I'm Coming From

In 1960–61, when I was an undergraduate student, the history degree at my university included a half-unit in historical method or historical theory – I fail to recall the exact title. Only one text was referred to, R.G. Collingwood's *The Idea of History*, in which the tutor believed that all wisdom upon the subject was to be found. Since the tutor in question was, unfortunately, also a wretched teacher, it isn't surprising that these sessions failed to make very much impact. Happily this did not destroy my interest in the subject – though it prejudiced me for a long time against Collingwood.

Such was our introduction to the problems associated with the study and writing of history and practically the only reference point our class group had at the time. However, although not utilised by our tutor, Marc Bloch's *The Historian's Craft* happened to be upon the shelves of the departmental library, so we did at least have access to another perspective and were aware, though only very vaguely, of the existence of the *Annales* school of historiography. Then in 1961 our situation was transformed with the appearance in the university bookshop of E.H. Carr's *What is History?*,[1] the short text which has been the introduction to historiography for a couple of generations of subsequent English-language history students and in many cases continues to be so. For myself and my colleagues at the time it constituted a revelation, introducing us to the epistemological and ethical problems associated with the historiographical enterprise, the uncertainty and slipperiness surrounding the notion of 'historical fact', the problematic nature of causality and other associated concerns.

As matters transpired, Carr's text proved to be the herald of a historiographical transformation which, within the Anglophone world at least, produced enormous upheaval in the nature of the discipline in the following decades – revolution both in subject-matter and methodological approach. Another two years saw the appearance of Edward Thompson's *The Making of the English Working Class*, which, I will go on to argue, formed the pivot of the developments about to take place. Three years after that the *Times Literary Supplement* published a famous special number under the title of 'The New History, which was principally concerned with methodologies – the benefits to be gained from linking historiography with other social science disciplines and the virtues of quantification and statistical techniques. Simultaneously in the United States social and cultural developments of profound importance were occurring, soon with far-reaching impact upon historiography's institutional, methodological and theoretical character.

The 1960s were of course also the decade of the left; a political and cultural climate more congenial to Marxism in the West than at any time since the 1930s or possibly throughout the twentieth century; and Marxist historiography shared in the trend in terms of attention and credibility. Marxist historians of repute there had been in the earlier years of the twentieth century, but these had been isolated and singular individuals. I can recall, as an undergraduate at the end of the 1950s, that our class on Tudor and Stuart Britain was recommended a text by Christopher Hill, but the recommendation was accompanied by our tutor's warning that this was a Marxist author, to be handled with care. Not long afterwards, though, Hill's *The Century of Revolution* was published, which we all read and which appeared to most of us as a new and refreshing approach to historical understanding.

I continued to follow with interest the methodological and substantial debates which began to emerge, and in particular the polemic around the Nairn-Anderson thesis regarding the evolution of British politics and society since the seventeenth century, in which I felt that Thompson, for all his erudition, got the worst of the argument. Naturally I was gratified to note, in the Anglo-American sphere, the increasing academic credibility of Marxist interpretations (though these of course were not uncontested) and the contribution which the British Marxist historians made to that process. I looked with interest too on the veritable revolution in historiography occurring during the late 1960s and the 1970s, exemplified in new approaches, new historiographical constituencies, new institutions and new journals, convinced that developments such as feminist historiography and the general widening of the field of accepted historiographical discourse could be incorporated without difficulty into an expanded Marxist framework.

That confidence was, admittedly, shaken by the appearance in English during the 1970s of the writings of the French structuralists, followed by those of their English disciples. Assuming that Althusser had novel and innovative things to say, I attempted to read his translated writings, only to find them impenetrably unintelligible, and those of his English-language epigones only marginally less so. Not surprisingly therefore I received with great enthusiasm what appeared to me then and still does, Thompson's effective demolition of structuralist claims in *The Poverty of Theory,* published in 1978. The year after that text appeared Thompson participated in a famous debate with his structuralist opponents during a History Workshop conference in Oxford. The debate, which I attended, took place in the interior of a church, then under renovation and whose internal walls were still covered in scaffolding. The event was packed out, and many attending perched themselves on the scaffolding, no doubt in blatant contravention of health and safety regulations. The thought struck me that this was what it must have looked like in Byzantine churches when the citizens gathered to debate the nature of the trinity and the relationship of Christ's humanity to his divinity – with equivalent outcomes, for the debate was a dialogue of the deaf: Thompson taking a wholly intransigent stand, citing Marx's aphorism that to leave error unconfuted amounted to intellectual immorality, with his antagonists responding in similar style.

If the 1960s and 1970s were historiographically disputatious, that was minor stuff compared to what was to come. Structuralism transmogrified into poststructuralism (here the Anglo-Saxon world was catching up on processes that had already developed in its French homeland) with the concept of postmodernism making its way into intellectual discourse[2] – I'll deal later on with their definitions. My own attitude towards the new tendencies was generally one of suspicion and hostility, though I was always willing to acknowledge that the approach contained useful historiographical insights. Although I couldn't help on one occasion responding favourably to a speaker who described postmodernism as an academic virus which turned all intellectual products into an indistinguishable mush – this at a time when there was a medical panic in Britain around a flesh-eating bug; and also to Richard Evans's remark that some of the barbarians are loitering around the gates with distinctly hostile intent – nevertheless the uncompromising reassertion of traditional historiographical conceptions by G.R. Elton, Arthur Marwick or Gertrude Himmelfarb, to cite its most high-profile defenders, living and dead, is unsustainable and proceed by simply ignoring or distorting the arguments of the new style.

To say that my own standpoint derives from the Marxian tradition would not be very enlightening as at least some of the advocates of the postmodern tendency would advance a similar claim, convincingly or otherwise. Postmodernism is a concept exceptionally hard to pin down, but I think it would be a fair and relatively uncontroversial assertion to note that in all intellectual disciplines it relates to questions of the possibility and the status of knowledge and interpretation. To be more precise therefore, as will become apparent throughout this text, I remain attached to a conviction of the centrality of scientific method and the scientific tradition of the past four centuries. In other words I believe that verifiable knowledge is possible, though mostly provisional and always incomplete. So far as historiography is concerned, my argument is that it rightly shares the scientific tradition in that it obeys at a very general level the same rules that are followed by the natural sciences – though it has other peculiarities which distinguish it, some of which it shares with other social sciences, some of which are specific to itself. Moreover historiography must be judged as a progressive science in that we constantly learn more, and more accurately, though the relationship between knowledge and the object of knowledge always remains problematic – these are key issues to be explored below. If I had to define my own position in a couple of words I would term it neo-realist.

The historiographical debate of the last third of the twentieth century has generated a truly enormous literature – in English alone, quite apart from other languages. For any single individual to master it all would require many years of concentrated study – if indeed such an aim was even practicable. The literature has been no less controversial than it has been extensive. The question that presents itself sharply and inescapably, therefore, is whether there can be any point in adding yet another volume to that mountain. Evidently I would not have written this one if I didn't think the answer should be 'yes', and my justification is as follows. I attempt, from a particular standpoint, to indicate in a very summary fashion the general course of modern Western historiography and relate it to the social and political circumstances of its times. Second, I try to tackle some of the epistemological issues from angles which, so far as I can establish, have not been previously developed and relate these to political and ethical questions.

I feel that some apology and explanation is appropriate for the fact that the discussion here is confined to Europe and North America. Asia, the Middle East, Africa, Australasia and Latin America are all wholly neglected.[3] The pragmatic reason for this is that to have included them would have made the text many times longer than it was intended to be and would have fractured its unity – quite apart from considerations of time. A more theoretical consideration is that for better or worse, regrettably or otherwise, it has been the scientific protocols originating from Europe which have come to dominate the field in this area of intellectual endeavour as in so many others.

The manner in which this volume proceeds is as follows. The following three chapters outline the main lines of development in Western historiography since the establishment of its 'scientific' character in the early nineteenth century. The first deals with the principal lines of historiographical evolution in Europe and the United States up to the 1960s, the second sketches the transformation in historical studies and, no less importantly, in historiographical consciousness which has taken place since that time, with the sub-discipline of social history as their particular seedbed, and the third addresses the conceptual conflicts of the 1980s and 1990s. My account diverges from the standard narrative of historiographical development in the significance it attaches to the Marxist tradition within historiography and the centrality which it attributes to Edward Thompson's writing.

Chapter 4 then proceeds to examine the present-day institutional matrix in Britain and the US in which historical research and writing is conducted and the implications, both material and theoretical, which this framework has for the kind of historiography which gets produced.

Chapter 5 is an argument about how we get to know what we know and how we understand and communicate it – and in particular the consequences for historiography of different positions in this debate. The argument has a specific target, namely the generically termed 'postmodernist' stances identified with the particular line of thinkers and their interpreters referred to above.

The remaining two chapters explore some of the implications and consequences which arise from the critical interrogations of the relations between historical evidence and its interpretation – implications which affect both historian and audience. I argue for an understanding of this relationship which concludes that while a conceptualisation of what happened in history, a measure of understanding thereof and an appropriate moral response are all certainly difficult and problematic, they are by no means altogether out of reach. In the course of doing so I attack what appear to me to be certain wholly fallacious and pernicious conceptions.

The Conclusion attempts to place in historical context the issues discussed and to reveal the ancestry of the trends which go under the name of deconstruction, poststructuralism or postmodernism in certain artistic/political movements, persisting in a number of recognisably similar forms throughout the twentieth century until, in later decades they were enabled by the turn of political events to find an insertion in certain of the social sciences, including history.

Finally, I must acknowledge all those whose contribution has been in one way or another vital to the production of this volume (acknowledging no less my own sole responsibility for all its shortcomings). They include first of all my students and colleagues at Caledonian University and more widely, whose dialogue and argument has made it possible for me to define my viewpoints more clearly (however inadequately) than I could otherwise have done. Secondly the authors and controversialists from whom I have learned and/or with whom I have argued in my own head; finally and centrally all the inimitable staff at Pluto Press, especially my endlessly patient editor, Anne Beech.

1
The Tradition Established

At the beginning of the twenty-first century it is unnecessary to waste too much time arguing about the importance of historical understanding in human affairs. Readers of this volume may well be familiar with the cliché that those who forget the past are condemned to repeat it; though it is no less true that those who remember it all too well are equally liable to find themselves repeating it – probably even more disastrously than the ones who forgot.

Setting this paradox on one side for the moment, it is impossible to doubt that any understanding of current realities in the Balkans, in Northern Ireland or in Russia is impossible without at least a basic knowledge of the history of these places – and not only of their most recent years, but of the ancient identities and millennial hatreds which inspire close neighbours to murder each other or young men to fire mortar bombs into school playgrounds filled with children. It is not however, as these examples suggest, only a question of understanding the past, but more specifically of how the past is perceived and interpreted by the communities involved.

What is implied here is the distinction suggested by J.H. Plumb in *The Death of the Past*[1] between 'the past' and 'history'. The former notion refers to the unexamined traditions, myths and historical presumptions current among historically conscious communities, whether of a 'natural' or an 'elective' sort – for example, villages in south Armagh on the one hand or Trotskyist sects on the other. The latter term, Plumb's 'history' proper, refers by contrast to past realities understood by means of critical historical investigation which is not intended to perpetuate tradition but to establish the historical truth (insofar as that slippery concept has any determinate meaning – of which more later).

'The recovery of the past' however, and its transformation into 'history' are not innocent phrases but come bound up together with all sorts of technical, procedural, philosophical, political – and historical – baggage. The essential technical procedures and canons of relevance by which historians operate were established at the beginning of the nineteenth century, and the date is not accidental: the 'historiographical revolution' was one aspect of the experience of modernity starting to overtake Europe during that era. Modernity is defined as 'a mode of ... experience of space and time, of the self and others, of life's possibilities and perils – that is shared by men and women all over the world today'.[2]

The aforesaid canons and procedures, adopted in due course and by force of example in every historically literate culture (being analogous to experimental procedures in physical science), have remained the foundation for all subsequent serious historiography and it is impossible to imagine that they are ever likely to be superseded – despite some contemporary efforts in that direction – since they incorporate the intrinsic logic of investigation into past realities in any sphere of human activity or relationship. In spite of that methodological bedrock however, the evolution of historiography over nearly two centuries has been far-reaching and multifarious. Its development has been driven partly by the emergence of contradictions and unforeseen implications within the procedures and partly by the transformation of the social world, bringing forward fresh agendas and demands for the exploration of hitherto disregarded pasts. The pre-eminent site of these investigations has always been in higher educational establishments – even when the area of historiographical concern was far removed from the academy – for it was in them that the apparatus was most readily assembled and future generations of practitioners trained and equipped.

Applied in its early days to political history in the most restricted interpretation and focused upon lives of 'great individuals', the new methodology expanded in time to embrace economic, demographic, social and cultural dimensions and learned to mobilise as historical evidence materials that would have been despised and discounted by the pioneers of 'scientific history'. Entire historiographic schools, each with its apparatus of academic personnel, textbooks, journals and conferences, have been instituted not merely in accordance with particular fields of study such as economic history, but on the basis of the kind of evidence taken account of and the methodological applications preferred by their adherents.

Historical transitions are never abrupt, and the new style had a number of precursors, but the name pre-eminently identified with the codification of the new procedures is that of the Prussian Leopold von

Ranke. However the significance of what he did and inspired is only properly understood in relation to that other Prussian, Ranke's partial contemporary, the remarkable philosopher G.W.F. Hegel. Hegel's was above all a philosophy of history, with History, in the guise of the World Spirit, the moving force of all development. 'History for Hegel "is mind clothing itself with the form of events or the immediate actuality of nature". In other words, history is mind or spirit as it manifests itself in nature, in the external world.'[3] Pantheistic notions in the past had identified God with Nature; Hegel identified him with History – History itself it must be emphasised, not a separate divine consciousness directing its course.[4] What came to be known as historicism, the ruling ideology of Ranke's successors, 'the evaluation of reality as a historical process of spiritual formation'[5] has actually more of a Hegelian flavour. Hegel's philosophy proved so influential, and continues to be so at several removes down to our own time, because it grasped the understanding that history was not a chapter of accidents, a ceaseless costume drama always featuring the same personalities, garbed in togas or doublets as the case might be, but a developmental process with a powerful, complex and intricate logic to it and one moreover that was driven by struggle and conflict. As Alex Callinicos notes, Hegel realised that emergent modernity could not, in light of the collapse of traditional norms and presumptions brought about by the French Revolution, be justified by an appeal to any concept of divine providence – if it did have any meaning then that could only be established through a philosophy of history.[6]

The philosophy in question did not spring out of nowhere (disregarding its formal roots and relationships in Hegel's predecessors and contemporaries: Kant, Fichte, Herder and Schelling) but represented an abstraction from the material realities of economic transformation, social upheaval and political revolution currently tearing and shaking Europe. It is very important to keep in mind that while we ourselves in the year 2000 know what the outcomes were, for the citizens of the late eighteenth and early nineteenth centuries Europe was pregnant with unforeseeable possibilities, and nobody was capable of imagining into what kind of future they might issue. It was possible on the one hand, like the ultra-reactionary de Maistre, to conceive of the French Revolution as being quite literally the work of the devil, permitted by God to rampage for a space of time; or on the other hand, like Robert Owen, to envisage Utopia as appearing just around the corner.

It is notorious that Hegel in his later years came to regard the Prussian state, a monarchic absolutism operating within a legal framework, as the culmination of the historical movement.[7] Truly in this case the philosophic mountains had laboured and brought forth a political mouse. Hegel, while not repudiating his philosophical system, had opted for conservative safety within a rigid hierarchical and authoritarian regime, erasing the revolutionary ardours of his past with the justification that this monarchy, through the transformations and reforms which had been imposed upon it in response to the revolutionary turmoil, upheld the legal and property rights instituted by the Revolution and subsequently carried across the continent by Napoleon. It was however still possible to make a distinction between Hegel's *system* and Hegel's *method,* and to read revolutionary implications into his dialectic. This is what his radical followers, the Young Hegelians, proceeded to do.

Unlike Hegel, Ranke's relationship to the politics of his time was unambiguous, for as well as being the outstanding historian of his generation he was also a paid agent of the Prussian government, secretly commissioned in the 1830s to use his growing academic prestige to publish attacks upon radicals and democrats. Fear of the heritage of the French Revolution and the manner in which historical speculation or models drawn from the past had been used to underpin revolutionary ideology were among Ranke's primary intellectual motivations.[8]

There are features of Ranke's approach which parallel those of Hegel as well as ones which are sharply distinguished from it, and no doubt the philosopher, along with more obvious revolutionary social theorists like Condorcet, was one of Ranke's targets. If he regarded Hegel as having arrived at the right political conclusions (similar to his own), he thought of him as having done so for profoundly wrong metaphysical reasons. Ranke excoriated historians or philosophers who presumed to advance grand explanatory schemes of historical development: his best-known remark is that he had no such ambitions but merely aimed to 'tell it like it was': *wie es eigenlich gewesen.* His conception represented a polar opposite to that of Hegel, for behind the rather disingenuous claim to have no philosophy and to be purely concerned with narrative and explanation stood a rigid belief that states and societies were justified by the mere fact of their existence; they represented whatever happened to be right for their time (here Ranke and Hegel were in accord) – but the historian scorned the notion of any process of dialectical development. All eras and all (traditional) institutions were equally valid in the sight of God.

Such a perspective implied the presumption that different historical epochs were also incommensurable, that the standards of any of them, including the present one, could not be applied to any of the others – a point of view termed 'genetic relationism' or 'historicism' (though the latter term has so many different or even contradictory meanings that it is all but useless) – and insisted therefore that the past could not be and must not be judged according to the values of the present. The political implications are readily evident and were even more so in the early decades of the nineteenth century, for they thereby justified and endorsed the feudal garbage of institutions and practices from monarchy to serfdom, against which the reformers struggled – an inheritance from the past, on this reckoning, might be regarded as no less valid than a social or political innovation, possibly even more so.

> Ranke, a German conservative writing after the storm and stress of the French Revolution, was weary of history written for, or permeated by, the purposes of revolutionary propaganda ... Written history that was cold, factual and apparently undisturbed by the passions of the time served best the cause of those who did not want to be disturbed.[9]

Ranke however was not a mere apologist for the status quo, but in his general outlook as well as his historiographical insight was a thinker of some substance (rather unfairly dismissed as insignificant by Marx and Engels in their correspondence) even if his thought was contradictory and incorporated a lot of bad faith. Although he strenuously repudiated any idea of writing history in the service of what we would now term contemporary ideology, that is exactly what he was doing himself, in the conviction that a true account 'like it was' would validate the rightfulness of the traditional institutions under examination and, by association, also those prevailing in his own time. It has been pointed out that *eigenlich* in Ranke's time had overtones it has now lost – it could mean 'essentially' as well as its current sense of 'actually'.[10] Challenges recorded in history from radical sources could also be viewed as part of the divine plan and were certain to meet ultimate defeat. History for him possessed a near-mystical character:

> God dwells and lives and can be known in all of history ... Every deed attests to Him, every moment preaches his name, but most of all, it seems to me, the connectedness of history in the large ... stands there like a holy hieroglyph ... May we, for our part, decipher this holy hieroglyph! Even so do we serve God. Even so are we priests. Even so are we teachers.[11]

And states were described by him as 'the thoughts of God'.

Nonetheless in Ranke's case as with Hegel it was possible to distinguish between system (and for that matter purpose) and method – with or without such revolutionary conclusions as the Young Hegelians drew. Procedures used to demonstrate that the history of the Catholic church (dismissed out of hand by the revolutionaries as a record of malign superstition and despotism) was in fact a great deal more complex, could equally well be employed to debunk the pretensions of rulers and aristocracies. They could likewise be used, once the idea of doing so had germinated, to demonstrate that the lower orders, or women, or persecuted minorities – wholly beneath the notice of Ranke and his disciples – possessed histories as complex and relevant as those of their masters and betters. The twentieth century witnessed a constant broadening of the categories of individuals and/or communities considered appropriate for historical research.

The canons and procedures in question have been explained and elaborated often enough, and so we will dwell upon them here only very briefly. To some degree they represent no more than applied common sense. The first and central principle is that the past must be reconstructed, retrieved or whichever term one wants to employ, only on the basis of evidence which was generated (by human agency or otherwise) at the time in question or by individuals who participated in the events under scrutiny. These are termed primary sources, generally written evidence. Historiography is distinguished by the key significance which it assigns to the documentary record or written sources – as distinct from other explorations of a historical nature, especially archaeology. (The distinction of course is artificial so far as the content of historical development is concerned; it is purely one of method and in many instances documentary and archeological evidence can be profitably combined.)

By contrast, secondary sources are accounts which have been compiled on the basis of primary (or original) sources – or of other secondary sources – and cover everything from the most profound exposition of new knowledge to the routine monographs and articles written by historians, and at the further end, the merest ephemeral trivia. Not that the status of a primary source is by any means clear cut. As an example we may take the gospel narratives of the New Testament, composed at least several decades after the events they purport to record, by individuals who lacked first-hand knowledge of them.[12] These represent primary evidence for the outlook and thinking of the early Christian communities among whom they were compiled, but only secondary evidence for the personality and career of Jesus of Nazareth. In many instances of course, particularly for remote eras, secondary sources are all that historians possess and they simply have to make the best of them. In those cases even where the primary source does exist (again the biblical texts are a good example) the original version of the document may very well not do so (the Dead Sea Scrolls are a renowned exception) and what remains extant are copies of copies of copies. Leaving the remote past for any other century, including the twentieth, the same principles apply no less. Newspaper reports, having been subject to editing, are secondary sources for the events they record; the original reporter's notebook, if it had survived, would be a primary source. A document can, as we have seen, be in different dimensions, either primary or secondary. The notoriously mendacious history of the Soviet communist party compiled in 1938 under Stalin's editorship could scarcely qualify even as a secondary source for the CPSU's actual history, but it provides an indispensable window into the Stalinist mentality.

The insight regarding primary sources represents the conceptual bedrock of the Rankean system: the notion of genetic relationism partially follows on from it as close acquaintance with the primary sources causes the realisation to dawn that the past is indeed a foreign country and that its inhabitants did things very differently from ourselves. In addition the Rankean approach incorporated techniques for the critical appraisal of texts, for establishing their authenticity if that should be in question, for understanding and evaluating their overt meaning and for extracting from them information which the creator of the source might not even be aware of revealing. Research according to Rankean principles tended (and tends) to be directed towards archives rather than published texts, as the sources found in the former – records, memoranda, letters, etc. – can be regarded as 'rawer' and possessing a greater degree of authenticity.

Such, in short, was the Rankean method, which soon came to be termed 'scientific history', and it cannot be seriously disputed that it represented a genuine and unquestionable advance and achievement in the recovery of the past. If an advance of this sort is measured by the fact that all subsequent practice operates under its influence, then Ranke was indeed the founder of modern historiography and established a sharp dividing line between 'before' and 'after'. The great historiographical classics, from the works of Thucydides to Gibbon, are evaluated as successful history by the degree to which they spontaneously anticipated or foreshadowed these canons; when they fail to do so their merit is literary rather than historiographical.

Other aspects of Ranke's approach and practice are a different matter. His concentration upon high politics and governing institutions such as secular states or the Papacy reflected both his own reactionary bias and also the availability of archives (state archives were being increasingly opened to investigators at the time) upon which his methodology could be exercised. The final aspect of Ranke's legacy to the future which deserves to be noted is the overwhelming – indeed nearly exclusive – location of serious professional historians within the higher education system. He operated from the University of Berlin and it was there he trained his immediate successors.

Before the end of the century a class of professional historian academics was in existence throughout the orbit of Western culture and the principles of the Rankean methodology were the accepted foundation of their practice, whatever divergences of approach or outlook might be added onto that.[13] Ranke himself had the happy fortune to live to see the triumph of his conceptions, remaining active until his death in 1886, when he was over ninety. A lot of contingent factors went into the explanation of this triumph – the reform and rationalisation of the university system throughout Western Europe, partly based on the German model, the development of a similar system in the United States, the ease of international academic and intellectual intercourse during a prolonged interval largely free of major wars – but centrally and most importantly the evident power and efficacy of the principles themselves. In Britain Lord Macaulay was the last of the great historians in the literary mode: the succeeding generation, exemplified especially by Lord Acton and the constitutional historian Bishop Stubbs, was wholly Rankean in its methods, though not necessarily in its historiographical perspectives.

> ... the result was a distinctive and remarkably time-specific tendency which focused on the British experience at the expense of the world outside, one that concentrated on types of constitutional history rather than on social, cultural or intellectual studies, and that often imbued that study with linear logic leading from past to present, so that history became a matter of identifying broad processes working themselves out over hundreds of years and connecting the present of Victorian Westminster with a past running through the Glorious Revolution, Magna Carta, the Witanagemot and eventually towards the forests of Saxony. The doctrines associated with this history were congratulatory: the story celebrated English (as opposed, mostly, to Scottish, Welsh or Irish) liberty ...[14]

In France, Numa Fustel de Coulanges and Gabriel Monod were energetic promoters of Rankean methodology, and despite the embittered international relations between that country and Germany following 1870 it was two French historians, Langlois and Seignobos, who produced its most complete and elaborated codification.[15] It prevailed too – supposedly in a particularly unimaginative fashion – in the United States.

> [the founding] editor of the *American Historical Review* ... in the 1890s ... described the period as one of 'second class work', in which professional historians would be most usefully employed in 'laying up stores of well-sifted materials' which a subsequent generation would synthesize ... [this] conception of the historian's task – the patient manufacture of four-square factualist bricks to be fitted together in the ultimate objective history – had enormous professional advantages. It offered an almost tangible image of steady, cumulative progress.[16]

Such unqualified triumph of the Rankean *method* did not mean however that the late nineteenth century lacked energetic disputes among its historians, sociologists and philosophers as to what history was *about*, or the extent to which it could or could not be assimilated in other social sciences ... 'a systematic understanding of source materials helped generate new questions about their use and limitations'.[17]

It was not an unconnected fact that the emergent national sentiment of hitherto disregarded nationalities in nineteenth-century Europe was based so distinctively upon historical perceptions. The power of history as a social force was making itself felt. Benedict Anderson has defined nations as 'imagined communities' – it could be equally true to say that they derived their status and legitimacy from imagined histories. It would indeed be tempting to assume that the sense of nationality developing among Germans, Czechs, Hungarians, Poles, Romanians, Irish and others, was founded purely upon historical myth, but though myth was undoubtedly a component and flourished in populist discourse, that conclusion would be too simplistic. To be at all plausible for the most part and certainly to sustain any intellectual credibility, the constructed histories required to be based upon genuine documentation subjected to the Rankean tests of authenticity.

However, the authenticated documentation is one thing, what you do with it is quite another: selective concentration in certain areas combined with deliberate or unthinking blindness in others will produce historical accounts that have all the appearance of Rankean 'objectivity' sustained with batteries of footnotes, but are nevertheless conveniently tailored to satisfy specific ideological agendas (one night say, in Plumb's terms, the past masquerading as history). Such indeed was the path followed by Ranke's successors among the German nationalist historians. Ranke had no particularly nationalist agenda. As a servant of the Prussian monarchy in the 1830s he was indeed in political opposition to the German nationalism which was at that time one of the monarchy's principal enemies. Nationalism prior to 1848 was generally regarded as a subversive force with left-wing connotations in opposition to Europe's dynastic regimes. Later, his non-nationalist 'objectivity' was an attribute which greatly assisted the spread of Ranke's influence outside Germany. By contrast German nationalist historians such as Sybel and Trietschke adopted his method but repudiated the spirit in which he had deployed it, criticising him for his lack of nationalist fervour.

The same was no less true in parallel ways for nineteenth-century historians in other countries – including English ones developing a nationalist focus upon the glories of the British Constitution, conceived as 'liberty broadening down from precedent to precedent',[18] and most of all among those subordinated European nationalities trying to establish recognition of their historical credentials,[19] while in the United States at the turn of the century , as Peter Novick explains, a 'useable' national past was constructed in the academy in face of insurgency by Populists (agrarian radicals), Wobblies (militant syndicalists) and socialists in the world outside, by devising an understanding of US history designed to reconcile memories of the Civil War trauma. A consensus of Northern and Southern historians, supposedly basing themselves upon strict Rankean handling of the sources, manufactured what emerged as the accepted understanding that slavery might have been regrettable and attempted Southern secession an error, but that both were understandable and excusable in view of the racial inferiority of 'the negro'. Such consideration of the relation between methods and purposes points to some of the central problems and ambiguities that are encountered with any attempt to reconstruct the past.

However the notion that the historical facts were there to be discovered and that the facts spoke for themselves – even if it was mostly assumed that they spoke with national accents – dominated historiographical thinking during the later nineteenth century[20] and in the years up to the outbreak of the First World War. Lord Acton, as editor of the *Cambridge Modern History*, and a member, if an uncomfortable one, of an international church, famously expressed his confidence that there existed a single true version of historical reality and that his contributors were capable of putting aside national prejudice and thereby attaining to it[21] – even though the renowned Wilhelm Dilthey, who had been Ranke's student, was arguing that historical understanding required historians to draw not only upon the archive sources but upon their own inner intuitions and understanding, *Verstehen*, to produce *Einfuhlung* or empathy.[22] In disputes over whether historical facts were to be handled by means of inner experience or subject to more scientistic analysis as the economic historians would have preferred, or else in the violent disagreements over the role of cultural forces postulated in the work of Karl Lamprecht – both the subject of bitter controversy in 1890s Germany – there was unquestioned common ground on the solidity, rigidity and accessibility of the historical fact. E.H. Carr has remarked that the cult of facts prevailing at this time may have had something to do with the fact that the facts appeared in those years to smile so propitiously upon the universe of expansionist Western culture, where of course the history was being written.

Following the traumas of the Great War, the Russian Revolution and the succeeding decades of economic and political instability, attitudes changed among the community of historians. On the one hand previous European and global history now had to be understood, even if only implicitly, as a long prologue to the great catastrophe which had overwhelmed the modern world – which itself had been the prologue to the calamitous economic breakdown that quickly followed; and so what had beforehand provided a generally accepted story of systemic progress had turned into a hotbed of rival interpretations. On the other hand new forms of evidence started to be investigated and fresh methods of dealing with them to be developed. Historiography had already proliferated far beyond the original political/diplomatic focus of Ranke's project. By the early twentieth century economic history, social history and cultural history were already in the field, not to speak of the historically-orientated social theory represented by Max Weber – even labour history, as the growing movements of the Socialist International loomed upon the historical stage. All, so far as they had any pretensions to be serious or scientific, however, were constrained, whatever else they might disagree about, to subscribe to the basic Rankean methodology.

The historians' enterprise did not cease to conform to ideological agendas, and in the 1920s (let alone the 1930s) these were far more apparent and strident than ever before. German historians and their sympathisers in the US diligently scrutinised the available documentation to demonstrate the injustice of the terms imposed by the Treaty of Versailles, particularly that ascribing responsibility for the war to the German state. French historians did the reverse. In the UK, where the labour movement was viewed for a short period as a real threat to the established order, the newly developing discipline of economic history brought to the fore individuals whose work aimed (among other things) to shore up the ideological credibility of capitalism by demonstrating that its early development in the industrial revolution had improved the living standards of the masses rather than worsened them as hitherto generally believed. Previously (though recognised as a valid academic discipline) economic history had been accorded only a very subordinate place, but during those years emerged with strength, acquiring its own society and journal. Its rise was undoubtedly connected with the economic crisis, as well as the resonance which socialist critiques of capitalism and its historical career were finding in the circumstances of the depression. Sir John Clapham's classic, *An Economic History of Modern Britain*, endeavoured to refute the indictment of capitalism's history and to demonstrate the inevitability of its progress.

What was to prove the most important historiographical departure of the interwar decades in Europe did not have any overt political agenda – though it is possible to suspect that at several removes it might be viewed as an alternative to Marxism. The *Annales* school of historians was named after the title of their journal and established from the late 1920s particularly by Marc Bloch[23] and Lucien Febvre.[24] The concern of the *Annalistes* might be termed sociocultural history in the broadest possible sense, embracing environmental and geographical determinants, demography, social structures and *mentalités* – ways of behaving, thinking and seeing among particular historical groups of subjects. It was a strikingly innovative and hitherto unconventional approach which was to become the dominant school of French historiography after the Second World War and was to extend its influence far beyond. In the words of Peter Schlötter:

> If historians today understand and practice their profession in a way different from their counterparts one hundred years ago, this change in self-perception is in no small part due to a scientific and historical event tied to the name *Annales*, and so to the periodical which Lucien Febvre and Marc Bloch founded in 1929 under the name *Annales d'histoire économique et sociale*.[25]

Despite its novelty, the '*Annales* paradigm' as it has been termed, did not spring out of nowhere but can, like Max Weber's much more individual undertaking, be seen to have its intellectual roots at the end of the nineteenth and beginning of the twentieth centuries in the historiographical disputes over how scientific historiography could be – in the sense of bringing the particularity of human behaviour within the scope of overarching generalisations (not the Rankean science of source criticism) – thus imitating 'harder' human sciences like geography, economics, anthropology or psychology. The *Annalistes* aspired to produce an integrated geographical, environmental, anthropological, economic, social, cultural and psychological (though scarcely political) history, though as Michael Bentley insists 'the point lay not in deriding documentary scholarship but transcending it by extending the subject, comparative and disciplinary base'.[26] Their project resulted in what he describes as 'the most exciting form of historical thought between the great wars of the twentieth century'.[27]

The German historical profession, the prime inheritors of the great tradition, was consumed by the political catastrophes of these years and was responsible for no innovative development. Its leading representative, Frederick Meinecke, who had during and before the war, like the majority of his colleagues, celebrated the Wilhelmine Reich and Bismarckian *Realpolitik*, turned his attention, again like the majority of his colleagues, to trying to comprehend what had gone wrong – within the same ideological and conceptual framework as they had previously sustained. In political terms the German profession was rigidly reactionary and never doubted that the rightful destiny of Germany was to dominate the continent, or at the very least East-Central Europe.

> ... a majority of those teaching history at German universities in the 1920s and 1930s were strict opponents of democracy ... they hated the Weimar state which had replaced the Empire they glorified and which symbolised defeat and military weakness ... they longed for a renewal of an authoritarian and externally powerful state ... historians at German universities actively and voluntarily helped to legitimise Germany's claim to European hegemony.[28]

Most of them accommodated the Nazi regime all too readily, though a few, to their credit including Meinke, either suffered persecution or kept their distance.

By and large the Rankean system (though certainly not the method), under pressure ever since the later nineteenth century, was upon its deathbed following 1914. What is observable in these years is its dissolution; both in the sense that it became recognisably impossible simply 'to tell it like it was' and in the proliferation of new approaches to history which transcended the archival and political focus of Ranke and his successors. All serious historians nevertheless continued to employ the Rankean *method* – for as indicated, not even the *Annales* school broke with that. In this respect historians at large might be appropriately termed neo-Rankeans, as indeed most of them continue to be. Nonetheless it was during the course of these years that the first real epistemological questioning began to be voiced, in a definitively more radical fashion than Dilthey had done, on the extent to which historical method could attain to historical truth, the degree to which the past, manifested only in the traces which it had left behind, was accessible to contemporary consciousness.

In this respect, the writer from the era who has left the most lasting impact was the English historian R.G. Collingwood (though his meditations were not published until 1946). Collingwood envisages a progression from the classical historians to 'scientific history', by which he does in fact mean the Rankean method, though oddly Ranke himself is mentioned only in passing and does not figure in the list of historians specifically discussed.[29] He acknowledges a debt to Dilthey, whom he describes as a 'lonely and neglected genius' but regards the latter's approach as too unhistorical. Collingwood's crucial innovation is that despite his commitment to the notion of scientific history he did not adhere to the naive notion of the 'fact' that had prevailed prior to 1914 and was aware of the theoretical (as well as the practical) problems associated with the retrieval of the past. His solution is drastic: it is to assert that since documentary sources convey only the thinking of their creators, all that can be known with certainty about the past is the thoughts of its actors – a peculiar notion, one might feel, for a historian who was also an archaeologist. As it happened, Collingwood was a relatively isolated figure, regarded with some irritation by many of his colleagues – though he also had loyal disciples – and his ideas had little impact upon British historiography in his own time.

The US

Matters were quite otherwise in the United States in relation to the conceptual basis of historiography, where amid violent and bitter dispute a rival epistemology, implicitly if not explicitly opposed to the Rankean (though it may have persuaded only a minority of American historians) almost contrived to gain the official endorsement of the American Historical Association (AHA).

Peter Novick in his admirable volume has left us a detailed and fascinating picture of how events developed. He stresses the reaction that set in among many US historians against the way in which they had been manipulated by the government, following American intervention in the First World War, to produce mendacious patriotic propaganda. '... viewing the venture in the large, the participants could not escape the realization that one could quite easily be flagrantly propagandist without violating the norms of scholarship narrowly conceived'.[30] Confidence was shaken that 'objectivity' could be attained simply by careful and scrupulous attention to source criticism.[31]

> One senior American historian, Clarence Alvord, confessed after the war that he had always 'conformed to the canons of my science ... walked along the straight and narrow road of approved scholarship .. learned to babble the words of von Ranke' ... This had all been very fine, he said while the world was a safe place to live in and and when people had been able to believe in ordered, rational and inevitable progress. But now 'all the spawn of hell roamed at will over the world and made of it a shambles ... The pretty edifice of ... history which had been designed and built by my contemporaries was rent asunder' ...[32]

Not only that particular edifice. National politics became more fraught. A postwar 'Red Scare' resulted in the widespread persecution of radicals; presidents were discredited by incapacity or corruption; immigration, instead of being encouraged, was choked off; majority public opinion reacted against the Treaty of Versailles, was terrified by the Bolshevik Revolution; and isolationist feeling strengthened. Within the profession fierce conflict erupted around the theses promulgated by Harry Elmer Barnes absolving Germany from responsibility in starting the war and laying the blame instead upon the Entente, though Barnes was so extravagant in his denunciations of opponents – he was in fact mentally deranged – that he alienated even his supporters. All this though, however ferocious, was still within the Rankean paradigm: both sides were claiming through documentary research to uncover and cite the true facts.

Economically, still worse was to come. The catastrophic slump beginning with the Wall Street Crash of October 1929 appeared to shake the foundations of American society. Throughout much of it the uninhibited *laissez-faire* culture hitherto celebrated as America's glory was discredited, or at least called into question. Across the Atlantic the fascist threat loomed, with American would-be imitators on the scene and the airwaves. Radical movements resurfaced and even the Communist Party attained a degree of credibility.

Greater turmoil now shook the profession, its intensity magnified by the existence of a centralised sounding-board in the shape of the AHA, a body with importance and power in the US context that had no equivalent in any other country. Two figures in particular became the focus of controversy, with the profession divided for or against – the terrible twins Carl Becker and Charles Beard. The principal source of dispute was their epistemological stance, though both were doubly controversial in that their politics, though not socialist, derived from the populist left – its outlook captured in the slogan 'the people against the interests' – and Beard was triply controversial for an oeuvre that interpreted the trajectory of US history in economic rather than constitutional terms – a strong version of economic determinism. Becker was not widely read among the general public but Beard, sometimes in collaboration with his wife Mary, was a very popular writer, and a survey of textbooks made in the mid-1930s showed his 1913 text, *An Economic Interpretation of the Constitution* to have become virtual orthodoxy,[33] while the first two volumes of *The Rise of American Civilisation* (1927), written with Mary, proved an instant and continuing best-seller.

Without doubt it was their epistemology which represented the most acute source of conflict and had the farthest-reaching consequences, and for the purposes of this volume it is that we are concerned with. Although they themselves did not accept the designation, they were categorised by their opponents as epistemological 'relativists', who denied the actuality of a past that was in principle the same for all potential observers and capable of being reconstructed by historical research. Instead they posited a state of affairs in which every era would have its own version/interpretation of the past and each would be right for its particular time. The emphasis was on interpretation – even they did not deny that the evidence for particular events was to be assembled via good Rankean principles. It could be argued indeed that they were more consistent Rankeans than Ranke himself in that they extended the principle of genetic relationism from the ethical to the cognitive dimension. Both were responding to an awareness of the conceptual problems involved in historiography and the inadequacy of Rankean assumptions. Becker was by temperament a detached sceptic, but Beard was a reforming activist (a co-founder of Ruskin College) eager to institute a democratic historical understanding in a democratic society – the appropriate form of history to his age as he saw it. Both, especially Beard, pursued careers somewhat at a tangent to the academic profession, though both were well enough established to become presidents of the AHA, from which platform they issued their provocative epistemological pronouncements.[34]

Without doubt their approach was influenced, if not in any systematic or declared fashion, by the home-grown American philosophical doctrine of pragmatism, and both had friends in that circle, the most important in the interwar years being the philosopher and educationist, John Dewey. Pragmatism is defined by its conception of truth, meaning in vulgar terms 'what works', or in more pretentious ones, what can be instrumentally validated. This is emphatically *not* to assert that a lie is true if enough people can be made to believe it (though the doctrine lends itself to caricature in those terms). Rather it is to assert that hypotheses are validated by their effective application in practice and to rule out as philosophically illegitimate or meaningless questions about the 'fit' between reality and concept that causes the answer to be effective.

Setting aside the fact that Engels had noted much earlier than C.S. Pierce, pragmatism's founder, that 'things in themselves' become 'things for us' once we have the understanding to manipulate them to our purposes (and that this represents a necessary test for hypotheses or theories in respect of material nature) a pragmatist view of truth can lead to very strange and contradictory consequences, nowhere better illustrated than in the role of John Dewey himself when he chaired the unofficial commission which examined the Stalinist charges against Trotsky, the centrepiece of the Moscow show trials.

Again, it is not simply a question of the accusations being lies (though of course in 'normal' understanding they certainly were) – for in a Stalinist 'frame of reference' that was not necessarily the case. From the Stalinist standpoint any political opposition amounted to treason, so anyone who had engaged in that was automatically guilty, and in that the authorities were perfectly sincere. It was simply, then – in *their* frame of reference – a case of the inquisitors ferreting out (or in Trotsky's own case, presuming, since he was absent) the conspiratorial treasons which *must* automatically have followed.[35] In a thoroughgoing pragmatist perspective it is hard to see why the Stalinist position should not be treated seriously, but Dewey's commission, using traditional standards of evidence, quite properly acquitted Trotsky on all charges. In the end the 'truth' in this instance turned out to be what the naive understanding of truth has always been; conformity with a reality independent of its proponents. Becker, Beard and their disciples were soon rejected, but they foreshadowed a challenge which three decades later was once again to shake the foundations of Western historiography – and appropriately enough, once again a pragmatist philosopher, this time Richard Rorty who has achieved eminence comparable to Dewey's, was to be called to aid this new generation of relativists.

Marxists and socialists

Although neither Marx nor Engels wrote what would be recognised as specifically historiographical text, apart from Engels's *The Peasant War in Germany*, their own outlook was of course a profoundly historical one and indeed they sketched one of the most influential ever models of long-term historical development, summarised in *The Communist Manifesto.* A virtuoso historical analysis of contemporary events, made in the framework of class relations, is found in *Class Struggles in France* (relating to the 1848 revolution); and especially *The Eighteenth Brumaire of Louis Bonaparte.* The first volume of *Capital* is as much a work of history as of analysis – and this by no means exhausts the list.

It might therefore have been expected that when Marxist labour movements became consolidated in the later nineteenth century they would give rise to a powerful historiographical tradition; but this by no means turned out to be the case – the tradition on the contrary was feeble and unimpressive and produced little of lasting merit. Possibly that was because the pioneers had simply been too successful, so that their concepts, interpreted principally as a species of economic determinism, were picked up and applied in the manner of a ready-made formula to understand historical reality without actually studying it. It was the practices of such vulgarisers which is said to have caused an exasperated Marx to exclaim in his later years that he was no Marxist.

Hardly any of the major figures of the Second International, the (mainly European) association of labour organisations founded in 1889, gave significant attention to historiography other than in a purely instrumental sense as a justification and rationale for political positions. although the concept of historical materialism was certainly discussed seriously, most notably by Georgi Plekhanov in his *The Monist View of History* of 1882 and in N.I. Bukharin's *Historical Materialism*. Of those few leaders who undertook explicit explorations into the past, Karl Kautsky wrote, speculatively, on the origins of Christianity and on Thomas More's *Utopia*; more importantly Jean Jaurès, the leader of the French 'Possibilists',[36] produced a study of the French Revolution (something Marx himself had once thought of undertaking) combining the most exacting standards of academic historiography with new interpretation in terms of class relations and conflicts. He however represented a solitary example attuned to Rankean method – which is not to say that figures like Lenin or Rosa Luxemburg did not possess an acute historical consciousness; however, they had more pressing matters to contend with and their historical consciousness was focused on the understanding of their contemporary reality.

If Marxist historiography prior to 1914 was largely stagnant, its fate following 1917 was for the most part horrendous. At the time of the Revolution no strong tradition of Marxist historiography existed in Russia any more than anywhere else, but a hopeful attempt was immediately put in hand to construct one (though representatives of the non-Marxist pre-revolutionary profession were permitted to retain their posts and their titles).[37] Central to this endeavour was the energetic and resourceful M.N. Pokrovsky, who received Lenin's personal stamp of approval, dominated the Soviet historical profession during the 1920s, became the chief historiographical interpreter for the regime and whose sixtieth birthday was celebrated officially with extravagant acclaim.[38]

The reason for the renown and promotion is not hard to recognise, for in Pokrovsky the regime had a serious and able historian who combined his historiographical abilities and organisational skills with an impressive understanding of Marxism. He also wrote well and accessibly – his popular *History of Russia*, which was translated into English, is very readable. Whatever judgement might be made of his interpretation of Russian history, which in essence was that the pre-revolutionary regime even from pre-Romanov times had rested upon capitalistic foundations (commercial at first), it was based upon thorough archival research using Rankean principles and was an arguable interpretation of the state's development. It was also vigorously hostile to any nationalistic celebration of the history of Russia and its state forms.

Pokrovsky died in 1932, which was fortunate for him because he was at that point still the celebrated doyen, though only just, of the country's historical profession.[39] The reaction set in almost immediately afterwards and the 'Pokrovsky school', as the authorities termed it, became the focus of denunciation and repression. He was purged posthumously, if not in his own lifetime, and his lieutenants and disciples were swept away to labour camps or their graves. The reason is evident enough – namely that the Stalinist system was being thoroughly implemented in all areas of Soviet culture and historical science, like every other element, was mobilised to serve the immediate purposes of the regime. As far back as 1928 Stalin, with the full weight of Party authority behind him, had intervened in historical practice by declaring that certain established facts about Lenin must not be recognised as facts – but at least that could be interpreted as a politically sensitive issue. By the mid-1930s any adherence to scholarly standards whatever was suspect, and all historiography relating to Russia, even that pertaining to pre-revolutionary times and past centuries, was required, in the best Orwellian style, to demonstrate from historical analysis that whatever current policies the regime might be pursuing they were unquestionably the correct ones.[40] That included the reinforcement of Great-Russian nationalism and presenting Stalin as the heir not only of Lenin but also of mighty Russian state-builders like Ivan the Terrible and Peter the Great. Only in relation to far countries and centuries could honest work be carried out. Soviet historiography, already in a very gloomy twilight of constraint and dogma, entered a deep night from which it never emerged – neither during the regime, nor subsequently.

In the countries beyond Stalin's reach the only one where a Marxist historiography of any significance flourished was France – not least because of the continuing influence of Jaurès's pioneering efforts and the importance of the theme which he had addressed. The source of its inspiration was, not surprisingly, the French Revolution and the study of that cataclysm was largely the subject matter. The emphasis of this historiography was to interpret the course of the Revolution in terms of class relations and class conflict – in essence the seizure of state power and the transformation of French society by the revolutionary bourgeoisie at the expense both of the historically superannuated aristocracy and the lower-class *sansculottes*, who were first mobilised behind the upon attack the *ancien regime*, then subsequently betrayed and repressed. It also applauded the role of the Jacobin left led by Robespierre and the Republic of the Year II over which these revolutionaries presided. By confining itself to the revolutionary years the school avoided conflict with the French Communist Party (whose interpretations of the Revolution ran parallel) with which it was was on the whole closely aligned, whilst maintaining an academic distance. Its two principal luminaries – both prodigiously energetic – were Georges Lefebvre, at one stage also a colleague of Bloch and involved with the *Annales*, and Albert Mathiez, dedicated above all to Robespierre's rehabilitation, who was briefly a member of the Parti Communiste Française (PCF), but left in 1923 before its outlook had hardened into dogma.

The most theoretically sophisticated variant of academic Marxism during the 1920s and 1930s was that of the Frankfurt School, which stressed the importance of Marxism's Hegelian antecedents and had a strong Hegelian, as well as Freudian, orientation.[41] The interests of its representatives however were philosophical (and to a lesser degree sociological) not historiographical; though the aphoristic theses of Walter Benjamin on history are among the most profound comments ever made upon it. However there was a single work which appeared during those years which can be regarded as the source from which a another alternative Marxist tradition did emerge. That was Trotsky's *History of the Russian Revolution*, a masterpiece of contemporary history and interpretation drawing upon the author's own central involvement with an event of momentous historical significance. Though it lacked the scholarly apparatus of footnoted references it was nevertheless, as Isaac Deutscher was to note, one of the most remarkable European history texts of the twentieth century and even the *Daily Telegraph* reviewer admired its expression of 'the Marxist dialectic in human language'. Although a Trotskyist-inspired tradition of historical writing was to be established, which in the postwar era would assume great importance, in the 1930s it had only one other representative apart from Trotsky himself, namely the Trinidadian C.L.R. James, then making an impact at the beginning of his historiographical career with *The Black Jacobins*, his account of the Haitian slave revolt.

In the United States Marxist historians had little if any purchase within the academy, where even the mild progressivism of Beard and Becker was deeply suspect in a largely racist and antisemitic profession.[42] W.E.B. DuBois was an African-American who inclined towards the Communist Party of the USA (CPUSA), though he did not join it until 1961 when he was in his old age. From a position partly inside academic institutions, but more often not, he spent the early years of the twentieth century demolishing the racist myths that formed the conservative orthodoxy of the profession. In the 1930s his insights were beginning to be picked up by a few professionals. He was a militant political activist as well as a writer, a founder of the National Association for the Advancement of Colored People (NAACP) and concerned not only with the situation of Black people inside the United States but also on an international scale.

Not connected, so far as I can discover, to any specific political party, but a writer, educator and organiser for a variety of US working-class organisations and unions, was Leo Huberman, who defined himself as a Marxist, though he would probably be better categorised as a radical socialist with an intense consciousness of the reality of class struggle. In the words of Harvey Kaye, 'Huberman embodied Gramsci's conception of the "organic intellectual"...'.[43] As early as 1932 (he was born in 1903) Huberman, drawing on Beard's work, had written *'We The People'*, which proved an immediate publishing success. In 1936 he produced *Man's Worldly Goods: The Story of the Wealth of Nations*, a lively and accessible economic history stretching from the Middle Ages to the twentieth century, which sold even better.[44] A significant market for left-wing historiography clearly existed in the US at this time which was in no way satisfied by the academic establishment except, in a partial sense, by Charles Beard.

In Britain, radical and labour historiography of a non-Marxist provenance, some academic, some not, was published widely in the pre-1914 and interwar years. At the 'academic' end of the spectrum the most significant representatives were Sidney and Beatrice Webb, John and Barbara Hammond, G.D.H. Cole and Raymond Postgate, and especially R.H. Tawney.[45] In the long run their example was undoubtedly to contribute to the emergent social history of the 1960s. The particular trend in this line of historiography was to expose the iniquities inflicted by the ascendant capitalist class on their industrial victims, and encapsulated in the title of the Hammonds' volume, *The Bleak Age*. Of these texts the most influential and renowned was probably Tawney's *Religion and the Rise of Capitalism*, and though this was Weberian in inspiration rather than Marxist, that did not save it from being denounced by reactionary historians in the 1950s as the fount of all error among history students. Also, prior to the First World War there flourished an unsophisticated but lively populist historiography, often written by working-class autodidacts. Raphael Samuel has explored this in detail in *New Left Review*, and elsewhere he writes that:

> Seventy or eighty years ago [by contrast to the focus on the subjective and individual prevalent in the late twentieth century] the whole attention of people's history was turned on impersonal historical forces, located by some in climate and geography, by others in tools and technology, by yet others in biological necessity. Its leading feature was a kind of multi-layered determinism, in which contingency could be disregarded while necessity ruled in its stead. History was conceived of as an orderly, logical development, an inevitable passage from lower to higher stages ... As a Welsh miner

> told the Ruskin students: 'We weren't interested in whether so-and-so had sugar in his coffee or not. What interested us was how and why societies change.'[46]

That autodidact tradition however was largely dead by the 1930s.[47]

Between the time of von Ranke and the outbreak of the Second World War, historiography had expanded significantly if not dramatically in terms of the number of researchers and writers, it had found its institutional focus in the university milieu and the archive, and the range of styles, subject matter and forms of enquiry had multiplied. For all that, the profession remained very much dominated by people with whom Ranke would have found instant empathy both in research tradition and political outlook. Above all the methodological paradigm which he had established of the meaning and purpose of historiography, if weakening, continued to be generally dominant, even among those who diverged on subject matter, political outlook or investigative approaches. Arthur Marwick commented that generations of historians went into action incanting the formula *wie es eigenlich gewesen*.[48] All that was to change entirely in the next half-century.

2
War, Cold War and the 1960s Revolution

Paradoxically, in view of the erosion of the Rankean tradition that had been taking place in the first four decades of the twentieth century, in the West the immediate effect of the Second World War and the political developments which followed was to revalidate the tradition and strengthen it. Once again, with the mobilisation of all national resources, it became necessary to establish a cult of historical fact – facts which confirmed the righteousness of the embattled West and damned the record as well as the current behaviour of the contemporary enemy.

In Britain for example, Herbert Butterfield had made a considerable impact in the 1930s with a brief polemic entitled *The Whig Interpretation of History*, in which he had subjected to ridicule the notion or practice of viewing the past as in some manner designed to lead to the happier circumstances of the present – specifically finding the embryo of the twentieth-century British constitution in the Anglo-Saxon Witanagemot or even the German forests of the Dark Ages. Subsequently, in the course of the War he published *The Englishman and his History*, in which by implication he retracted most of what he had argued in the earlier text.

In the US, as Peter Novick puts it, 'The coming of World War II saw American culture turn towards affirmation and the search for certainty. American mobilisation, intellectual as well as material, became permanent ....'[1] Novick gives several typical examples, just prior to and during the war, of harsh public criticism directed against historians for relativistically undermining the patriotic moral fibre of American youth by trying to discredit the certitude of right and wrong positions; and in the course of those years the relativistic current was driven underground.

It was however during this period, in 1942 in the US, that an important development occurred which, though it did not challenge the status of the historical fact, had significant things to say about the potential for handling them. Under the title 'The Function of General Laws in History', published in the *Journal of Philosophy* rather than a historical journal, Carl Hempel advanced the subsequently much discussed notion of 'covering law', arguing that the protocols of scientific investigation and proof defined by Karl Popper could and should also apply to historiography. Roughly speaking a covering law has the form, 'If ..., then ...' and it has to be said that applying it to historical events in any precise manner has proved to be exceptionally difficult and unrewarding. Nevertheless, in principle it should be possible to do so, and a couple of examples will illustrate this.

In a monetary economy a sudden and rapid rise in circulating medium without corresponding growth in output will result in price inflation – a well-established and incontestable relationship. It ought therefore to be possible, again in principle, to specify, in those historical circumstances where such an injection of specie or banknotes or other form of money has taken place, what the economic, social and possibly even political consequences are bound to be once the defining initial conditions have been accurately established. In practice, however, whether it is a matter of the input of silver bullion to sixteenth-century Spain, or hyperflation in the Civil War Soviet economy, or 1923 Weimar Germany, so many unpredictable non-monetary variables come into the picture that all that can be said with any certainty is that such circumstances will prove very disruptive for the society which undergoes them. Again, in modern economies the existence of business cycle and even, roughly, its timing are well attested phenomena. It should therefore be possible for the downswing and upswing of every business cycle in the past two centuries to be fully and consensually explicable in terms of covering laws – in reality there is no consensus whatever among economic historians, there are simply too many variables. If such is the case with examples where large aggregates are involved and simplifying assumptions can reasonably be made about behaviour, how much more impossible it becomes when the events in question are conceptualised as 'war' or 'revolution'. Hempel was nevertheless quite right to point out that historians constantly use generalisations framed in terms of a covering law, but do so in an impressionistic and intuitive fashion. It would seem that they are fated to continue to do so; for instance in formulations such as 'God is with the big battalions'.

Cold War

The US and Britain

Ideological conformity in the US became, if anything, even more intense during the years of the Cold War than it had been during the fight against the Axis, in part no doubt because from the point of view of authority and the majority of the public there was now in addition an 'enemy within' in the shape of domestic communists and their stooges and/or sympathisers. In the US radical academics and writers, not least historians, including Leo Huberman and W.E.B. DuBois, were relentlessly hounded through the McCarthy and other official committees. All communists and many others in addition were evicted from academic positions. Only two historians of any note remained publicly CP members during those years, Herbert Aptheker and Philip S. Foner, and they were employed in party-related bodies, not educational establishments.[2] Any others in the academy who might have expressed Marxist or leftist sentiments were intimidated into compliance with the governing consensus.

Nonetheless, there was still defiance, if not within the groves of academe. Foner and Aptheker continued to publish, if not with any major publisher. In 1949 although the times were scarcely propitious for left-wing initiatives, Huberman, together with the economist Paul Sweezy, founded the Marxist journal *Monthly Review*, which continued to publish in spite of McCarthyite persecution and remains extant. Sweezy was later to become widely known in connection with the Dobb-Sweezy controversy, an argument about the historical character of capitalist development which is referred to below.

The anti-communist witch hunt in Britain was a much milder affair than in the US, but that did not mean that it was insignificant. Communist or Marxist academics in those days were very rare in the British higher educational system, although a few historians, subject to various forms of discrimination, did succeed in holding on. For the most part, however, the massive complacency of the British historical establishment remained undisturbed, in that political assumptions about the virtues of the British state system and historiographical ones respecting the character of historical facts and methodologies both continued unquestioned. The profession in the 1950s was dominated and overawed by the figure of Lewis B. Namier, a Central European emigré of ultra-conservative political instincts.[3] These were reflected in his attraction to the field of eighteenth-century British politics – he admired that era for its social stability and dominance by the landed elite as contrasted with the contemptible paroxysms of democracy and nationalism indulged in by nineteenth and twentieth century Europe.

Namier, on account of his arrogance and snobbery, was not popular with his colleagues – he was referred to behind his back as 'constipation Namier – the big shit we can't get rid of' – but his particular approach to the subject, which he had begun to develop in the 1930s, made an enormous impression in the postwar years to the extent that some academics were known to suggest with confidence that before long all history (at least political history) would be written in the Namier style. His technique consisted of minute and detailed archive-based structural analysis of the networks of interest and patronage linking members of the English governing elite during the eighteenth century, particularly the 1760s. Namier suggested explicitly that what emerged from his studies furnished the real explanation for the course of British eighteenth-century politics (and by extension the same for other times) and that both party labels and ideological positions were irrelevant – except that they would be dangerous if taken seriously. 'His credo was actually a vulgar psychologism.'[4] In the intellectual climate of the time that was not necessarily viewed as a serious disadvantage. Undoubtedly Namier stood as the pre-eminent representative of British historiography in his day, and aspiring historians strove to imitate him. Christopher Hill did not, but as an undergraduate in the 1930s was nonetheless impressed by Namier's 'historical imagination'.

Isaac Deutscher was also a Central European emigré, also a historian writing in English (which was not his first language or even his second) but of an altogether different stamp from Namier. In his youth in the 1930s he had joined the Trotskyist movement but, though continuing to be inspired by Trotsky, broke with it, dismayed by its attachment to political unrealism and subsequently belonged to none of the multitude of sects into which the movement splintered. He was never an academic historian and indeed was blocked by establishment prejudice, exemplified in academics such as Max Beloff and Isaiah Berlin, from being awarded even the most lowly of academic positions which would have enabled him to concentrate on his researches. Instead he was obliged to make his living and so devote large amounts of his time and energies to journalism, as a commentator on Soviet and East European affairs. In short articles he explored many dimensions of contemporary history, but his emphasis was upon the biographical mode and his masterpieces were his biographies of Stalin (1949) – still the most readable and perceptive account of the tyrant, if now a bit dated – and of Trotsky himself, published in three volumes between 1954 and 1963 and still unsuperseded.[5]

Deutscher's use of the available documentary sources[6] was impeccably Rankean, and so to some degree was his stance towards his protagonists – to avoid rhetorical justification or condemnation, but instead to understand and explain. In a sense his stance was the ideal one for an engaged historian – his commitments were clear and indeed saturated his entire approach, but in reaching any conclusion the evidence always had priority. His literary style resembled Trotsky's own, clear yet eloquent, and deployed with a grandeur appropriate to its subject. Later history has shown many of Deutscher's judgements, particularly on the prospects of the Soviet bloc, to have been seriously flawed, but they were always advanced in good faith and he was without doubt an exemplary Marxist historian, possibly the most outstanding of his time.

He was not, however, the only one at work in Britain at that time, though the others then would have regarded him as untouchable, for their source was the Stalinist tradition.[7] Ironically it was their work which was to form the seedbed for the Marxist historiography which was to be most influential in the late twentieth century, partly in itself and partly for what it gave rise to. This was the Historians' Group of the British Communist Party,[8] which began to flourish in the postwar years. Its roots however go back to the late 1930s when the CP, in line with the Popular Front strategy of uniting all progressive forces under communist leadership in resistance to fascism, was endeavouring to present itself as the distilled embodiment of British radical traditions throughout the centuries, commencing with the Peasants' Revolt of 1381 if not earlier. In such circumstances it became possible for A.L. (Leslie) Morton to write and publish in 1938 under the Party's imprimatur[9] his *A People's History of England*, intended to be a popular interpretation of English history as a tradition of the common people's resistance to and revolt against their masters, a tradition which had reached its culmination in the twentieth-century labour movement and, implicitly, in the Communist Party, though that last point was tactfully unstated. Although written with popular intent and based on secondary sources (how else would it be possible to cover two millennia?) this text maintained scholarly standards of argument from the evidence rather than the writer's ideological disposition, and Morton's later work was to demonstrate that he could use original sources as well as anybody.

Of a very different temper, but no less significant, was the volume appearing in 1946 by Maurice Dobb, one of the very small number of the Party's academic luminaries,[10] under the title *Studies in the Development of Capitalism*. In a densely-referenced text Dobb traced the emergence, growth and triumph of capitalism as a dominant economic and social form from roots in the medieval centuries; interpreting the driving force behind it as the relationship and conflict of social classes,[11] thereby treating its progress as inherent in the dynamic social structure of exploitation and struggle (principally in England) rather than being explained by the impact of extraneous forces such as trade relations (though Dobb certainly did not neglect these). Later, in the 'Dobb-Sweezy Controversy' the latter challenged Dobb's interpretation of capitalism's development and instead attributed greater importance than Dobb was prepared to concede to the impact of extraneous forces. Clearly this raised issues of the greatest consequence so far as Marxists were concerned and has been continued by the argument between Robert Brenner who adopts a position in line with Dobb's, and among others, Emmanuel Wallerstein, whose approach is closer to Sweezy's.[12]

In their different ways these volumes were both considerable historiographical achievements and they provided compass points for the Historians' Group which was established in the Cold War years,[13] a time when communist leaderships demanded that their intellectuals be mobilised along very strict criteria to fight the 'battle of ideas'[14] – and yet ironically, the Historians' Group, unlike that for the Party's writers, was little affected.[15] John Saville has suggested that this immunity derived from the fact that while literary expression and certain areas of natural science were close concerns of the Soviet leadership, whose views were transmitted through the British CP hierarchy, Stalin and his minions were comparatively indifferent to discussions of British historical development so long as it kept away from sensitive twentieth-century concerns – which the Historians' Group avoided.[16] Consequently a thriving internal culture of dialogue and discussion was able to continue[17] and the Group was able to reach out to a wider constituency when certain of its members took the initiative which resulted in 1952 in the journal *Past & Present*, not published by the party or its affiliates and never intended to be an exclusively Marxist enterprise, but initially carrying the subtitle *A Journal of Scientific History* – which proclaimed its allegiance in a general sense. It has subsequently gone on to be recognised as one of the world's leading historical journals. According to Raphael Samuel 'the present flourishing state of English social history [he is writing in 1980] was incubated in the Communist Party Historians' Group ...'.[18]

The idyll came to an abrupt end in 1956, not because of an onset of Stalinist repression directed against those historians, but with Khrushchev's 'secret speech' denouncing Stalin in February and the subsequent turmoil in Eastern Europe culminating in the suppression of the Hungarian revolution by Soviet invasion in November. A number of the members of the Historians' Group were in the forefront of the internal dissent which demanded an accounting with the Stalinist past of the communist movement in general and the British CP in particular. They included Christopher Hill, Rodney Hilton, Royden Harrison, Raphael Samuel and, above all, John Saville and Edward Thompson.[19]

All of them were subsequently to produce historical work of the highest calibre, and it was after 1956 that they produced it. The efflorescence however should not necessarily be attributed to their abandonment of the Party, for Eric Hobsbawm had similar achievements though he remained a member. It was the later work of Edward Thompson, however, which was to set the trend with which we are concerned and in due course to revolutionise English-speaking historiography.

Continental Europe

On the European continent, East and West, while patterns varied enormously, without question it was in France that the richest historiographical culture was to be found. The *Annales* school found institutional embodiment in Paris at the centre of French academic culture and under Febvre's leadership rose to dominate the historiographical landscape. His successor, Ferdinand Braudel, was a historian of no less accomplishment and dynamism who effectively maintained the profile of the school. One commentator notes the astonishing eclecticism of subject matter combined with fidelity to the methodology and objectives of the founders, particularly Febvre. The list of contents of issues, in 1960 for example, included Yoruba (Nigerian) farming practices, Bosnian gold mines, North African camels in Roman times, the eighteenth-century Chilean economy, technical experiments in antiquity with mechanical harvesters, medieval conceptions of time, the concept of the Baroque, Plato, Galileo and Newton. Apart from recognised historians, contributors in the same year included Claude Lévi-Strauss on history and anthropology and Roland Barthes on Racine.[20]

The inheritance of the French Revolution and the continuing great popular strength of the Communist Party in postwar France – despite being driven from its positions in central government and suffering the domestic consequences not only of the Cold War but of the Algerian war as well – combined to give the left, Marxism and Communism, greater intellectual credibility and respectability than anywhere else in Europe apart from Italy, where historiographical and philosophical dynamism, though certainly not absent, was less pronounced. A number of the most promising figures in the rising generation of *Annalistes*, including Braudel's eventual successor, Emmanuel Le Roy Ladurie, were in fact PCF members and involved in the bitter political infighting which followed the events of 1956.[21] The historiography of the French Revolution also continued to thrive. In *La Révolution Francaise*, published in 1951 Lefebvre reached his full stature by drawing together his earlier studies into a grand synthesis, while his acknowledged successor as the doyen of Revolution historiography, Albert Soboul, began to demonstrate his command of the theme from the 1950s onwards.

The singular character of German history meant that historical research in that country – both the Federal Republic, i.e., West Germany, and the German Democratic Republic – would be directed primarily towards understanding the circumstances which had led up to the catastrophe of 1933–45. The Third Reich had exposed, in the heart of 'civilised' Europe, an experience of depravity without historical precedent, which for years left German historians in a state of ideological prostration,[22] but here too the 1960s saw innovation – in West Germany, for East German historians were constrained by the crude official Marxism, academically compulsory, which insisted that German fascism was nothing more than the unmediated expression of predatory and aggressive drives on the part of German monopoly capital.

Not that these predatory and aggressive drives should have been ignored as they tended to be by the West German profession, for they were certainly part of the story, even if by no means the whole one. In the early 1960s Fritz Fischer created a sensation and made himself an extremely controversial figure 'the gadfly of Hamburg', by new research in a very traditional field – diplomatic and political history. His scrutiny of the sources was impeccably Rankean, but from the standpoint of the conservative German historical establishment it came up with the wrong answers – to the effect that the elites of the Bismarckian Reich had indeed been chiefly responsible for launching the war of 1914–18 and that there were clear continuities thereafter to 1945 on the part of these same elites. This was heretical indeed – the official consensus was that the *Kaiserreich*, whatever its shortcomings, represented an intrinsically sound political system and the Third Reich a hideous aberration brought about through the weakening of the political system by the Versailles Treaty.

Whether through Fischer's initiative or otherwise – West Germany was also shaken by the student revolt – radical young historians began to use social history methodologies to interpret German politics, particularly middle-class ones where the main reservoir of reaction was located, from the foundation of the state to the 1930s. Most prominent was what was known as the Bielefeld School, from the new university in that town, and with Jurgen Kocka and Hans-Ulrich Wehler as its major representatives. Certain British historians, such as Tim Mason, were involved in the same field of research and labour historians extended similar approaches to the pre-1914 German labour movement, exploring some of the tensions between the day-to-day realities of working-class life, its attitudes and practices as contrasted with the previously accepted picture that had appeared through the prism of official Social Democratic ideology. In due course the conclusions of the Bielefeld School – that German political evolution up to 1914 was especially pathological and deviant from the West European norm – came under attack, but by critics such as Geoff Eley, using a similar social history approach to those the school had pioneered but reaching the opposite conclusion – that prior to 1914 Germany was socially not too different from its West European counterparts and the subsequent pathologies had been due to realities specific to the interwar period.

Between Western and Eastern Europe no meaningful comparison is possible. Following the onset of the Cold War and the subordination of the East European states to Moscow, Soviet prescriptions were imposed not only in economic and political affairs but in cultural ones too. (The Yugoslav political breakaway in 1948 did not dramatically change the nature of social arrangements in Yugoslavia, though it severely tightened the Stalinist grip in the others.) Stalin's death in 1953, and his posthumous denunciation by Khrushchev in 1956, may have lightened the burden of repression – Deutscher noted that occasional historically truthful references to Trotsky began to appear in the Soviet press – but in essence not a great deal changed. The possibility of doing honest historical work in distant centuries and on distant countries was improved, but to be an accredited academic of any sort in the Soviet bloc required loyal commitment to the regime and acceptance of the vulgarised doctrine of 'Marxism-Leninism' which constituted the ruling ideology. On historiographical issues of any sensitivity, party control remained absolute.

The following quote, though it comes from an intransigently hostile source, undoubtedly reflects the reality in the main if not in detail:

> The most distinctive feature of the Soviet system is that it subjects everything to plan. Some call this socialism; others prefer to give it

> another name. Be that as it may, the rule knows no exceptions. Hence, in the Soviet Union, scholarship is subordinated to a plan and is regulated and organised, as are industry, agriculture, or transport. What is more, this organisation and planning of scholarship is not confined to outward forms only – institutions, equipment and personnel – but extends even to the choice of research problems and to the method of solving them.
>
> There exist special state institutions – in the Soviet Union all institutions are state institutions – within which research is concentrated. Outside these establishments no one can pursue scholarship. Within their precincts the exercise of individual initiative is impossible, as in other areas ... Soviet historiography has no significance in itself, nor has any other branch of learning in the Soviet state.[23]

The last comment is undoubtedly an exaggeration, for the work of the Soviet historian of medieval and early-modern England, E.A. Kosminsky, was respected even in the West, but the main argument remains unaffected. Shteppa's volume prints the text of a Soviet official statement of 1960, which summarises the official position of the time and includes the following paragraph:

> A central task of historians of the USSR is to combat bourgeiois ideology and expose bourgeois reformist and revisionist historiography. Soviet researchers must rebuff hostile ideology in all areas of historical scholarship, above all those concerned with the history of Soviet society and recent history. Needless to say, this does not mean lessening the attention paid to current problems or to earlier periods of history. The reactionary forces of the capitalist world, which are falsifying history, must not be permitted to gain control over the study of remote epochs.[24]

Officially represented Soviet history comprised, in the words of one commentator, 'a creation myth with a happy ending'.[25] By far the most significant material emerging at that time was the *samizdat* history being written by dissidents such as Roy Medvedev,[26] which the regime harassed but refrained from persecuting so intensively as to destroy it. Alexandr Solzhenitsyn, whose position was different in that, apart from his expulsion, he wrote history in a fictional mode, is referred to below.

The 1960s revolution

Like any revolution this one had multiple sources including dissatisfaction with the prevailing historiographical tradition. It was also certainly related to the far-reaching changes in intellectual and general culture with which the decade is associated in popular memory. It marked a revolution in the objects of historiographical attention, in methodology and in the theoretical understanding of the discipline. Its impact was least felt in France, where the earlier revolution represented by the *Annales* paradigm was still in spate, and greatest in the Anglo-Saxon world where it was heralded by E.H. Carr's volume, *What is History?* Someone with a taste for rhetoric might define it as the first blast of the trumpet.

Carr never suggested that one could ever dispense with the Rankean method. Although new forms of evidence might be deployed ('the landscape is a historical document', Febvre once remarked) and new methods of handling it might be devised, the principle of starting with the contemporary sources and subjecting them to critical analysis and comparison as the basis for any eventual conclusions remained the cardinal rule. What was revolutionary was his attack on the status of the 'historical fact'. The argument deployed by Carr in the earlier chapters of his book presses this home with the aid of striking metaphors and analogies. He briskly and elegantly demonstrates the mythical nature of the historical fact and the impossibility of producing a comprehensive factual and neutral account of any set of events.[27] All the evidence in all the original sources put together for even a tolerably well-documented event – say, the Bolshevik Revolution – will still leave out an infinite amount of detail, which will forever be missing from the surviving record, and the accidents of war or other destruction may eliminate critical items of what has been recorded. The evidence when promiscuously collected together – say in the notebooks or the computer files of the historian or their research team – will not mean a great deal in its raw state. It will only take on meaning when selected, arranged and put in order by the historian. In other words it will be a construction, designed to answer certain questions and not others, but far from being an arbitrary construction: its framework will be determined by the character of the evidence and will carry more or less conviction according to how it handles that evidence. That is the essential nature of historiography.

Paradoxically perhaps, if in one sense there is always too little evidence because so much always gets left out, in another sense there is usually too much. For any individual to master all the surviving evidence for any but the briefest of historical episodes of the last half-millennium (and many before that) is an effective impossibility. Moreover, Carr points out, there may be in existence records of events which are assumed to have no bearing on the area under study and which no historian bothers about – until it is revealed that they are after all important and alter the understanding of particular developments.

Carr has sometimes been accused of being a Marxist, particularly by Arthur Marwick.[28] The claim is wholly unfounded. It presumably derives from the fact that Carr was inclined to mock historians and commentators who regretted the Bolshevik revolution and who indulged their imaginations with more congenial scenarios of what might have happened in 1917 had matters developed differently. His *magnum opus*, the massive multi-volume history of Soviet Russia from the revolution until the early 1930s, also, while exempt from any deliberate distortion of the evidence, tended to accept the inevitability of the regime and view it with a detached sympathy.

Carr addressed a number of aspects of historiographical theory (his later chapters are less convincing than the earlier ones) but the text that was to provide the greatest intellectual momentum to the revolution, though it had plenty of theoretical implications, made its definitive impact in terms of the conceptualisation of its subject matter and thereby the shift in focus it implied for the objects of historical study.

E.P. Thompson and *The Making*

Edward Thompson had been a member of the Communist Party Historians' Group, though not one of its most active, and indeed his interests were more literary than historical in what was then the strictly understood sense. He was employed during the 1950s as an extra-mural tutor by Leeds University and had been engaged in lecturing to adult classes in scattered towns and villages throughout the area on the English literary tradition.[29] Prior to 1956 he had published one book and that, significantly enough, was a biography of William Morris, the late nineteenth-century romantic poet, writer, artist and pioneer socialist.

Thompson drew upon that background and experience in compiling the monumental text in which he became engaged once the battles inside the CP had subsided with the defeat of the dissidents.[30] *The Making of the English Working Class* was published in 1963 (coincidentally by Gollancz, the same house as had published Morton's classic 25 years earlier). It represented something dramatically new in historiographical approach and method and, in the context of political, social and cultural developments of the 1960s, was to set the agenda for the most significant developments of the next several decades, though not purely by historiographical achievement. 'It was also the example he set ... He was a man of feeling, reason, and commitment, and he set for us the standard of what an intellectual should be.'[31]

The argument being presented here is that *The Making of the English Working Class* is the starting point for not one but several new historiographical traditions, all of which carry the marks of their source but which do not necessarily follow its current – some of which indeed flow in opposite directions to it.

To understand the enormous impact of this text, which has some claim to be, historiographically, the most influential of the twentieth century, it is necessary first of all to explore the manner in which it is constructed and how the text, running to over 900 pages, operates at several different levels. First of all, it should be stressed, Thompson abides by the basic Rankean rules. The breadth and depth of his original sources are most impressive. The core of these are found in archival documentation: Thompson has carefully searched the state archives relating to government repression of the radical movement in the late eighteenth and early nineteenth centuries, and along with information on the machinery of repression, has derived from the reports of spies and reformers, critically handled, valuable insights on how the radicals operated.

Published material and archive documentation, where extant, of the radical and trade union organisations themselves, has likewise been exhaustively consulted. So have memoirs and press reports from the establishment media as well as that of the incipient and emerging working class. In addition, reports of court proceedings, parliamentary debates (where available) and so forth, all play their part.

However, as Carr remarked, to praise a historian for using the best available source material is like praising an architect for using well-seasoned timber – it tells nothing about the manner in which they've handled it. Again in this respect, Thompson adheres to the basic rule of Rankean procedure. His sources are never taken at face value but are always critically interrogated, and the probable reliability of whoever created the document in question is assessed. Moreover, Thompson explains to the reader how the assessment is made – for example a government spy reluctantly conceding the virtues of the opposition is likely to have greater veracity than one who is manifestly playing up to the prejudices of his paymasters.

When, as in some instances, the historian is faced with a seemingly unbridgeable gap in the evidence Thompson is ready to concede the point. In certain important areas of his examination this is unavoidable. The Luddite movement, because it operated so deep underground and on the basis of oral communication, is particularly badly documented, and its surviving participants left no memoirs. Here there is an impenetrable barrier to historical investigation and it has to be acknowledged that this important episode in the history of working-class formation will always remain in obscurity. All that is possible is to advance more or less convincing hypotheses on the basis of such fragmentary evidence as remains available. The most exacting critic could not fault Thompson for treatment of source material.

Construction

The second aspect of this text which is relevant to our argument is the manner in which it is constructed. Its opening chapter is a dramatic narrative, an account of the emergence of the radical political movement in London in the early 1790s, inspired by the French Revolution. Thompson then proceeds to trace the sources of oppositional impulse, finding them in the background of religious nonconformity, the traditions of the 'freeborn Englishman' and his common law, and those of plebeian riot against particular intolerable impositions on the part of authority. The remainder of this section then goes on to recount the repression and eventual obliteration of this political movement in the course of the 1790s.

The next section of *The Making* changes key altogether. Under the heading of 'The Curse of Adam' it examines in detail the conditions of labour in the principal economic sectors of the late eighteenth century, giving particular attention, as it should, to agriculture, which constituted the largest economic sector of the period – and deals with some of the contemporary responses to these conditions, such as the practice of Methodism.

The section which follows is the main substance of the book, in four chapters and seventeen sections, with the heading of 'The Working Class Presence'. It covers the political developments associated with the emergence, or as Thompson would have it, the 'making' of a self-conscious working class between the imposition of the Combination Acts in 1799 and the 1832 Parliamentary Reform Act. It is linked to the earlier sections by Thompson's argument that the radical tradition established and then driven underground in the 1790s supplied the core of working-class political consciousness for subsequent decades and the realities of the life of the labouring poor, discussed earlier, its foundation. In a sense the book as a whole recapitulates the design of its opening sections, a specifically analytical and descriptive assessment (in the first place radical traditions and in the second labouring conditions), followed by an analytical narrative of sociopolitical developments.

Not surprisingly, *The Making* came under substantial attack from mainstream historiography, which severely queried Thompson's interpretations, particularly his assessment of the deterioration of living standards during the early nineteenth century, and his sarcastic comment that overall economic growth had translated itself for the working population into a few square yards of cotton, tea in place of beer and a great many articles in the *Economic History Review*. His description of Methodist ecstasy as 'psychic masturbation' caused grave offence. He was accused of treating the embryonic working class in a highly romanticised fashion, indeed of identifying one which had not really existed at the time in question, in short of having radically distorted the mass of evidence and documentation he had deployed.

For historians on the left *The Making* could not fail to be welcomed as an enormous achievement. Nevertheless from this angle too it was open to criticism, and not only in detail. There were two main aspects of criticism; they were linked, both were important and one was absolutely central.

The first concerns the time-scale upon which the interpretation is based. Thompson's claim is that the English working class was formed (or made) before heavy industry, especially engineering, had become seriously established, when the railway network had scarcely begun to be laid and before even machine textile production had reached its full development. Moreover, even within the time-frame with which he is concerned, the factory and mining labour forces are almost entirely neglected and their role downplayed: the concentration is upon handicraft and artisan production. Can this therefore really claim to be an account of the making of a working class in which heavy industry and mining played such central roles? Indeed few historians could now be found who would be prepared to accept that the English working class was 'made' by 1832. In that particular respect Thompson's argument falls down, but this, as we shall see, doesn't matter all that much.

The other aspect remains a major source of debate. Thompson is insistent that the working class was not (as both right-wing and left-wing standpoints had tended to assume) something that was secreted by the growth of machine industry in the manner that a silkworm secretes silk, the outcome of a mechanical process (in both senses of the term), but came about, was *made* by the conscious action of the human beings involved. As he puts it, 'The working class was present at its own making.' Thompson (implicitly rather than explicitly) rejects Marx's distinction (a Hegelian echo) between a class 'in itself' – a section of a population which can be recognised as a class because of a common relation to the means of production, but whose members do not have any consciousness of a common identity – and a class 'for itself' where the members recognise themselves as such and pursue conscious common aims. Thompson's controversial standpoint is that definition of a class *must* include class consciousness – in his view an agglomeration of individuals defined only by a common economic relationship does not constitute a class. The argument is explicitly presented that the working class can be regarded as having been made by 1832, regardless of later developments in the economy, because by that date all the necessary components had come into being which enabled this class to recognise itself as such, the final one having been the struggle for the franchise which culminated in that year and whose potential was betrayed by the middle classes.

'The Poor stockinger ...'

An important, and possibly, as it turned out, the most important target of Thompson's reinterpretation, was the then current 'Whig interpretation' of labour history, whether in its labourist or Marxist versions. This explicitly or implicitly viewed the labour movement as holding to a central line of advance issuing triumphantly in the trade union structures, the Labour Party and the welfare state of the contemporary era; a process now complete in essence (though doubtless capable of further improvement) in the labourist version, or still to be consummated in the Marxist one with a fully-fledged socialist hegemony. Along the way, according to this narrative, a variety of false starts and false prophets were encountered, but they were always transcended and the true destiny reasserted. The present was viewed as the natural and appropriate outcome of the past.

Thompson attacked this conception head-on; he was concerned with turning the spotlight on the losers as well as the winners in the historical process, for as he put it, they suffered the reality of their times and we did not, and in these times it was of course impossible to evaluate their situation or their potential in the light of later outcomes. Hence he was concerned to rescue 'The Poor stockinger, Luddite cropper, the "obsolete" handloom weaver, the "utopian" artisan, and even the deluded follower of Joanna Southcott' from, in the phrase which has gone ringing around historiography since the 1960s, 'the enormous condescension of posterity'. Placing them back upon the historical stage might easily have been done in an antiquarian mode, and these individuals or groups displayed as curiosities for amusement or pity – that would still have been condescension – but Thompson's approach was different. He presented them as both having historical validity in their own right and as contributing, no less than the successful winners, to a historical process which was the conscious creation of the people who made it and whose outcome was entirely opaque for the individuals who were engaged in it. Thompson was engaged in demonstrating the hopes, the vision, the creativity of obscure anonymous individuals, though he by no means neglected the 'stars' of the developing labour movement. It remains a powerful and affecting picture of what happened in England as class relations were restructured in the crucible of early industrialisation.

Whether or not Thompson had correctly interpreted the process of working class formation (or whether in fact any correct interpretation is possible) turned out to be largely irrelevant to the importance of this book – its long-term significance is rather to be found in the fact that it inspired agendas quite different from those pursuing the answer to that particular question. By 'seeking to rescue', and doing it in the context of a magnificent and awesome narrative and analysis, Thompson had in fact taken the initial step in putting a new conception of social history at the centre of historiographical debate.

The practice of 'history from below' was not a new one. It is to be distinguished from the history of subaltern classes and social layers which is merely descriptive of their plight, such as the Hammonds' writings in the early twentieth century on the town and the rural labourer during the industrial revolution, for it also means examination and the search for understanding of the action and resistance of such people in their confrontation with their circumstance and their exploiters and superiors. Since the 1950s George Rudé had been writing and publishing on the eighteenth-century urban crowd and particularly the Parisian *sansculottes* of the revolutionary era. In 1964, the same year as *The Making* appeared, so did Eric Hobsbawm's *Labouring Men*, a compilation of articles, many of which had been written in the 1950s. These were to be important texts, to which subsequent historians would make frequent reference, but it was *The Making*, with its sweep and grandeur, as well as Thompson's very distinctive style, much influenced by the Romantic tradition, which was to make the impact that put this new approach at the forefront of historiographical development.

Nonetheless, as even the two examples noted demonstrate, E.P. Thompson was not the only Marxist historian of major significance who was coming to prominence in British historiography during these years, for various members or former members of the Historians' Group were writing voluminously and starting to make a major impact. Christopher Hill was transforming the understanding of the seventeenth century and along with Hobsbawm and Rudé the writings of Victor Kiernan, Rodney Hilton and Maurice Dobb were appearing on history syllabuses.

Consequences

As emphasised earlier though, it was not merely a battle of the books. *The Making* made its appearance at the same time as the currents of political radicalism which were to characterise the 1960s began to flow. Thompson had been a leading participant in the original and British New Left, which had died shortly before his masterpiece appeared in print. It was quickly succeeded however by a *new* new left which was far more numerous, diffuse, eclectic and international and which gave the 1960s their distinctive political flavour.

In the developed West, in Europe and the US, Marxism of one sort or another (often spiced with anarchism) became the intellectual flavour of the decade along with the more concrete *praxis* of demonstration, riot and similar manifestations – which in France came close to overthrowing and did succeed in demoralising, an authoritarian regime. Mark Poster suggests that for the first time the events of 1968 allowed Critical Theory descended from the Frankfurt School to articulate with actual social forces – and advance a post-Marxist critique of society.[32] The personnel of this new left were drawn from diverse social locations, ranging from ghettoised urban African-Americans to Italian industrial workers, but the greatest number were students from lower middle-class backgrounds finding their way into an expanded higher education system. No single cause or circumstance will explain the climate of radicalism[33] and of course far from every student was affected. However, that the climate existed cannot be gainsaid, and one measure of this is the ready market, continuing into the 1970s, that existed for Marxist texts, which publishers snapped up as fast as they could be offered (not to speak of the numberless radical journals in circulation). These texts included editions of the Marxist classics, hitherto neglected texts by the classic authors and new writing by the new radicals. A specific and notable instance of far-reaching importance was the appearance of editions in numerous languages of Antonio Gramsci's works, which proved influential in many directions and appealed particularly to left-wing social historians; for his ideas, especially in relation to the concept of hegemony, provided an explanatory framework for the operation and intricacies of relationships between dominant and dominated classes much more sophisticated than anything hitherto available.

Britain

The generally hostile academic reception of *The Making* at its first appearance did little to diminish its popularity at large and it received the accolade, when published in a paperback edition, of appearing as the 1000th Pelican text in the renowned Penguin series. Apart from its intrinsic merits it had the virtue for left-leaning academics of focusing, in a particular and welcome manner, the interest in social history which was germinating in any case.[34] In 1966 at Ruskin College in Oxford, History Workshop (taking its name from the Theatre Workshop of Joan Littlewood) was established under the inspiration of Raphael Samuel, with principal collaborators Anna Davin, Alun Howkins, Tim Mason, and Gareth Stedman Jones. Ruskin College, which was attached to Oxford University but autonomous, had had a stormy history of its own since its foundation by nineteenth-century philanthropists, but served in the 1960s principally as a route into higher education, usually under trade union sponsorship, for working people who had missed out on the standard modes of entry in their earlier years.[35]

Samuel was one of the original New Left historians, a charismatic and unforgettable personality. His conception of historiography was that it should be a living and creative process linking the past with the present and encompassing the joint skills of academically trained historians, researchers, archivists, curators, students who were beginning to do original historical work – indeed all who had an interest in history, professional or amateur – and, where applicable, the subjects of the historical study themselves, via their criticism of and dialogue with the researchers and academics. He himself has indicated the kind of problems that had to be overcome:

> ... it was nearly closed down after a few weeks of existence, because of the then Principal's anxiety that the students were listening to each other's talks, instead of to a lecture; he was also dismayed that they were attending to questions remote from the examination syllabus ... at Ruskin then the very activity of primary research was a forbidden luxury, reserved for those who had been given the accolade of a university degree ...[36]

There was to be nothing sloppy or impressionistic about this mode of working – on the contrary the most rigorous standards of documentary criticism were to be observed, while at the same time 'theoretical perspectives ... certainly shaped the direction of its work'. Naturally, the focus was upon the history of working-class communities. From 1967 regular annual conferences took place at Ruskin, but when at the 1969 meeting Sheila Rowbotham proposed that people working on women's issues should get together later in the day, the suggestion was at first received with incomprehension. In spite of that, however, her initiative resulted in the organisation of a Women's Liberation conference in Britain the following year, generally regarded as the start of the organised movement in Britain, for which History Workshop, or at least its feminist component, could take the immediate credit.

For feminist historiography *The Making* represented both an inspiration and a challenge. It had pioneered a new style of historiography as well as opening up a new continent of historical experience for investigation, it had demonstrated what could be done – but it was only a matter of time before it was pointed out, quite properly, that *The Making* is unthinkingly male-centred. Women, though not by any means ignored, play a relatively marginal role in its record and interpretation of the epic accomplishment – it is surely unthinkable that in reality they were so absent and their contribution so insipid. Indeed the woman who features most prominently in Thompson's text is Joanna Southcott, the absurd early nineteenth-century prophetess who imagined herself pregnant with the messiah. Now to be sure 'the deluded follower of Joanna Southcott' (and presumably Joanna herself) features among those to be rescued from condescension, yet what does it indicate about the book's structure to single her out in such a fashion as the only woman to be given extended attention?

There were other symptomatic absences in that volume. Thompson also rescues another deluded group, the Cato Street conspirators of 1820, and gives them their honoured place in the record. As it happens, Davidson, one of the conspirators (most of whom ended their revolutionary efforts on the gallows) was black, which Thompson notes in passing, but mainly to the effect that he was not a Deist. From a different angle, working-class tories, people from the same social strata as Thompson's protagonists who were nevertheless upholders of the establishment, not inconsiderable in number, are virtually excluded from his definition of 'the people':

> ... whatever group you take as the hero of your epic – bourgeoisie or proletariat, or the blacks or womanhood – the result is always mystification. A history constructed around heroes and villains makes it impossible to understand how the past happened as it did.[37]

It is important to emphasise that these points do not reflect in any sense upon Thompson's integrity as a historian, nor do they amount to an accusation of bad faith. *The Making* is already a very long book, and of course it would be impossible to include everything. As Carr was so concerned to insist, the historian can only utilise a fraction of the evidence at his/her disposal, the more so when the canvas is as broad as the one with which Thompson was dealing. To highlight those absences therefore, is only to note that like every text, *The Making* is constrained by the time and culture in which it was written, when the issues which subsequently came into dispute were simply not present on the agenda.

Nonetheless the fact that the absences are precisely the ones indicated is not accidental, they are symptomatic and themselves a piece of historical or rather historiographical evidence. They are indicative too of a particular slant of Thompson's interpretation, namely that the narrative of the English working class's 'making' is constructed in terms of heroic models of historic accomplishment against adversity.[38] A feminist reading of *The Making* uncovers its limitations, as it would of any work of history written prior to the 1970s – and many subsequently. It is however one of the strengths of this landmark publication that it has been among the inspirations for the approaches which identify and analyse its weaknesses.

The US

Meanwhile in the United States social, political and intellectual changes of a momentous nature were in process. *The Making* had an enormous international impact, and as Peter Novick remarks, its publication occurred at just the appropriate movement to exert far-reaching influence upon the explosive developments about to occur in US historiography, linked as these were to developments on the streets. 'Surely no work in European history has ever so profoundly and so rapidly influenced so many American historians.'[39] Two separate though overlapping phases of development can be identified, both with a highly radical and disruptive thrust, both with American history as their focus, both contemptuous of received historical 'truth', both terrifying to establishment historiography – but nonetheless advancing differing and sometimes even incompatible agendas.

The beginning of the 1960s marked a change in the political climate. The 1962 Cuban nuclear stand-off, even if it had produced 'success' for the US had also brought home the apocalyptic dangers of uncontrolled nuclear sabre-rattling. The nuclear test ban treaty followed shortly afterwards, the first really significant agreement between the two sides since the onset of the Cold War – but at the same time escalation of the Vietnam conflict put US policy in an increasingly unfavourable light and the revolt against racial segregation and discrimination began in the southern states. As the CPUSA came to be perceived at large as more of an irrelevance than a menace, radicalism of an increasingly left coloration started to grow fashionable in the circles of educated youth.

It was therefore wholly appropriate that the initial focus of historiographical conflict was the hitherto received interpretation of the Cold War.[40] Studies by both academics and journalists delving into recent history uncovered evidence supporting the few lonely figures of the previous decade who had argued that US aims and actions were less than wholly disinterested; that America's commitment to freedom and democracy was ambiguous to say the least; and that the USSR no less than the US might have had legitimate security concerns. Before long, as academic establishments across the country erupted into student protest over a range of immediate grievances[41] and beyond that the implications of the Vietnam war penetrated onto the campus – not least with the potential liability of male students to be conscripted for a dangerous and unethical military enterprise – critique broadened to embrace the totality of US government and of bourgeois institutions. Government lying in the 1960s inspired scepticism about all official truth (and sometimes truth of any sort).[42] Novick quotes a statement by Barrington Moore which sums up the attitudes of uncompromising suspicion which had developed: '... in any society the dominant groups are those with the most to hide about the way society works'.[43] A new version of the American past was created – no longer a story of freedom and broadening opportunity, but one in which government, corporations, academia and a corrupt union establishment worked together to keep the mass of the public in subjection.[44]

As will tend to occur in circumstances of revolutionary expectations – and these undoubtedly existed among the campus radicals – tensions and differentiations made their appearance between those eager to draw the most extreme conclusions for both theory and practice ('Many believed that they might be on the eve of the American October')[45] and others of a more cautious disposition. In historiography the rift showed itself between an older left-wing generation with a professional loyalty to the discipline and the academy and a group younger opponents, graduate students or recently recruited faculty members, who in effect regarded higher education as a bourgeois conspiracy with structures designed to neutralise and assimilate radical elements. In the words of one of their prominent figures: 'Disgorge the bait of tenure and the problem of making a living can solve itself year by year.'[46] As he was to say later on: 'I sure wasn't going to ... score brownie points with senior conservative historians for the rest of my life to prove that, even though I was a radical, I could be a good historian too.'[47] Instead what he and others demanded was a 'relevant' historiography that would serve the interests of the disadvantaged and exploited.

Lynd was a senior figure among the ultra-radical historians. He was born in 1929, though he had come late to academic life, and he was selected as the figurehead, the presidential candidate in opposition to the establishment, for what was regarded as the strategic campaign to capture the leadership of the American Historical Association in 1969. Not that Lynd's opponent R.R. Palmer could in any way be accounted a conservative – he had written a sympathetic collective biography of the French revolutionary leaders of the Year II. In the event the radicals' project failed totally, not least due to poor tactics and organisation on their part. The older left historians were aghast at what they saw as the attempted destruction of the academic community and formed a bloc with the establishment. Even an anti-Vietnam war resolution was rejected (though one was passed without much fuss a few years later). The outraged feelings of this group was expressed by Eugene Genovese, who had been in his time a CP member and recalled all too well the intellectual excesses of Stalinism: 'The demand for ideological history, for "class truth" for "partisanship in science" has ended in the service of a new elite, a new oppressor.' He denounced the radicals in the most vituperative terms: '... fantasies of a revolutionary apocalypse – of a grand denouement that features the overthrow of the American state by an invincible army of acid-heads and suburbanites'. A sentiment echoed by E.P. Thompson himself:

> ... this New Left had elements within it that could be seen at once by a historian as the revolting bourgeoisie doing its own revolting thing – that is the expressive and irrationalist, self-exalting gestures of style that do not belong to a serious and deeply-rooted, rational, revolutionary tradition.[48]

Lynd, it should be said, accepted for himself the implications of his ideological stand and remained outside the academy.

The white heat of the fury died down in the subsequent decade, but it left its mark. The great majority of the young left graduates in history, whether they were on the activist or the 'disciplinary' wing of the trend, entered the field of social history and in the two decades between 1958 and 1978 in the US the annual output of theses in social history quadrupled, '... thoroughgoingly conservative social historians would be about as numerous as Republican folk-singers'.[49] Social history was unquestionably the cutting edge (and not only in the US), though the Genoveses insisted on the centrality of the economics and politics of class relationships and deplored 'massive attempts by social historians to deflect attention to the bedrooms, bathrooms and kitchens of each one's favourite victims'.[50]

For all that these radical historians, who were mainly white, male and middle class, envisaged a committed historiography that would champion the interests of the oppressed, they did not challenge the Rankean methodological paradigm which insisted that a reasonably veracious version of the past, in principle open to anyone, could be reconstructed by locating the appropriate evidence and interpreting it according to rationally-founded criteria. They simply presumed that the evidence they sought would be more revealing and their interpretations truer. These assumptions were to be put under scrutiny in the second phase of the historiographical revolution, associated with the infusion of identity politics into American historiography, just as the initial one had been with the politics of the traditional left.

Prior to the 1960s Black historiography had been as much an academic ghetto as the actual ones in which most African-Americans had lived, despite the endeavours of historians like DuBois and Genovese to make Americans as a whole conscious of this dimension of their heritage. The Black insurrection, commencing in the South then spreading to the North in the late 1960s, with massive urban rioting and radical politics such as represented by the Black Panthers, put Black historiography centrally on the map. Growing numbers of African-Americans, now finding it possible to gain entrance to major universities with the collapse of segregation and affirmative action programmes, were attracted to the profession. Controversy, sometimes bitter, was generated, particularly around what meaning should be attached to the slave experience and subsequently to that of segregation, what these had done to African-American families and what degree of Black resistance there had been. Methodologically however there was an even more significant development; the denial by African-American historians that anyone who was not Black was equipped to research and write about

Black history (even in relation to slaveowners) and the intellectual harassment of White historians who violated this prohibition – one of whom, Robert Starobin, even committed suicide. That incident was a particularly dramatic pointer towards an issue soon to feature prominently in historiographical debate – the question of the perspectives and the identity or identities from which the historian writes. The presumption that historical knowledge was a neutral datum that was in principle equally available to anybody – that, 'identity might propose but documentation disposed'[51] – could no longer be taken for granted.

The same question was raised with no less force in relation to the other main form of identity politics and practice which emerged in this period and soon made its mark on the academic milieu,[52] the women's movement. As in Britain, with the expansion of higher education in the 1960s and early 1970s, in the US the opportunity for women to pursue academic careers improved – though mainly at the lower levels. The feminist upsurge of the era, while certainly an international phenomenon, undoubtedly found its most intense expression in that country. Its implications were profound for every sphere of culture, and historiography was no exception. As Novick puts it, feminism was 'a transforming vision with revolutionary implications for the understanding of all human activity' and American feminism, more so than its British counterpart, maintained an 'avowedly perspectival' posture.[53]

Women's history was one thing, *feminist* historiography was something else. The former aimed to bring historical women, whether individually or collectively, into the historical light, out of the darkness in which male historiography had banished them, and this was the form of historiography which predominated among feminist historians in the early 1970s, of whom Sheila Rowbotham in Britain and Gerda Lerner in the United States are especially noteworthy examples. Although continuing to flourish, from the mid/late 1970s onwards this approach came to be overshadowed by the latter one, which had as its implicit or explicit agenda the reinterpretation of all history in a feminist perspective – and in the eyes of certain theorists that was a perspective incompatible with all accepted historiographical norms whether from the right or the left.

It would be misleading to suggest that Marxist-influenced social history was the only significant new form of historiography to make its appearance during those years. The US was also home to the strongest development of quantitative methodology[54] which marked an important new departure, assisted by the growing improvement in computer technology. It certainly produced significant new knowledge, but its leading proponents were infected with historiographical hubris and seduced into overplaying their hand by proclaiming the supremacy of 'cliometrics' – an assertion that the *only* valid way of carrying out historical research was by mathematical modelling, whether, for example, in the form of economic input/output measurement or the investigation of population records or voter preferences – all else was impressionistic fudge.

> The common characteristic of cliometricians is that they apply the quantitative methods and behavioural models of the social sciences to the study of history ... Cliometricians want the study of history to be based on explicit models of human behaviour. They believe that historians do not really have a choice of using or not using behavioural models since all attempts to explain historical behaviour – to relate the elemental facts of history to each other ... involve some sort of a model. The real choice is whether these models will be implicit, vague, incomplete and internally inconsistent, as cliometricians contend is frequently the case in traditional historical research, or whether the models will be explicit, with all the relevant assumptions clearly stated, and formulated in such a manner as to be subject to rigorous empirical verification.[55]

Such arrogance paid its price: having had one of their most elaborate texts systematically demolished,[56] they not surprisingly suffered a speedy descent into unfashionableness. Quantitative history naturally continues, but with a more modest demeanour.

The cutting edge

By the early 1970s, however much history in the traditional mode might continue to be written by what Arthur Marwick designated 'the straight-line professionals', the Western historiographical landscape had been transformed from its condition a decade earlier. A new historiography had taken centre-stage. Nothing of a comparable scope had occurred previously in the twentieth century or for that matter since the Rankean revolution. Regarding the new developments, two characteristics stand out. In the first place a recognisably left-wing orientation, mostly Marxist or quasi-Marxist, was evident both in terms of the people involved and the angle from which they approached their historical tasks. A left-wing intellectual and youth culture flourished and the new historians found an audience ready to hear what they had to say. Second, the transformation had taken place primarily and overwhelmingly through the medium of social history, whether or not a marriage was proposed with sociology as a discipline, as happened from time to time.

All the major developments described above had been in one way or another linked to social history (even when it was termed 'history from below') directly or indirectly. Had my summary been extended to other Western countries in Europe or elsewhere the same tendencies would be revealed. Here undoubtedly was the cutting edge, and some practitioners were incautious enough to assume that the ultimate, definitive form of historiography had been achieved at last. In all this historiographical upheaval, however, one central element of continuity remained: new subjects of history might be brought into the light, new sources to record their histories might be revealed, but up to the early 1970s the Rankean *method* remained unchallenged and behind it a Rankean epistemology – the presumption that historians individually or collectively could construct a coherent and accurate account of whatever was under study.

Then from the middle of the decade the revolution changed direction, and some might even suggest that it came to a stop. As left-wing agendas in the political domain crumbled or were unrecognisably transformed, a growing mood of disillusion with social history manifested itself even as it continued to be practised and its insights absorbed into the historiographical mainstream. Most strikingly a challenge was mounted, more radical than any yet experienced, to the foundations of all historiography as previously understood and accepted; to suggest that in pursuing historical knowledge or truth historians were chasing a phantom and that historiography as practised up to that point was a fundamentally misguided or even sinister enterprise. How that challenge originated and developed forms the subject of our third chapter.

3

Continuing Revolution or Counter-Revolution?

The material circumstances of the revolutionary years of the 1960s and early 1970s when historians (and academics of all sorts) enjoyed a seller's market did not last. The postwar global 'long boom', already faltering for several years, was finally pushed over and succeeded by recession following 1973 and the dramatic rise in oil prices occasioned by the Yom Kippur war. Instead of expansion, contraction became the governing reality for the higher education sector. The academic job market tightened dramatically and crisis supervened. Membership of the American Historical Association fell by a third in the 1970s, and by the early 1980s history PhDs in the US by a half, from a figure of over 1200 per year. At AHA conferences security measures had to be instituted to prevent applicants for the limited number of appointments on offer being sabotaged by rivals, while the Association felt compelled to advise graduating doctorates to think very carefully about the profession that they aimed to pursue.[1]

The British picture was not essentially different except in one important respect. According to Novick's account, one consequence of the crisis was to create in the US a new branch of the profession – the 'public historians'. These were individuals disappointed in their hopes for academic employment who instead took their skills into other sorts of organisations – commercial, governmental, community, voluntary – where historical analysis of one sort or another was required and funds were available to hire a historian. By 1980 there were enough of them in the US to make possible the establishment of a specialist journal, *The Public Historian*. The development was not universally welcomed among the US profession, even as a palliative to the employment problem, for fears were voiced that the historiographical integrity of such practitioners was likely to be compromised by the need to satisfy their clients, or by identification with the client's objectives, so that slanted and mendacious history was likely to be the outcome – fears not alleviated when some public historians publicly spurned the pretensions of academic objectivity as a sham and declared that identification of such a kind was no more disreputable than that of a lawyer defending a client.[2]

Outside the US no comparable occupational group evolved. British historians to be sure, if on a much lesser scale, engaged in similar activities, but nearly always as consultants from an academic base. There were, however, plenty of able but disappointed history graduates who would have preferred to pursue an academic and research career and were certainly equipped to do so, but who were unable to secure even part-time or temporary positions and had to content themselves with different sorts of employment – if any could be found.

The perceived attack on academic standards and liberties during the Reagan/Thatcher years would no doubt in itself have been enough to produce a strong climate of demoralisation, especially when accompanied by significantly deteriorating research and teaching conditions for the academic historians in post as relentless contraction was imposed on per capita resources. For those inclined to the left, however, there was worse to come. By the late 1970s it was clear beyond any real doubt that the radical wave of the 1960s and after had exhausted itself and that nothing momentous could be expected either from the established parties of the left, communist or social democratic, or from the disparate scatter of alternative leftist elements. The 1980s and 1990s went on to underline that lesson in the sharpest possible manner. Social polarisation intensified in the West. Some of the great tyrannies fell, but nothing remotely recognisable as socialism succeeded their regimes, whether in Russia, Eastern Europe or South Africa. The women's movement faded as an active force. Environmental awareness increased but environmental predation continued unabated.

It would be a crude distortion to suggest that the development of historical theory and interpretation during those years was normally connected in any straightforward or simple manner to events taking place on the social and political plane though it would come as no surprise to discover that periods of economic recession are likely to be linked with the advance of cultural pessimism, but it can be argued much more convincingly that such events formed the matrix in which the perception of historiography was formed; that they rendered certain options more attractive and likely to win favour, and others less so. Even the great *Annales* felt the force of changes in the intellectual climate. In

1994 the subtitle was changed from *Economies. Sociétés. Civilisations* to *Histoire. Sciences Sociales*. One should perhaps not read too much into an altered subtitle, but it does seem to suggest a lowering of historiographical sights. Under the influence of what has been referred to as the 'fourth generation' (following the exemplars of Febvre and Bloch; Braudel; Le Roy Ladurie), according to one sympathetic commentator a recession set in:

> The new *Annales* was trendy, following fashion rather than leading it. At the same time, the editors were in danger of departing from the philosophical perspective which had been 'essential since the journal's creation', namely the ambition to write total or global history by reconstituting 'all the social realities' which are in the background of any historical problem.[3]

In one area at least the link between political developments and the historiographical response was plain and unmistakable. With the French intelligentsia moving rapidly rightwards the ruling interpretation in France of the French Revolution, the neo-Jacobin version descended through Mathiez and Soboul, mostly shared by Marxists, was comprehensively challenged and generally regarded as having been overthrown. The attackers, of whom François Furet was the leading proponent,[4] using as their starting point the detailed investigations of British historians Alfred Cobban and Richard Cobb, and at first noting Marx's own reluctance to see the Revolution in this light, argued the implausibility of explaining the events between 1789 and 1794 in terms of a 'bourgeois revolution' and a key development in the unfolding of historical progress – for the revisionists claimed in essence that the revolutionaries were not bourgeois and the bourgeoisie not revolutionary. As the left's position, both politically and intellectually, darkened still further, so the revisions became bolder and the entire Revolution condemned as a bloody debacle without sense or purpose, with the Terror of 1793–94 implicit in the events of July 1789. Nobody was under any illusion that what was being attacked through the anathema pronounced against the French Revolution was the Russian Revolution and the entire left project of revolutionary social transformation. The communist left had used the Revolution to validate its own politics, the resurgent right now used it to discredit them.

Soviet historiography shared in the general decrepitude of the regime despite a brief moment of renewed hope in the initial stages of the Gorbachev reforms. R.W. Davies writes that: 'It would be wrong to conclude that the period up to the appointment of Gorbachev as General Secretary was one of complete stagnation.'[5] He cites some exceptions, but is in no doubt that they were marginal and the ruling philosophy in historiography was encapsulated in a Central Committee resolution of 1982, '... it is impossible to tolerate the publication in certain journals of works in which the history of the fatherland, the socialist revolution and collectivisation are presented with serious departures from the living truth'.[6] As Elizabeth Waters notes, 'the profession was in bad shape to meet the challenge of perestroika',[7] but nevertheless there was hope among the younger generation that the historical taboos of the past would be cast aside, a truer picture of the Soviet record would emerge and individuals still written out of the script would be restored to their place:[8] 'there is a ferment of ideas, often distinguished by originality and even profundity'.[9] 'Nikolai Bukharin in particular ... for a time commanded wide enthusiasm. In 1988 he was the hot essay topic for students of Soviet history at the Moscow Historical Archive Institute.'[10] But as the process of revision acquired its own momentum in the context of a collapsing economic infrastructure, the heroes of yesteryear were quickly transformed into the demons of today. Waters writes that the switch came quite suddenly in the spring of 1990:

> ... the popular press began to approach [Lenin] from a very different angle, as a man capable of cruelty and lacking in scruples ... Lenin's star has fallen so rapidly – from being the epitome of all things positive he has become a scapegoat for all social evils.[11]

After 1991 and the dissolution of the USSR the Russian historians favoured by the new regime and allowed favoured access to the archives – for these did not become generally open – spared no effort to discredit in every particular the Revolution and the Soviet 'experiment'. In their use of sources they may have been less mendacious than their Soviet predecessors, but in their ideological pronouncements they were scarcely less unanimous.

It is hard to imagine that, if instead of experiencing near-total defeat, the left had been advancing confidently and forcefully in the last quarter of the twentieth century the debates around historical understanding and the status of historiography would not be very different from what they actually are. That, it should be stressed, says nothing about the ontological status of the concepts and ideas in question. A standpoint has to be evaluated on its merits, not on its source of origin – and defeat of the left, as Marx was prompt to warn, is at least as likely as victory to generate truthful perceptions. My argument will rather be that the experience of defeat encouraged certain courses which are also, as it happens, largely though not altogether misconceived in their approach to historiography.

Adventures of the dialectic – social history in the backwash

Social history as developed in the 1960s, it is necessary to recall, had been the wellspring and fountainhead of all the new historical initiatives. In the late 1970s, on the face of things, its position was strong and consolidated. New texts reflecting its popularity and influence were spilling from the presses in a variety of countries, and what might be termed historical sociology, represented by writers such as W.C. Runciman, Michael Mann and Ernest Gellner, was achieving growing prominence and profile. New and important journals were founded at the end of the decade, either specifically in this field or closely aligned to it. They included in the UK the emanation of History Workshop, *History Workshop Journal* (*HWJ*), appearing at the beginning of 1976 and *Social History*, whose title is indicative enough, and in the US the *Journal of Social History*; *Comparative Studies in Society and History*; the *Journal of Interdisciplinary History*, whose emphasis was in the same direction and *Radical History Review*, the publication of the somewhat oddly titled Mid-Atlantic Radical Historians' Organisation (MARHO). Journals of similar orientation were also being established in Europe. In the words of Joyce Appelby at her 1998 AHA Presidential address, 'The new social history swept all before it for a decade and more.'

Yet scarcely had the discipline achieved this apotheosis than the foundations of its conceptual framework came under sustained internal attack in Tony Judt's renowned/notorious article in *History Workshop Journal* No. 7, of Spring 1979. The editorial in that number declared that he addressed 'a major intellectual and political confusion between social history and socialist history' Judt did not spare his language, and the article opens with the one-sentence paragraph: 'This is a bad time to be a social historian.' Other snippets of choice phraseology from his article are 'the astonishing use of sources alone should have consigned it [a particular article] to the editorial waste-bin'; 'A large part of the ignorance on display'; 'The subtle admixture of socio-biology and bad history is seductive'; 'It is hard to tell whether it is the pulp novel or biography which accounts for this sort of twaddle.'[12] These examples are far from unrepresentative.

Joan Scott and Louise Tilly, later renowned as feminist historians of a postmodernist temper, supply two of Judt's minor targets, but neither feminism nor structuralism are ever mentioned, and ironically in view of what was to come, a major thrust of the attack is directed against what he views as a strain of anti-Marxist positivism running through this historiography – the use of abstract and empty sociological jargon, dismissal of the existential realities of past lives and obsession with statistical validation, in short a pursuit of 'scientific' findings at the expense of significance. One particular significance which he alleges to be denied is that of political reality, political domination and class struggle, strongly suggesting that his targets are addicted to modernisation theory and Parsonian structural-functionalism – the reigning sociological fashion in the US during the 1950s and early 1960s.

> The next step is to place ideology, along with every other dimension of human thinking, in the category of epiphenomena. This daring move dispenses altogether with the need to discuss ideas. We should not be surprised to find Edward Shorter in the forefront of the move to this end. Logic and rationality, he claims, 'are just other words for ego control, the psycho-structural state of mind whence expressive sexuality flows.'[13]

Judt quotes the famous phrase used by the editor of the *Journal of Social History* that, 'When the history of menarche is widely recognised as equal in importance to the history of monarchy, we will have arrived'; and responds, 'Until monarchy and its implications are firmly placed back where they belong, in that position from which they have been dislodged by the non-history of eg, puberty, menarche ... social history will remain ... bereft of any social or theoretical value.'[14]

The institutional walls of social history did not fall at the blast of Judt's polemic and in the meantime continued pretty much as before. Indeed his article seemed to provoke very little response in the pages of *HWJ* itself – at least few were published. More contributors to the journal at that point were involved in a discussion which was simultaneously running on the theme 'Towards a socialist history'. Nonetheless a growing realisation began to form by the early 1980s, with the progress both of the discipline and of events in the wider world, that social history was not destined to marginalise all other forms of historiography, neither was it going to hold the intellectual high ground in the interests of the left even though conservatives like Geoffrey Elton or Gertrude Himmelfarb might continue to regard it in a threatening and demoniacal light.

Instead, Anglo-American social history, whether in its Marxist or more liberal or ideologically neutral variants had emerged by the beginning of the 1980s as a recognised sub-discipline within the wider historiographical community. The veteran Marxist historians had become eminently respected figures on both sides of the Atlantic, and in Britain Eric Hobsbawm made a significant public impact with his analyses of the background of Thatcher's rise and his participation in the debates then raging upon the British left as to the best political response. Practitioners of social and Marxist historiography continued to produce new knowledge and in some instances their volumes were a *tour de force* of insight and analysis. Yet the work was taking place within a climate of long-term historical defeat and the apparent total debacle of Marxism at the end of the 1980s. A further consideration that has been advanced refers to an internal dialectic within the discipline, itself producing a sense of its demoralisation. Social history, it has been suggested, was implicitly premised upon the assumption of progressive development, the 'forward march of labour' in Europe and, in the US, the creation out of diverse ethnic strands of an all-embracing democratic republic – *'e pluribus unum'*. If the debacle of the left called the former myth into question, how could the latter stand up to the realities of Black historical experience? In either case, whether in the present or in prospect, there was little to celebrate.

It was in such circumstances that in the 1980s a marked turn was occurring away from social history to cultural and intellectual history, with society treated as 'social text', as what remained of the Western left sought an approach that might furnish a key to unlock the manifest blockages in the political and social domains. Culture should be regarded not as what the *Annalistes* termed the 'third level', what remained once the more serious business of economy and society had been dealt with, but as constitutive and formative – the matrix outside of which economy, society and politics had no meaning. These theorists, their approach strongly influenced by developments in anthropological theory, exemplified Judt's complaint about neglect of state power (though for different reasons to those he had specified) which is not to say that the individuals who made the turns necessarily posed the matter to themselves in quite those terms. The founding figures are Robert Darnton and Roger Chartier in France (other notable figures include Gareth Stedman Jones in Britain and Luisa Passerini in Italy) . Darnton is probably the most generally known of these historians, having proclaimed:

> ... the arrival of a new method for the historical analysis of *mentalité*, one sensitive to the complexity of meaning generated by human beings. This new, intensely hermeneutic sensibility is founded not on behaviourist assumptions and quantitative methods but takes as its principle 'the notion of reading'. Darnton will read for 'meaning – the meaning inscribed by contemporaries in whatever survives of their vision of the world'.[15]

No historian could possibly take exception to that, but the character of Darnton's most famous essay, 'The Great Cat Massacre',[16] illustrates well the problems with this approach. In this Darnton discusses the account of an episode in which a group of mid-eighteenth-century Parisian printing workers are said to have embarked upon the slaughter of their employer's cat along with every other one they could catch in the neighbourhood. From it he draws far-reaching conclusions about the cultural mentality of French artisan workers at the time and even claims that it prefigured the more bloodthirsty episodes of the French Revolution. An interesting hermeneutic critique of Darnton's interpretation is advanced by Harold Mah,[17] but a more glaringly obvious point would occur at once to any Rankean – namely that Darnton erects a skyscraper of speculative interpretation upon a pebble of evidence. The account of the 'massacre' is derived from a single questionable source, a former printing worker who, as Mah points out, had ulterior motives for writing it. It is an open question whether the great cat massacre ever actually occurred.

Language and discourse are most evidently intrinsic to cultural practice and relationships, so a cultural turn was therefore well adapted to becoming a linguistic turn and finding inspiration in the writings of Hayden White, Michael Foucault or Jacques Derrida, to exchanging outlooks and methodologies with cultural and literary studies. Taken together with claims of radical cognitive differences between men and women or between different ethnicities, the components of the postmodern[18] discourse were well in place. To understand this properly however it is necessary to trace the linkages.

The French connection

At first sight it must appear rather odd that the notions which have underpinned the the turn in Anglo-American historiography about to be examined derived in the most part from France. It becomes explicable in the light of the singular part that French culture and politics played in the intellectual life of postwar Europe and which in due course fitted certain aspects for transatlantic export.

From the onset of the Cold War in 1947 the Communist Party was politically isolated and under siege, but it continued to exercise a widespread influence impossible to quantify but certainly very great, over the thinking of the French intelligentsia, and Marxism in a more general sense exercised a wider influence still. The deformation of French politics by colonial war up till 1962 further polarised society, and, if anything, strengthened the basic solidarity of an embattled left regardless of its internal divisions.

During the late 1940s and the 1950s the dominating, one might say the hegemonic, influence on the intellectual left (French culture as a whole, and influential far beyond France) in spite of frequent raucous opposition from the right and from the Communist Party, was the group around the *Temps Modernes* journal, especially Jean-Paul Sartre and Maurice Merleau-Ponty (the latter by the 1950s an ex-associate).[19] It was Merleau-Ponty who initially endeavoured to interpret twentieth-century history (and incidentally justify the Moscow trials) within the existential framework which characterised the group and the version of Hegelianism propounded by Alexander Kojeve in the 1930s – but Sartre was the more significant writer.

The philosophical text which established his reputation, *Being and Nothingness*, published in 1943, was a study of consciousness and the relation of individual consciousness with things, the body and other people, and was essentially the product of Sartre's thinking during the 1930s. Its focus was intensely individualistic. In the course of the War and Occupation, however, he was, as he himself acknowledged, seized by history, and was to spend the remainder of his life trying to comprehend it as a totality and to act politically in line with that understanding. In the period between 1945 and 1952 he and his colleagues tried to adopt left-wing postures independent of, though not hostile to, the world communist movement and the PCF. From 1952 to 1956, in response to the situation in French politics, Sartre, though he never joined the party, wholly identified his positions with those of the communists.

The events of 1956, particularly the Soviet invasion of Hungary in November, marked a break. Sartre condemned the invasion, cooled his relations with the CP and set out to accomplish the intellectual totalisation of history in a Marxist framework on which he had been reflecting during the course of the 1950s. The result was the *Critique of Dialectical Reason* (the title is a deliberate echo of Kant), which appeared in 1960 – a historical anthropology rather than a work of historiography – aiming to identify the conditions in which historical action can take place. (The second volume, which would have engaged with historical events and processes, was never completed.[20])The text contains interesting insights but overall can only be considered a heroic failure. It was flawed both in its intrinsic approach of speculative argument and the fact that it was largely composed under the influence of the stimulant drugs which the author used to push his work rate beyond all rational limits.

The general sterility of CP Marxism in France and the failure of Sartre's project of universal historical comprehension opened the way for the emergence and rise to prominence of structuralism as an approach to the human sciences that was deliberately and explicitly anti-humanist in the sense that social (and individual) behaviour was seen as being determined by the structures in which individuals were placed, leaving no scope for autonomous agency. Structuralism derived from a theory about language, which saw it as a closed system or structure in which elements of language relate to each other in a structure of signifiers (words) and signifieds (concepts) rather than, as we naively assume, extra-linguistic objects (referents).

A further implication is that other forms of social practices and interactions such as mythological systems, governmental or economic ones, or even subjective individuality, can be interpreted as analogous to language understood in this sense. Behind the chaos of observed social interaction there exist deep structures of an abstract sort, often themselves linguistically determined, which compel the manifest empirical realities to assume certain specific forms – for example the capitalist mode of production has a certain necessary abstract character, present throughout the various diverse and contingent social formations in which it exists. Marxism, whether in relation to philosophy, economics, sociology or history, undeniably constitutes a theoretical approach whose primary focus is upon social structures. Structuralism however was more than that. It was a theory of how structures (not merely economic; not necessarily social, possibly also discursive and linguistic) have a stronger ontological reality than human individuals. Indeed it could be said to reverse Mrs Thatcher's notorious phrase that 'society does not exist: only individuals and their families'; asserting instead that 'there are no such things as individuals, only structures'.

The anthropologist Claude Lévi-Strauss was the first of the major structuralist writers to rise to prominence, but for political significance its most renowned representative was the philosopher Louis Althusser.

Althusser was actually a member of the PCF, though not an orthodox one. Politically he was Maoist in inclination,[21] though personally tolerated because until very late in the day he was discreet, humbly acknowledged the theoretical strictures he received from the Party leadership and refrained from turning his theoretical disagreements into political opposition.[22] It is something of a puzzle to understand how he reconciled the extreme voluntarism of Maoist politics with the tenets of structuralism, which denied any significance to human agency. However there is much about Althusser's philosophy that is difficult to understand: his theoretical writings are almost impenetrably dense.

Althusser declared that individuals are primarily the 'bearers' (*träger*) of the structures which determine their reality and moreover that this insight could be reached only by means of theoretical analysis, 'theoretical practice', to which empirical evidence was irrelevant. As he phrased it:

> No mathematician in the world expects that his theories have to be applied before they are declared verified by the facts. The truth of its theorems are completely furnished by the internal criteria of mathematical practice. We would say the same of all the sciences.[23]

Hirsch encapsulates 'Althusser's structuralist renovation of traditional Marxism' as 'a consistent pattern of an almost transmogrified form of Hegelian essentialism'.[24]

The classic weakness of structuralism and not the least of the reasons for the brevity of its popularity was that it was a form of totalisation that could not account for change: it could not convincingly articulate, despite Althusser's statement that the class struggle is the 'motor' of history, a mechanism that produced the constantly mutating character of historical reality, which in recent centuries at least has been its most distinguishing aspect.[25] Structuralism turned out to be a short-lived phenomenon, but the detour through this philosophical experience was far from irrelevant – for it supplied the foundation for the far more significant poststructuralism which came increasingly to the fore and was to exercise a much greater impact on English-language historiography and its theoretical articulation.

Once again it is not a question simply, or perhaps even primarily, of intellectual lineage. In between the student insurrection and political upheaval of May 1968 in Paris had intervened, when it had appeared briefly that the most romantic visions of the most extreme political romantics were within measuring distance of being realised on earth. Lévi-Strauss was dismayed, at least intellectually. 'Imagination to power!' was scarcely a structuralist slogan and he regarded the *gauchistes* as Sartre's philosophical children rather than his own. Althusser maintained a low profile. By contrast many of the leading names of the poststructuralist wave to come were attached to the non-communist left during these weeks.

After the inevitable denouement of disappointment (it would have been the same even if the Gaullist regime had fallen) followed the no less inevitable bitter disillusionment. That too played its part in discrediting structuralism's pretensions to scientificity – theoretical practice had shown itself to have little leverage upon practice in the real world. What we may term a poststructuralist consciousness had already been germinating among certain French literati, the most significant being Jacques Derrida, Michael Foucault and Roland Barthes, during the 1960s; its dispositions were embodied in a few small intellectual circles, notably the situationists, and the aftermath of 1968 provided opportune conditions for it to blossom. It took from structuralism the emphasis on the centrality of language but repudiated any idea of producing scientifically guaranteed knowledge, the 'restricting claims of objectivity';[26] to the contrary the emphasis was upon the irreducible fluidity of meaning or even the proposition that meaning inevitably defeats itself in relation to texts no less than to the non-textual world (if any such thing existed).

While major names on the whole maintained a token allegiance to a loosely defined left, their French intellectual disciples, in many cases reacting with vehemence against their shattered hopes, made a complete transition to the political right. The anti-Soviet atmosphere in which they had matured politically was distilled into a vituperative hatred of all things Marxist and indeed against left-wing principles of any sort. This however was not the route taken in the main by Anglo-American followers of the poststructuralist trend, and is not our concern.

Anglo-American responses

Instead, as poststructuralism, together with the looser concept of postmodernism, made its way into English-language intellectual discourse and the themes of Derrida, Barthes, Baudrillard, Bachelard, Foucault, Kristeva, Irigaray et al. were picked up across the Channel and across the Atlantic by a new generation of academics and writers, a general left-wing orientation was preserved, in forms adapted to these very different academic and intellectual milieux and in senses which would have scarcely been recognised in any earlier left culture. The postmodern tide flowing from France first reached the areas of literary and media studies, where it prevailed mightily (with a number of delectable academic scandals along the way), then inundated cultural studies more generally.[27] Part of the attraction was that by attacking the conceptual foundations of science and philosophy it claimed a warrant for literary critics to put themselves on (at least) an equal footing with scientists and philosophers. 'Theory is now ubiquitous within the academy and most academics are at least familiar, if not altogether comfortable, with the presentation of complex and at times bizarre notions in difficult languages and opaque styles.'[28] Or as Novick phrases it, '... it was all but impossible to have a serious critical encounter with much recent work in European intellectual history without being fluent in Derridese'.[29] Unable 'to break the structures of state power, post-structuralism found it possible instead to subvert the structures of language'[30] – and from the early 1980s the style began to make its way into historiography.

Here to some degree however we are running together structuralism and post-structuralism, though outside their French setting the distinction is less important. Structuralism enjoyed a brief delayed vogue in British left wing academic circles during the early 1970s as translations of Althusser's work became available and the echoes of 1968 still sounded more sweetly than they did on the continent as the British state itself was shaken by industrial conflict on the mainland and revolt in Northern Ireland. It was in 1978 that E.P. Thompson, under the title *The Poverty of Theory*, launched a polemical assault upon Althusser and his British acolytes. He denounced (rather than criticised) Althusserian structuralism, demonstrated that it was a caricature of historical materialism and declared it to be no more than a theoretical codification of Stalinism, a possible source of inspiration for the Khmer Rouge and most emphatically not to be considered in any sense whatever an element of the left. By contrast he vindicated the approach which he had embodied in *The Making*, that people do indeed make their own history (if not in circumstances of their own choosing), that they exercise thereby independent agency and that they do so through the assimilation of human experience in all its dimensions.

In his theoretical strictures Thompson did not mention, and at the time was probably unaware of, the volume which had appeared two years earlier and was to become central to the historiographical debate, Hayden White's *Metahistory*. This seminal text was more structuralist than poststructuralist in inspiration ('for those who care about such things', as Richard Evans significantly put it) and is examined below in Chapter 5. What we are concerned with at this point is its impact, which though slow in making itself felt was eventually very considerable in affecting the terms of the discussion. The essence of White's postulates was that the literary form in which historians framed their work largely determined the manner in which they interpreted their empirical material. It can without too much distortion be regarded as the founding charter of historiographical postmodernism, for if its arguments are taken seriously they provide a warrant for anybody wanting to maintain the impossibility of any verifiable truth being located in history and that radically variant interpretations of historical evidence are both incommensurable and equally legitimate, for historiography is essentially a literary enterprise. In the words of Stanley Fish:

> 'It [uncontrolled interpretation] relieves me of the obligation to be right (a standard that simply drops out) and demands only that I be interesting (a standard that can be met without any reference at all to an illusory objectivity).'[31]

Fish is a literary critic rather than a historian but his point would apply no less to historiography if White's thesis is justified – and that point remains valid even if few have consciously employed the latter's categories as a guide or model for their own historical writing. Novick suggests that he has had little *practical* effect outside the sub-discipline of European intellectual history and not all that much within it,[32] but the conceptual ripples from his texts have spread in ever-widening intellectual circles.

A poststructuralist writer (though he denied that he was one) who *has* influenced the content of certain historical work to a considerable degree and historical theory to a greater one is Michael Foucault on account of his methodology (which bears comparison with that of White), his conceptual innovations and the fact that in his writings he applied these to the historical sweep of the past several centuries and did so in a forceful and provocative style. Deconstruction is a term appropriately applied to Foucault's handling of history, as it is to the way other poststructuralists deal with literary texts. In spite of the complaint by some of his admirers of a 'wilful disregard of Foucault's work' by the historical mainstream[33] references to it are to be found everywhere, not only in discussions of historiographical theory but in social history texts. Even as early as 1978 he was among the 100 most cited authors in the *Arts and Humanities Citation Index*.[34]

Why postmodernism?

Whether in historiography or in other disciplines the great majority of poststructuralists/postmodernists would regard themselves as being on the left in some sense of that overworked term. Certainly this is the perspective in which they tend to be seen by the political and academic right wing, which views them as subverters of Western values and Western culture. The postmodernists (we will now operate with this portmanteau, albeit unsatisfactory, term) certainly see themselves for the most part as standing in opposition to the powers-that-be, and one of the most frequently cited vindications of the postmodern sensibility is that it gives a voice to previously marginalised and subordinated subjects. Although a few exemplars of postmodernism, particularly Lyotard and Baudrillard, have given it a quietist slant – if all certainty has collapsed, what's the point of struggling, so enjoy the ride – the implications of such a posture have in general been very little pursued.

Postmodern, deconstructionist writing with few exceptions almost always contains at least the hint of an activist dimension, the suggestion, if no more, that adoption of its perspectives would produce benign social or cultural consequences. Frederic Jameson may not be a postmodernist in any simple sense, but his writings have probably done more than anybody else's to give the notion theoretical credibility as the inescapable 'cultural logic' of the current era – and Jameson is a Marxist, though of a Hegelian temper.[35] Other central figures, including even key names such as Derrida and Spivak, also claim at least in part a Marxist lineage. The claim may well be spurious, but the fact that it is made is itself significant. It appears to me that postmodern stances towards the natural and human sciences – what one writer has termed 'this postist philosophical reflex'[36] – have attained credibility and popularity because they provide theoretical underpinning and justification for two distinct though connected responses to the dilemmas of present times, both of which can be viewed as politically radical in some form or manner.

In the first instance, they can appeal to proponents who aim to rescue particular categories of people – communities, cultures, collectives however defined – from the condescension of contemporary Western culture, and incidentally of course their histories likewise. Such an agenda is supported by theories which deny the validity of an accepted 'universal' definition of reality, which show how the dominant ideology has constructed 'the Other' and insist upon the equivalent appropriateness of ways of seeing and acting deriving from the margins. So far as historiography is concerned, it is in the area of feminist history that this approach has been most influential and it is also central to what has become known as postcolonialism.

The second form of response (linked to the first) which is sustained by the postmodern sensibility can be judged to be a form of displaced political activism. As far back as the 1970s Edward Thompson had accused the Althusserians of indulging in 'theoretical practice' as an excuse for evading engagement in practical practice. The postmodern outlook, as we shall see, explicitly renounces the overarching historical schemes, the 'grand narratives' which have sustained the left in its various shades since the nineteenth century. The global triumph of global capitalism is accepted as permanent and irreversible, as least over foreseeable time horizons. A form of Anglo-American postmodern, purportedly radical, politics and political commentary has grown up on this soil – one might mention the names of Richard Rorty, Anthony Giddens, Geoff Mulgan – but that is not our concern. In the historiographical arena (the same being true for cultural or literary studies), running through much of the writing coming from the postmodern direction is the hint or implication that by deconstructing categories and concepts, or else pursuing 'construction of identity within real lived power relations of class, gender and race',[37] one is somehow also doing all that is possible to confront the structures of power in the academy or in society and undermine the major source of strength of the imperialist West.[38] According to Appelby, Hunt and Jacob between 1976 and 1990 English-language publications on French history declined by half in the political and diplomatic spheres and by a quarter in economic and social history, while publications in intellectual and cultural history doubled. In France itself the proportions for political/diplomatic and economic/social decline were a quarter and a half respectively, while those in intellectual and cultural history doubled there as well.[39]

From the later 1970s an explicitly feminist historiography came to overshadow the earlier efflorescence of women's history, for 'simply to substitute women's history for mainstream history leaves us prisoners of precisely that pernicious status as "other" to which mainstream history has assigned us.'[40] Many names could be cited in this connection, but probably the most significant is Joan Wallach Scott, probably because she is both an aggressive theorist and a prolific and very able historian.[41] History written from women's viewpoints need not imply controversial epistemological claims:

> ... women's history challenges mainstream history not to substitute the chronicle of the female subject for that of the male, but rather ...

> to explore the varied and unequal terms upon which genders, classes and races participate in the forging of a common destiny.[42]

Someone recently has written a history of the world from a Basque viewpoint with the implication only that this corrects other versions of world history, not that it is incommensurable with them. But the tendency of feminist historiography has been otherwise. Novick quotes a statement which sums it up:

> If we assert that nineteenth century women in particular, and perhaps all women, constitute an autonomous female culture, we assert that women's separate sphere and experiences are the product, not of men's ghettoisation of women but of women's distinctive psychosexual and biological nature. We then unambiguously proclaim women's absolute Otherness.[43]

'Absolute Otherness' implies that feminist historiography cannot therefore be judged by the same protocols as have been evolved to operate in a masculinist and patriarchal profession, in other words that it cannot properly be subject to the reckoning of male Reason. Beard and Becker's relativism had returned in spades. The application of a similar style of reasoning to ethnic categories produced the phenomenon of Afrocentrism and its attendant historiography – indeed this ideological construct was erected largely on the basis of historical interpretations. This has been, however, very largely a US phenomenon. The arguments in relation to particularist historiography of various sorts are considered in Chapter 7.

A consistent thread which runs through all the dimensions of poststructuralism in historiography (and elsewhere) is the repudiation of 'totalisation' – of far-ranging historical explanations, especially those of a Marxist sort. These are condemned even as 'totalitarian' for imposing patterns of explanation upon the chaotic flux of the past, an illegitimate scientism. 'Essentialist' is used as a condemnatory term for any form of synthetic understanding or interpretation. Instead, 'Megill ... has shown to what extent postmodernists from Nietzsche up to and including Derrida want to extend aesthetics over the entire domain of the representation of reality ... Content is a derivative of style.'[44] Ankersmit proceeds to evoke for history the metaphor of a tree with a trunk, branches and leaves, to suggest that the 'trunk' and 'branches' are beyond conceptual reach and recommend therefore that the 'leaves' are the only proper object of historical study.

What this might mean in more prosaic terms is that historiography should focus exclusively on what has been termed 'microhistory' – the study of very limited and localised areas of investigation (with no necessary adherence to Rankean norms – plausible invention being permitted), since this is the only basis upon which even a provisional and aesthetically satisfying 'truth' might be established. Examples of this might include Emmanuel Le Roy Ladurie's *Montaillou*, Natalie Zemon Davis's *The Return of Martin Guerre*, or Carlo Ginzburg's *The Cheese and the Worms* – though it should be pointed out that neither Le Roy Ladurie not Ginzburg are postmodernists in any sense, both are impeccably Rankean in their methods and the latter has vehemently denounced postmodern metaphysics. It would possibly occur to a reader that it might be hard to get a grasp upon what was going on in Montaillou without some understanding of the role of the Catholic Church in thirteenth-century Europe; similarly, some centuries later, with the heretic miller of Friuli in Ginzburg's account; or the events in *Martin Guerre* without an appreciation of the reality of European peasant life generally in the early modern era. The same considerations apply to *any* microhistory – it can never make sense without being placed in all the contexts which draw down accusations of 'totalisation'.

In the course of the twentieth century's last two decades postmodernist or deconstructionist history has been increasingly taken notice of, but it was mostly (not entirely) statements of theoretical intent or explication rather than historical works exemplifying them that provoked attention – the world still awaits the deconstructionist equivalent of *The Making*. Indeed the enormous proliferation of historical theory, other than in certain restricted fields, has taken place to a large extent in isolation from what most historians have actually been doing (we will suggest some of the reasons why in the following chapter). Historians and historical theorists work in well-nigh separate disciplines in spite of the energetic efforts of some postmodernist historians, such as Patrick Joyce, to effect a junction.[45] But in the main when a historical journal features a discussion on postmodern themes, as occasionally happens, it is something of an event, as was the case with *Past & Present* and *Social History* in the late 1980s and early 1990s, in the latter case running through the first half of the decade. The *American Historical Review* from the 1980s was also giving the theme some attention, but this was relatively marginal. The developing debate however could be followed in detail within the pages of *History and Theory*,[46] a journal published from Wesleyan University and dating from 1960. It had begun by aiming to promote the 'new social history' in terms of linkages with sociology, but had developed in an increasingly theoretical mode, its editorial direction coming principally from philosophers. As early as 1981 Raphael Samuel was expressing disquiet at an emergent tendency[47] and in 1990 Bryan Palmer published *Descent into Discourse*, which I believe to have been the first full-length attack on postmodern theory in historiography.[48] In the following year Raphael Samuel produced an eminently sane and balanced assessment of the position so far reached in an article (it was intended 'to be continued' but, sadly, never was) that is seldom referred to in any of the subsequent discussion.[49]

Samuel acknowledges, with reference to *HWJ*, that while its method retains affiliations with conventional academic practice, perhaps 'we have been more deeply influenced by the deconstructive turn in contemporary thought than some of us care to recognise'.[50] The question of the labour process which had dominated early issues had all but disappeared, while issues of representation and identity politics had grown increasingly prominent. A look through the contents of issues of the journal since 1995 will show a further strengthening of this tendency; one which is even more marked in what might be reasonably regarded as *HWJ*'s equivalent across the Atlantic, *Radical History Review*. However Samuel's comment of 1991 still appears apposite a decade later:

> Historians, by contrast, though increasingly divided by the multiplication of sub-disciplines, have remained apparently immune to epistemological doubt. Under the influence of discourse analysis new problematics may have been taken on. But however novel the subject matter, the method of enquiry and mode of argument – as Joan Scott complains in her critique of feminist history – are quite traditional. At least for those engaged in writing and research, the fundamental worth of history, whether as a record of what happened in the past, or as knowledge-based representation of it, remains unquestioned.[51]

Another more metaphorical way of expressing the matter is that the main citadel of mainstream Rankean-inspired academic historiography remains intact, although the deconstructionists have managed to entrench themselves in some of the outworks. This warfare-derived metaphor is suggested by the bitterness and antagonism which has characterised some of the debate that has been conducted between the rival positions since 1990, reflecting in the historiographical field a still wider debate on the validity of the postmodern agenda throughout the human sciences.[52]

The spectrum of positions in historiography are nicely delimited. Bryan Palmer is the most uncompromising enemy of postmodernism in all its shapes and varieties. He is castigated by Richard Evans for a crude and vulgarised understanding of the issues. Evans is in turn castigated by Joyce Appelby and Lynn Hunt for similar vices on his part. They themselves are attacked by Patrick Joyce who accuses them of treating postmodernism as 'a sacrificial lamb thrown to the New Right',[53] and even Patrick Joyce is insufficiently dynamic for Keith Jenkins. In some (indeed in a not inconsiderable number of) respects the ferocity of the encounter was inescapable – two incompatible mental universes or visions of reality are in conflict; adherence to one means repudiation of its rival. In certain other dimensions, as both Evans and Appelby et al. have argued from their respective positions, a degree of mutual interchange and even reconciliation may be possible. The following chapters attempt to examine these themes in some detail and to do so from angles which have hitherto featured little in the discussion. The current institutional context is our starting point, for institutions have a life of their own, they reproduce themselves through their structures and personnel, and on their character depends whether historiography itself lives or dies and what kind of historiography flourishes or gets smothered at birth.

4
Institutions and Personnel

Quite clearly the character of historiographical production cannot be separated from the institutions in which it takes place, the constraints, demands and imperatives which are placed upon the producers as well as their relationship with their audiences, both actual and potential.

What we are dealing with here is what might be termed investigative historiography, productions which attempt to interrogate the past, answer questions and, to indulge a cliche, 'extend the frontiers of knowledge'. Our discussion therefore avoids productions such as school textbooks and narrative accounts aimed at a mass market – which (in the former case) hold no pretensions to do other than relate broadly accepted interpretations or (in the latter) demand the reader's confidence in the author's credentials without the necessity of arguing a case or considering alternative possibilities.[1]

To remain for a moment with mass culture however; of all the academic human sciences, history is the one which comes nearest to everyday forms of discourse – even technically sophisticated historiography can be quite readily taken on board by readers with the average levels of education found in advanced Western societies; and indeed a number of such monographs have become mass-market best-sellers. There exists in Britain a number of history (even subdivisions such as a medieval history and an ancient history) book clubs, and they are not aimed at an academic readership. There are no counterparts for sociology or economics for example, and the idea of such would be faintly ridiculous. In Britain too there flourishes the semi-popular illustrated historical monthly periodical *History Today*, successful since the 1950s through many changes of format – though an attempt in the 1980s by the AHA to establish an American counterpart had to be abandoned through lack of funds.[2] Historical discussions and presentations, often of a quite sophisticated sort, are regular features of mainstream TV broadcasting. There is clearly an interaction between academic and popular historiography, but our concentration here is upon the academic end of the spectrum, the environment in which questions are raised and new evidence interrogated.

The central institution is of course the university. The physical sciences, for all the importance of the university for those as well, have major research institutions outside the academic orbit and connected to commercial concerns, the human sciences do not, naturally enough, since they do not produce the same sort of commercial payoff. The establishment of the university as the central locus for historical research is a feature that is also attributable to the example of Leopold von Ranke – after his time major historians working independently of the academic sphere were a dying breed.[3]

This process is generally referred to as the professionalisation of history, though 'institutionalisation of historiography' might be more appropriate. After all it is far from clear why an individual working outside the academy and dependent for income upon historical output which will sell on the market isn't better entitled to be termed a professional historian than any academic. Nevertheless it is clear that since the middle of the nineteenth century the overwhelming bulk of serious historical output has been undertaken by people who have been employed by universities or equivalent institutions. Out of these has grown a web of institutional bodies and practices which form the context and the environment for historical production and which largely define the meaning and purpose of the discipline. The aim of this chapter will be to examine the manner in which the institutional reality affects or determines the understanding of what is meant by history, dictates the nature of its composition and forms the subjectivity of the historians involved. It is worth keeping in mind that, as with physical scientists, there are more practising historians alive today than have lived in all the past centuries taken together.

Scientific method has been referred to previously, in essence an achievement of the past four centuries, largely coinciding with modernity and of course intimately and reciprocally involved in its creation. It does not float free in the cultural atmosphere but is embodied in a tradition among its practitioners and the tradition in turn is embodied (although it did not begin in such a manner) in institutions concerned with developing it. The historiographical tradition constitutes one particular domain of that tradition of scientific method, with the academy as its focus. An image frequently canvassed in the past and now much mocked, is that every humble practitioner is adding a brick or bricks to the edifice of knowledge and understanding. It would be truer to say that every practitioner has behind him or her and draws upon, whether consciously or implicitly, a web of understandings and insights from the past as well as the present – history in other words is a collective enterprise in time as well as space – the same is true for any area of scientific endeavour.

The gravitational pull of the academy is enormously strong. Even the projects of radical and innovative (even counter-establishment) history such as History Workshop have come to centre there – even if the original home of History Workshop was a somewhat unorthodox institution it was still connected to Oxford University. There are of course practical and material reasons why this should be so; universities possess the facilities, equipment and personnel for pursuing historical investigations, regardless of whether these are of mainstream or unorthodox varieties, in a way which is simply unavailable in any other context. Clearly of course – and this applies to every country – not all higher education institutions are equal in the sight of the Lord, or, what is more to the point, in popular or academic perception. To gain an appointment as a historian (or any other sort of academic) at Oxbridge, is not the same thing as to gain one at, say, Preston, difficult enough though even the latter is.[4] As Russell Jacoby puts it (for the point applies with equal force to the US):

> ... these studies suggest that where one went to school and whom one knows, not what one does, are critical. Not quality of work but social relations permeate academic success. Of course, this can be exaggerated: a deadbeat graduate of Harvard University may fare no better than one of Middle Tennessee State University. There are no guarantees or automatic awards; yet an examination of academic careers indicates a decisive tilt towards the well connected. The professor at Black Hills State College in Spearfish, South Dakota, who received his doctorate from the University of South Dakota and who has published a fine book with the University of Nebraska Press, will be professionally invisible. The professor at Princeton University who received a doctorate from Yale and published a dissertation with MIT Press, will be an esteemed expert, regularly cited, invited and funded.[5]

Teaching

Except in rare instances however, historians do not devote the greater part of their time and energies to carrying out historical investigations. Rather they are occupied to a large extent in passing on accumulated historical knowledge and understanding, in a pre-digested form, to potential trainee historians, the undergraduate students on the programmes for first degrees, from whom will be selected those deemed to be equipped for serious training. The US situation differs from the British in that in the former accredited academic historians will conduct a large proportion of their teaching in the graduate schools, for which there are no real British equivalents. The nature of what is passed on, however, is significant. Historians do not, or at least they certainly ought not to, provide a series of facts and narratives to be ingested by rote. Instead they make their students aware of the disputed interpretations, the ambiguities and gaps present in any historical reconstruction – of the perpetually unfinished nature of the historical account while at the same time demonstrating (unless they have raised the banner of postmodernism) that historical knowledge is possible, even if difficult, to attain. They should do this both in their verbal interactions with their students and by the guidance they provide to the relevant texts (increasingly today in non-book form), whose study should indeed form the main content of the programme. The texts themselves should reinforce the message that what is being presented is never a finished body of knowledge but interpretations subject to infinite questioning and refinement.

This represents perhaps a somewhat idealised picture of what is going on. It is not without truth, but is far from being the entire truth. In actuality both undergraduate students and their tutors are subject to the pressures being felt throughout the Western world, and probably with greatest intensity in the UK, ironically,[6] where centralised government is in a stronger position than in the US to enforce an agenda, towards the commodification of higher education and its subjection to managerial and quasi-market forces. The tutors will be under intense pressure to accommodate the maximum number of students with the minimum expenditure of resources, and their mode of teaching and assessment will inevitably be affected – the tendency will indeed be to teach history as a finished body of knowledge to be absorbed mechanically, with only the most cursory gestures to the complexities of historical understanding, in a fashion which makes for ease of assessment.[7]

Students for their part are primarily motivated to pass successfully through the assessment procedures rather than to develop their historical temper. This, it has to be acknowledged, has always been the reality, but as pressures in the employment market intensify and the qualifications required for equivalent appointments are constantly enhanced,[8] it can only become more pronounced, as indeed it has been doing since the 1960s. In the outcome of the British final exams the student is stamped with a grading which is unalterable and will largely determine their life opportunities. Nor is this the end of the matter. In previous eras of happy nostalgic memory, students may have been pressured academically, but those in Britain and Western Europe (the US situation was always different) generally enjoyed tolerable financial security. At the beginning of the present century matters are very different. Unless they come from unusually privileged backgrounds most students are obliged to moonlight, to find part-time employment (usually of an ill-paid service sort) in order to fund their study. Moreover, the percentage of part-time students has greatly risen and is continuing to rise. They may be in a better financial position than their full-time academic counterparts but their struggle to cope with their academic obligations is made correspondingly more severe. In any event the current realities of undergraduate life are not likely to do much to cultivate the historical imagination of those who are exposed to it. That the obstacles are nevertheless overcome is a tribute to the determination and single-mindedness of those who do so.

From the other side of the relationship the academic teaching staff are likewise exposed to growing pressures and stresses, as repeated surveys make repeatedly apparent. The pay, though not unreasonable in absolute terms, is well below that of employees in comparable occupations and is constantly tending to slip further behind. Recent proposals regarding the UK are likely to make the situation worse by instituting a star system with far greater financial rewards for academics at the top of the tree of fame and recognition and inferior ones for those at the bottom, creating a pool of resentment, bitterness and division which academic managements, hurrying down the managerialist route, will prove only too happy to fish in.

Discontent over pay however, is almost certainly not the major grievance or source of stress and tension. Rather it is the proliferating jungle of bureaucracy and trivial paperwork which the expansion of higher education without equivalently expanding resources has imposed upon them. Teaching quality exercises, research assessment exercises (all enormously time-consuming), commercial-type targets and kafkaesque procedural labyrinths surrounding assessment and the introduction of new programmes, added to vacation times being constantly whittled away have largely destroyed what used to be one of the principal attractions of academic employment – personal control over working time outside formally scheduled interactions of teaching or meetings. Again, keeping the principal aim and purpose of a historical education in view amidst the swirl and pressure of these impositions and distractions requires a considerable degree of resolution and determination.

The tutor will, in the process of disseminating historical knowledge and inculcating an appreciation of the ambiguities and uncertainties of historical practice, be endeavouring to enable students to begin their initial steps towards developing that practice on their own account. Until the final year of their undergraduate programmes (and in the US probably not at all) that is unlikely to involve the handling of original source material except in the form of selections from prepared volumes of extracts. Rather the focus will be on critical reading of secondary texts and developing the ability to discriminate between historians' interpretations and distinguishing good argument from bad even when conclusions are less than fully substantiated. To take an example – the merits of Thompson's approach in *The Making* can be developed at length and from numerous different angles even while it is being demonstrated that his concrete conclusions do not stand up to detailed empirical investigation in some instances or conceptual critique in others.

Nowadays a great many history programmes include a separate course in historical method, which attempts to raise in specific forms the kinds of issues and problems that this text has been discussing. If these are well handled they do indeed introduce undergraduate students to the problematic concerns which have in the past three decades or so pressed themselves so strongly upon the consciousness of most historians and reinforce the understanding, which should be implicit throughout the entire programme, that historiography is always unfinished business, both empirically and conceptually. In the American graduate schools a course in historical methodology used to be central to the programme, but that appears to have become a victim of the theoretical conflicts and cultural wars. For all that, the tradition gets transferred by conceptual osmosis and the majority of US trainee historians still emerge as good Rankeans (as a glance at the *American Historical Review* or any mainstream journal will confirm) – though a significant minority do not.

No matter how they differ in detail, what all undergraduate history programmes are doing, however, and this, in the eyes of postmodenrists, is their principal weakness, is inducting their students into a historiographical tradition which, although it varies throughout the Western world according to national circumstances, possesses nonetheless an essential unity deriving from Rankean origins and certain common conceptualisations and understandings of historical development since the classical era, of which periodisation is probably the most evident aspect and deeply engraved into every historian's consciousness. Periodisations can be challenged, but, interestingly, the first thing a historian who is doing that has to undertake is an explanation of why the challenge is being mounted. Programmes and textbooks, while their periodisations differ in detail, tend to follow the traditionally accepted ancient, classical, late antiquity, medieval, early modern and modern segments. Similarly, though there are bitter disputes over questions of relative importance concerning aspects of historical development, these disputes occur within a broad area of consensus nevertheless. One might well write a serious socially and culturally grounded history of evolving fashions in clothes, or the development of children's toys, but anyone who tried to argue that either of these areas had the same determining influence on historical progression[9] as are legitimately, if disputably, ascribed to the economy or ideology, would never be taken seriously. It is presumed (probably correctly, but who can say for sure?) that ideology and the economy are matters of major import, probably of determining importance, even if their relative import is a matter of contention, but that fashion and toys are not; that they are no more than relatively minor aspects of the others. The undergraduate at honours level or graduate school will also learn, mostly through acquaintance with the critical apparatus in the texts that he or she is using, what are the protocols for establishing a claim or assertion and the chain of logic and argument which leads from source material to the printed page (or video clip or web page) of a finished text.

Postgraduates

The socialisation into a tradition which is instilled at undergraduate history levels (particularly outside the US) is strengthened, developed and brought to perfection (it is hoped) in the case of postgraduate, especially research, students. Indeed, postgraduate assessment is designed to establish whether it has in fact been brought to perfection and the candidate can be appropriately recognised as a member of what J.H. Hexter once called the 'historians' guild'. To even be admitted to postgraduate study, let alone to be funded for it, a highly appraised first degree is generally considered to be minimum requirement, in other words, evidence that the candidate has already well absorbed the values and procedures of the historiographical tradition. Postgraduate study, if it is a taught programme, will involve the absorption of further considerable elements of knowledge, but this will be undertaken from an enhanced critical and questioning perspective contextualised by keen and constant awareness of historiographical problems. In addition it will certainly involve a major element of independent work devoted to a particular problem or area of study and requiring intensive engagement with original sources, almost certainly archive ones.

When the postgraduate degree is being pursued by research alone (in the US it never does, in Britain it may do so, though nowadays a minimum of taught training is usually required), these procedures entirely dominate the entire enterprise. The student is required to select a theme, position it historiographically, identify the gaps in established knowledge (i.e., what cannot be located in the existing secondary sources) and then to use the information derived from primary sources in order to fill it. The undertaking is an arduous one – the many bitter complaints and even litigation by research students is witness enough of that. Financial pressures continue in most cases to exercise a baleful influence, for the funding available to a postgraduate student will seldom suffice to cover basic necessities, particularly if family responsibilities also come into the picture. Usually for full-time research students, however, there is another option available, though that brings problems of its own.

As part of their induction to the universe of professional history research students will normally be encouraged, perhaps even required, to join the ranks of casually-employed academics (in this being no different from their counterparts in other academic disciplines). They will be offered teaching and assessment responsibilities – remunerated at part-time rates – and while no one would deny that this does constitute valuable experience and a very useful background should they eventually have the good fortune to occupy a full-time academic post, it can be, and usually is, very time-consuming. All the more reason therefore in their research to stick to established methodological tramlines and practices, since less space is left for innovative thinking and exploration. The teaching they undertake will naturally be on courses devised and controlled by established academics and they will have to convey knowledge and discuss interpretation more or less according to prescription – the only dimension of real flexibility will be in the style in which they do so. In short, their success as part-time teachers (which can have long-term consequences when references come to be written) will be judged for the most part on how effectively they perpetuate the tradition among the undergraduate population.

The postgraduate researcher's focus is, however, necessarily upon their area of investigation, and in the case of history this is invariably a single-person project, for a postgraduate thesis appearing under two or more names – a collaborative investigation – is quite unheard of. The research thesis is intended to demonstrate that the candidate is capable of independent research and construction of new knowledge according to the accepted criteria of the tradition. It is an exercise which in principle will be repeated from project to project should the candidate become a fully-fledged academic historian.

The standard procedures are well established. The candidates, who will be assigned a supervisor or supervisors to provide guidance and to ensure that the appropriate procedures are followed, will have as their first undertaking to read all feasible 'secondary' – i.e., already published – texts bearing upon the area under investigation, and in this fashion to acquaint themselves thoroughly with all that is reputably established about the background of their theme. For example, suppose that the thesis is about the British seamen's strike of 1966 with particular reference to the position of the women who were related or connected to the men involved. In the first place it would be necessary to consult the various histories of the Wilson government as well as relevant texts relating to the development of the British political system, such as Keith Middlemas's. More particularly, material on the shipping industry for the relevant period (and much earlier) would be required, as well on the seamen's union, including both monographs and journal articles. Any journal articles which might exist on the strike itself would of course be especially relevant. These processes are made easier nowadays than they used to be, thanks to the existence of computer technology which can instantly scan library catalogues for relevant keywords. All such sources give pointers to potential other ones via their bibliographical apparatus. Uncovering secondary sources particularly relevant to the women's situation on this theme would be much more difficult – as far as I know none exist – though texts dealing with the position of British women in general during the 1960s would be relevant. A check must be made to determine whether any other unpublished theses exist in this or nearby fields. Finally, a search on the web to see whether any material not in printed form was available there would nowadays be obligatory.

Having exhausted the secondary sources (as far as humanly possible) the researcher would turn to those which hover in the twilight between primary and secondary, namely the newspaper press. Straightforward enough in principle, the actual process is enormously tedious and time-consuming on account of the number of newspapers requiring to be consulted and the exertion of searching through a span of several weeks in numerous bulky bound volumes, even if the newspaper, like *The Times*, should be indexed. Here however useful clues might be picked up on the particular dimension being researched – the women's position.

It is only after all of this, however, that the real work would begin, namely the plunge into archives of unprocessed documentation. In this case there are three clearly evident principal ones within the frame, namely government records from the relevant year available in the Public Record Office at Kew, and the records of the National Union of Seamen and the TUC so far as these are available. Two other archive sources which might be important and would have to be considered, however, are those of the Labour Party and the Communist Party lodged at the National Museum of Labour History in Manchester. The archives of local authorities in the seaports might in some instances also be worth considering.

Finally, since the events in question occurred less than 40 years ago, there are numerous people involved who are still alive. An element of oral history would therefore have to be introduced into the research. A selection of participants would need to be interviewed and their recollections considered if the project was to have any credibility. Clearly, given the constraints of time and numbers it could only be a selection and a lot of time would be needed locating potential interviewees and trying to ensure as representative a selection as possible. The researcher would have to acquire some knowledge of interviewing technique and of oral history, its potential and its drawbacks, before this part of the project could begin. However it is here that the most valuable data for this investigation would be obtained, for here the women can speak in their own voices and their role and situation can be brought to the forefront – and possibly in some instances the interviews might be supplemented on the part of the interviewees with offers to make available relevant private correspondence – though that of course should never be requested.

The purpose of all this arduous toil is only accomplished once the gathered evidence is processed into a historical reconstruction aimed at enhancing understanding of the events or possibly modifying previous interpretations. It has become customary for a thesis to begin with a chapter reviewing the evidence and sources employed, both primary and secondary, as evidence of the labour expended in the search and a guide to the material's strengths and limitations. This however is only a preliminary. The researcher, well before any serious research has begun, will naturally have worked out a plan of what the eventual product will look like, in other words will have begun the process of emplotment (to use a term to be discussed in the next chapter), which will of course be developed and very likely altered in the course of the writing and affected by the character of the evidence which is accumulated. Conceptually it is usual to distinguish the collection of evidence from its transformation into a finished piece of work, as though they were processes separated in time, but in reality they will almost always proceed simultaneously – the thesis will be constantly being rewritten and replotted as the pieces of the evidence jigsaw are moved around and, unlike material jigsaws, fitted in different positions and with different neighbours.

What the researcher is doing is selecting evidence (for much more will have been inevitably accumulated than will be useable) according to criteria which will always have to be explained, interpreting its significance (likewise according to criteria) and arranging the result into continuous prose incorporating both a narrative and an explanation/interpretation, very possibly in the form of an argument endorsing certain claims and rejecting others with greater or lesser assurance. To this will have to be attached a critical apparatus, substantiating every significant claim on the basis of identified source material. In principle this enables claims to be checked and occasionally this might happen in actuality – but rarely unless controversial assertions are being offered. In practice the professional good faith of the postgraduate is relied upon. I can recall when writing my own PhD thesis wearily ploughing through the fragmented records of the Glasgow Custom House and doing calculations on a pre-electronic calculator, having the discreditable thought that if I simply invented the figures it was most unlikely that anybody was going to double-check them. Invariably, in order to give a conclusive demonstration of strict adherence to what the cited evidence will support, the critical apparatus of the postgraduate thesis is far fuller that any real necessity requires – indeed it will almost certainly be considerably inflated just to be on the safe side.

Eventually, though seldom in the initially specified three-year period for full-time doctorate postgraduates, a thesis of around 100,000 words will have been produced that will represent, for better or worse, an original contribution to knowledge by following the specified procedures. Form as well as content will be taken into consideration. No formal requirement in the documentation accepting the candidate for postgraduate study is likely to specify that it must be written in prose, but it is scarcely likely to satisfy the examiners if it appears in alexandrine couplets (and would lead to severe censure for the supervisors). Moreover, a connected narrative or argument is insisted upon. The thesis must be coherent and structured – any candidate who wrote it in the manner of Foucault would be failed, unless their argument were exceptionally brilliant, in which case they would be given the opportunity to rewrite it in the approved manner. Provided all the conditions are satisfied the thesis is passed by its examiners and the candidate becomes accepted as a bona fide member of the historical guild (in the US a PhD is virtually an absolute requirement) – though that ensures no automatic further rewards.

In any event an enormous amount of time, resources and nervous stress has been invested in producing the doctorate, particularly if the candidate also has family responsibilities. In effect he or she has mortgaged their future to it. With every postgraduate history thesis or dissertation the tradition has been newly endorsed and reaffirmed. In the course of producing it the apprentice historian has been socialised and acclimatised to Rankean standards. It has been suggested that one of the reasons for the cultural continuity of psychoanalysis is that trainee psychoanalysts have to invest so much of their time and money in the training that they gain a powerful incentive never to break with it (though they may found new schools within the tradition) even if intellectually they realise later in their careers that it is nonsense. The same point could with some justice be made regarding academic historians in Western cultures, but it is important not to stretch the point too far. The manner in which psychoanalysts are socialised does not in itself prove that psychoanalysis is fraudulent – that must be shown on other grounds (which I believe it can be) and the way in which the historiographical tradition is inculcated does not in itself prove it to be unsound. It may still, regardless of the social and occupational pressures which it generates, nevertheless be valid (as I believe it is). Indeed it is inconceivable to imagine a science which was not embodied in a tradition of some kind interlinked with years of arduous training for its practitioners and which naturally creates a disposition in favour of perpetuating the tradition.

Employment

Achievement of the doctorate is, unhappily, not the end of the sad story, for while prior to the 1970s that qualification was virtually a guarantee of academic employment at some level, the contracting of the market ended that situation long ago, and other than in exceptional cases the best that even a brilliant PhD graduate can immediately hope for are temporary appointments, perhaps a string of them. Not much imagination is needed to appreciate the strains and tensions attendant upon having to live from year to year in the uncertainty of teaching or research contracts being renewed or secured elsewhere, but such are the nature of current circumstances and central to the growing casualisation of employment in higher education. Again the intellectual consequences are clear – the individuals concerned are put into a position where to diverge too radically from the mainstream consensus is also to put one's future employment prospects in peril when the time comes for renewal.[10]

In Britain it is not exceptional for such appointments to be made while the research is still in process if the individual is promising, and therefore for individuals pursuing research degrees (or at least in their latter years) to do so in their own time while engaged in employment at their institution (perhaps, if fortunate, with a concession on teaching hours to assist them to complete the degree). In which case an additional burden is created – not only does teaching performance have to come up to scratch and one's colleagues and superiors satisfied in other dimensions, but the anxiety over possible failure to complete can be an ever-present source of demoralisation.

Finally, through a combination of dedication, intellect and a large measure of good fortune the aspirant historian may at last achieve the glory of a full-time, putatively permanent appointment – which is not quite the same thing as guaranteed tenure – the security of such appointments varies from country to country and where it exists is normally awarded only after a probationary period.[11] Academic tenure is currently under pressure in both the UK and the US, the latter being engaged in developing a system of 'non-tenure track' appointments. Currently throughout the developed world (not to speak of other parts) historians face what is very much a buyer's market – there are far more qualified historians than there are such posts available for them, as departments face blocks upon any expansion for staff or even compulsory downsizing.

Even when established with relative safety, however, the historian faces a range of circumstances which surely detract from undivided attention to transmitting existing, and constructing new knowledge. The 'publish or perish' syndrome has been around for a long time, but of late has intensified dramatically, a feature in Britain symbolised especially by the recurrent research assessment exercise of the 1990s.[12] The grading system introduced here – together with the financial rewards and penalties for departments which accompany it – pushes historians (as with all academics) into frenetic publication and hastily accomplished research projects. The idea of the Research Assessment Exercise (RAE) was to stimulate both the quantity and quality of research output, but being inimical to well-thought out, long-term projects that require above all space and deliberation, its effect has been entirely counter-productive and its main impact has been to widen severely the divide between the most prestigious centres and all the others. Failure to perform acceptably in this sphere (that is, acceptably according to the imposed criteria) may lead to the dread fate of being stigmatised as 'research inactive' with the result that the unfortunate will be encouraged to move on or have their card marked for the future.

Accomplishing significant research, whether on an individual, collaborative, or a team basis, is difficult without the underpinning of significant resources, even if that should only be of time – but even time can cost money, if it means hiring someone else (probably a post-graduate student) to fulfil the teaching duties of the historian who has been released for more intensive research. Better still if research assistants and funding for travel and other expenses, such as clerical assistance, can be secured. What this means is that applications have to be made to research funding agencies of various sorts. Preparation of these is in itself a tedious and time-consuming operation, and moreover once again acts as a constraint, for to improve one's chances one is naturally best advised to stick to conventional methodological tram-lines.

Not only is it research which is subject to bureaucratic scrutiny but teaching too has assessment exercises imposed upon it, involving vast quantities of paperwork and producing eventual meaningless gradings. In addition, academics will be expected to take responsibility for areas of administration relating to their courses and to their department's research. They will be required, for example, to act as admission tutors, exam tutors and a range of similar highly responsible functions and large swathes of time are spent in writing research funding applications. Publishers have to be bargained with and conferences have to be organised. They will be obliged to become highly computer literate. It is natural that established historians will seek promotion in the academic hierarchy, either within the institution that they are currently attached to or by advancing upwards to another. Their success or otherwise in this endeavour will depend in most instances primarily upon research credibility as measured by publication output, but also upon performance in the various other dimensions sketched above. Once promoted, administrative burdens multiply, in Britain particularly in the older, more collegial, less managerialist universities, where head of department posts and deanships, even vice-principalships, are filled on a rotating basis rather than as permanent salaried appointments. Nor are such responsibilities exactly unknown in the US. Looked at from outside it sometimes appears surprising that any research at all manages to get done. In the whirl of audits, inquisitions, administrative duties and uncertain futures, the pressure to stick to safe and traditional courses and formats in teaching and research is all too readily understandable. It is always easiest to proceed along existing tramlines.

Archives

Without archives historians are all but helpless.[13] It is certainly possible to produce relevant and important historiography without the use of archival sources,[14] but the Rankean approach effectively requires that these are the central foundation for the production of articles and monographs in most historical areas. The initially striking fact in relation to archives is how numerous they are – so far as I am aware no count or estimate has ever been made, even for a single country. They range in size and importance from the imposing grandeur of state archives to the most humble collection of the papers of insignificant clubs or societies – and that is not counting the innumerable archives of private persons. (I leave aside theoretical discussions among archivists regarding what counts as a record.)[15]

Even a single modest public archive – say, to take an example with which I am familiar, the Museum of Labour History in Manchester – will contain much more documentation than any one person could examine in a lifetime. Searching among them at random would amount to no more than an exercise in futility. Historians have to know what they are looking for before they even begin to search – i.e., documentation referring to a particular theme or subject – and also where it can be found. The organisation of an archive is therefore all-important, and establishing such organisation is an archivist's central responsibility.

It is not, however, by any means the end of their responsibilities – being an archivist requires skills and judgement of the highest calibre. Perfecting the archive's organisation and listing its holdings in a useable catalogue is only the beginning – the archivist has to be constantly on the lookout for fresh relevant material becoming available which can be appropriately added to it. In some instances, depending on the nature of the archive, there may be routine accretion – possibly official records no longer in working use which are conveyed to the archive at regular intervals, such as British government records under the 30-year rule.

Often enough, however, it may be necessary to exercise initiative, as when important commercial records are in danger of being dumped upon the bankruptcy or takeover of the firm which generated them – and countless parallel kinds of instance for institutions or individuals.

Not only must the archivist possess a thorough and detailed historical knowledge of the archive in order to undertake these responsibilities, but a great deal of technical expertise is needed as well, for paper records are delicate material and even in the best of environments are subject to decay. The later the manufacture of the paper the faster it decays, thanks to increasing amounts of acid used in the mass-manufacture of pulp paper, so that even with careful preservation newsprint retains its original character for less than a century and otherwise crumbles much faster still.[16] The physical condition of archives is therefore of the highest importance – temperature, humidity and light intensity have to be strictly regulated. Care has to be taken to regulate the behaviour of researchers as well, so that their handling of documents does not damage them. Marking them would of course be unthinkable, but in addition in many instances it is also forbidden to use pens of any sort when taking notes, lest ink contaminate the paper – only pencils are allowed.

What is possibly the most sensitive aspect of all of an archivist's responsibilities follows on from the fact that with the best will in the world not everything can be preserved. Physical capacity is never infinite and in a well-established archive shelf-space is always at a premium. When new material is added, organised and catalogued therefore, some degree of weeding is very likely to occur (in the case of the Public Record Office (PRO) this will have already been done by the government departments concerned).[17] What to reject – and possibly destroy – requires the most precise and delicate degree of judgement. The judgement would appear to be simplest in cases where documents are duplicated – for example two sets of minutes for the same meeting – yet it is never possible to be wholly certain that two apparently identical documents really are identical, there could just possibly be important differences not evident to immediate inspection. Any other case is even more complex and there can never be complete certainty that the right choice has been made.

It happens from time to time that a historian for contingent reasons is presented with a coherent set of records that have not been lodged in any official archive – an individual dies, for example, and the heirs (for whatever motives) make their papers available to researchers. What is in question in these cases is a private archive of manageable proportions, that has not been catalogued and very possibly not even organised. That sort of thing however is the exception, and the overwhelming bulk of historical research is done in public archives of one sort or another that have been subjected to the processes sketched above. Our concern is with the theoretical implications (if any) which this holds for historical method.

One clear implication is that the reconstruction and understanding of the past rests upon the foundation of a highly elaborate technical apparatus devoted to the handling and preservation of the documentary record embodying the evidence upon which that reconstruction is based. The same in principle applies to the non-paper record – to the National Film Archive as much as to the PRO. Hence these records do not reach historians in an unmediated form – they have undergone a process of selection and arrangement even before the historians begin to exercise their own, and moreover the historians are compelled to follow the tracks laid down in the arrangement and cataloguing of the records. They can deviate if they want and look at apparently unrelated material, but then they are proceeding into what is, from the point of their project, a trackless wilderness, and if they come up with a lucky find that is pure contingency.

The point cannot be emphasised enough: the reconstruction of the past and the process of establishing knowledge about it is a collaborative enterprise; the evidence on which the reconstruction is based does not present itself neutrally and passively to the researcher's consciousness nor is it simply lying around waiting to be found – before the historian even gets to it it has been classified, arranged and put in order by other hands, and so another layer of selectivity has been interspersed between the initial selectivity on the part of the consciousnesses who generated the documentation and the further selectivity which the historian will inevitably exercise in dealing with it.

On the face of things such realities might appear to reinforce deconstructionist claims that the historian's products are pretty arbitrary affairs bearing little if any relationship to the reality of what went on in the past. Any such conclusion however betrays a simple slippage of logic. Because a reconstruction is and must be imperfect, provisional and subject to almost infinite amendment, it does not follow that it is necessarily inaccurate in essence and has not established a degree of reliable knowledge and possible understanding. The argument is that what we may term the intrinsic indeterminacy of the historical evidence is best viewed as a challenge to be confronted rather than an impassable barrier to knowledge.

Journals and Publishers

Historians' output (leaving aside their interaction with their students, previously considered) assumes two principal forms, though these are increasingly supplemented by various usages of the electronic media. The forms of text in question are either, like this one, the standard book (single or multiple authored and of various grades of scholarly achievement) or the journal article. Of these two it tends to be the latter (though this is a matter of considerable flexibility) which is accorded the greater prestige in the academic subculture. Any well-established historian as a matter of course will be expected to produce a constant output of books and/or journal articles, though for those at the beginning of their careers achieving publication can present considerable obstacles.

Academic historical journals vary enormously in character and standing, with the *Annales*, though somewhat diminished from its previous glory, probably regarded as being still upon the apex, followed by the great national historical journals established in the nineteenth century and in continuous publication since then.[18] Some journals are supported by academic/commercial publishers, some by university presses and some remain free-standing, though this is an increasingly difficult economic feat. Some are general in their scope and some are specialised. To be regarded seriously by the guild however, any historical journal must fulfil a certain condition, namely, that the articles published by it must be refereed – in other words they must be sent before publication anonymously to at least one outside reader expert in the area which the author is treating who will confirm (or otherwise) their academic credibility. What appears in the journal is consequently filtered in the first place by the editor(s) who judges whether a piece is worth having refereed, the referee, then the editor again who, if it receives a favourable opinion, still has to judge whether the journal has room for it. The implications of this practice for perpetuating the standard and accepted methodologies of historiography – let alone the maintenance of accepted interpretations – will be evident enough. It is hard to imagine that an article, whatever the merit of its content, would be accepted by a refereed journal if it were written in the style say, of Hunter S. Thompson or Will Self. Indeed, if E.P. Thompson had boiled down the argument of *The Making* into a journal article it is most unlikely that it would have been accepted by any of those being published at that time.

Journal editors receive for their consideration far more proposals and articles than they can hope to publish, and even the number of those acceptable in principle well exceeds their available space. The criteria of selection is therefore a very important consideration in whether a particular historical interpretation or extension of knowledge finds its way into the public domain.[19] We should therefore consider hypothetically what the criteria of selection are likely to be and, again, what possible theoretical implications this may carry.

A number of considerations will be taken into account in making an editorial decision. The editor will appraise the offered article in the first place for whether it throws new light on the field, either because it documents previously unknown aspects of the issue or because it reinterprets existing knowledge in a manner to alter or improve previously accepted understanding or to try to settle an issue in historiographical dispute. If it passes these tests it can be judged suitable for submission to the referee(s). These latter of course do not hang from branches – they are busy people doing their research and most likely writing their own articles or books – and they aren't paid (assuming that the journal has resources for such a purpose, which it doesn't). Securing appropriate referees can therefore be for an editor a matter of considerable organisational toil requiring in addition delicate diplomacy and he/she may have to make the best of what is available rather than come up with the most ideal expert.

A lot hangs upon the referee's opinion. He or she must assess (if it had been beyond the editor's competence to do so on a first inspection) whether the article presents a coherent argument and whether the evidence cited is reliable and appropriate to the theme. If the editor has been favourably impressed in the first instance the referee will be expected to confirm or refute that judgement. Naturally if the author is presenting a case which contradicts the referee's own historiographical standpoint, then the latter will have to exercise a lot of principled detachment not to allow this to affect their assessment of the argument's quality. Of course the editor will be aware of the temperament of the referees he or she selects (or is able to recruit) and will have endeavoured to try to avoid the situation of submitting a piece to a referee known to be opinionated and adamantly hostile to the writer's viewpoint – unless it happens that the editor is ill-disposed but, not being able to claim sufficient expertise, simply wants confirmation of his or her own prejudice.

Academic historical journals with few exceptions, like *History Today*, which aims at a more popular market, are generally read only by other historians (including students) and usually indeed only by historians in a particular area of study. They are not expected to be very profitable enterprises – though naturally their proprietors aim to minimise losses and at least break even as far as possible, which they do by means of their pricing policies, institutional subscriptions being much higher than individual ones. The most established of such journals, such as the *English Historical Review* and its equivalents elsewhere, have a guaranteed institutional market, for no university history department would have credibility without their presence on its shelves. Less eminent publications have to manage as best they can and find subscribers according to their merits. Competition is severe and expresses both the advantages and drawbacks of unregulated markets. It remains fair to say that a journal which consistently advances new interpretations, ably argued according to accepted criteria, and in addition publicises itself well, will attract growing interest and levels of subscribers. In this regard at least quality will tell, *Radical History Review* being an instance in question[20] or, in Britain, what is now *Labour History Review*. Understandably editors will wish, if they can, to focus their attention upon authors with reputation, who can be relied on to produce material certain to attract and stimulate their potential readers. Not surprisingly a large number of articles are commissioned in advance following informal discussion between editor and author, and the same is true of monographs, though here the overall conditions are rather different.

Before turning to that, however, another feature of the historical journal has to be mentioned, which is the reviews it carries of historical texts. Some journals are very comprehensive, for example the *English Historical Review* (the *American Historical Review* being stunningly so) and the *Economic History Review* in its field; a few, like *Past and Present*, eschew reviews altogether, and most lie somewhere in between. These review sections fulfil an important function in enabling historians to keep abreast with what is being published, but the greatest reserve has to be exercised in judging the content of reviews, for here the standard historiographical rules do not apply and reviews are notoriously used for returning favours between author and reviewer, seeking future preferment or venting spleen – which is not to say of course that there are not many honest and conscientious reviewers as well, who keep their prejudices well away from their word processors. Nonetheless, these reviews, or rather the prospect of being found upon the end of a damning one, does act as a form of cultural control upon historians, albeit a weak one.

Paradoxically, for unestablished authors it is actually easier to get published at book length than in leading historical journals, in spite of the much greater labours that must go into compiling a monograph of 100,000 words or more. Basically the reason is that from the author's point of view this is much more of a seller's market. Since most publishers cover a range of themes there are many more of them interested in historical texts than there are historical journals in specific fields, and all of them are on the look-out for new and innovative texts which will have market as well as academic potential, and which, unlike journal articles, can be promoted individually. Journal editors, unless their periodical is new and struggling, do not have to worry about such considerations and have in hand a surplus of submitted articles and proposals among which they can pick and choose. The great university presses on either side of the Atlantic are of course in a special position of eminence and will be sought after by the most eminent academics, including historians, but their very distinction makes them less inclined to be adventurous or experimental.

Many historical journals invite readers to submit finished articles: publishers by contrast do not as a rule wish to receive finished monographs without prior consultation. The standard procedure is for a proposal to be submitted – it helps if the historian is part of a network through which this can be done, along with a personal recommendation made in advance. As with a journal article the publisher's editor with whom the aspiring author is dealing may have the proposal evaluated by an outside referee, or often enough the decision may be made in-house – the informal rules are a lot less stringent than in the case of journals. The proposal may – and probably will – be amended in discussion between the author and the editor, and then the process begins of turning the proposal into a finished text, a process which involves all the questions of dialogue between historian and evidence to be discussed below, and also of course questions of the historian's own tenacity and commitment, not really germane to our discussion and certainly not of interest to our readers.

These differences in the conditions of publication as between journal articles and monographs are well known to the profession and are reflected in the greater credibility accorded to journal publication, which is generally rated more highly than a single-authored book – while pieces published in multi-authored texts are given only grudging credit and lie at the foot of the hierarchy, regardless of quality.[21] Mention must also be made of footnote citations in other historians' articles, for the number of these a historian receives will significantly affect his or her standing. For historians the *Humanities Citation Index* is the crucial volume, appearing several times a year with international coverage.[22] What was designed as a research tool however, can have invidious implications, as described by Russell Jacoby:

> Many citations to an individual's work indicates he or she is important; conversely few or no references implies someone is unknown and irrelevant. 'If citation indexing becomes a basis for promotion and tenure, for grants and fellowships' comments Jon Weiner, 'the implications for one's own footnotes are clear. In the marketplace of ideas the footnote is the unit of currency ... One should definitely footnote one's friends ... and do what is possible to see that they footnote you in return ...'[23]

Other institutional frameworks

The materiality of research and publication as outlined above does not by any means exhaust the organisational infrastructure through which historical understanding is advanced and disseminated. Institutes and centres of varying standing and level of resources play an important role in underpinning the networks of contact through which historians operate and in setting historical agendas. More important still, indeed absolutely critical for the direction of historiography, are the funding bodies noted earlier, to which historians are obliged to apply for the resources necessary to undertake their major projects, in the British case most importantly the Economic and Social Research Council (which has in reality though not on paper a certain historiographical remit) and the British Academy and its offshoot the Academic and Humanities Research Board.[24]

The crucial importance of these bodies does not need to be underlined. They cannot totally determine the direction of historical research, for researchers who are passionate enough about their project will usually find some means to carry it out regardless, but they can certainly affect it substantially, by deciding which initiatives will be made easy by the allocation of resources and which will not. The criteria on which such decisions are made and the advice on which they are based are therefore of the utmost importance and amount to another set of tramlines (possibly the most important of all) along which the direction of historiographical development has to run. Funding bodies do not make public the reasons why particular decisions are made, why one application is favoured and another rejected, but they do have to be convinced by the successful ones in a bitterly competitive environment where there are far more applications than funds available.

Clearly the criteria will include the strength of argument for the importance of the project being advanced and methodology which corresponds with accepted historiographical practice. Projects which are significantly deviant in the latter sense are not likely to be viewed favourably – but then they are not likely to be submitted in the first place.

Historians, as with every other academic discipline, have their cross-institutional associations, of which there are a great many, both general and specialist. In this connection it is necessary to mention the American Historical Association, for nothing like it exists in any other country. Peter Novick provides a detailed account of how in the late nineteenth century, inspired by Rankean principles, often misunderstood in a simplistic fashion, it was the moving force in the professionalisation of history in the US and its grounding primarily within the academy. Since that time its importance has remained central, embracing the overwhelming majority of US historians.[25] Election as its annual president constitutes an enormous professional accolade and the President's address to its conference the highpoint of the professional calendar. The Historical Association in Britain is not in any sense a parallel institution but a modest and demure network. It was set up in the first decade of the twentieth century, with its primary appeal directed to schoolteachers, in whom the AHA had little interest. Although it publishes an important academic journal, *History*, probably a minority, and perhaps a small one, of British academic historians are members, whereas a fair proportion of the membership are amateur historians, a category spurned by the AHA.[26]

The AHA conference is not merely an intellectual event but the profession's key job market, where appointments are advertised and hotly pursued – for many, perhaps the majority, attending, it is the primary function of the event. The format, if Novick is to be believed, is not such as to inspire a passionate and selfless devotion to Clio. Apart from the President's address it is much too big to operate in plenary sessions and in consequence falls into a large number of unrelated specialist sessions, generally characterised, we are told, by small attendances, lack of interest and speakers who gabble through their scripts at great length unless restrained by the chair.[27] All in all, it gives the impression of being the conference from hell, an outcome of the fact that the main purpose of attendance is not intellectual interchange but job opportunities and networking. Admittedly Novick's account dates from over a decade ago, but there appears no reason to believe that matters have changed greatly in the interim. Reports suggest that conferences of the AHA's literary equivalent, the Modern Languages Association, are if anything even worse in those respects.

Conferences of course come in all shapes and sizes, and many are perfectly serious and sober instruments for the advancement of knowledge and fulfil a genuinely important role for the collectivity of historians – though naturally they are also expected to be convivial occasions whenever possible, whether they are local, national or international. No historian with any pretensions to recognition can avoid substantial participation in them. The variety of functions they serve, quite apart from the ostensible one of disseminating the latest findings of research, include fringe benefits for hardworked academics (possibly in exotic surroundings); networking; personal display; and of course sex.

Such conferences are organised on the initiative of history departments or groupings or wider historical collectives like the AHA, and the launching of successful historical conferences is itself a cachet, bringing prestige to the institution. The organisers select a theme and either invite papers relevant to that theme or else already have in mind the paper-givers that they want to recruit. The former case provides the best opportunity for historians who are as yet unknown and unpublished, but it goes without saying that the paper – a summary of which they will be expected to submit in advance – should meet accepted historiographical standards, and there may well be competition, so it is advisable to ensure that incorporation of these standards is well displayed. To be sure, even if not delivering a paper it is always possible to get oneself noticed by asking penetrating questions of the speaker following their delivery, or advancing one's own judicious comments (what counts as judicious naturally also depends upon the accepted consensus of historians).

It has to be acknowledged that listening to conference papers, so far as the majority are concerned, is not a particularly life-enhancing experience. They tend to be read verbatim and lifelessly, and their content is available in any case in transcript. Nevertheless that content may still be important, and the conference paper is frequently the first airing for ideas or interpretations that eventually appear as journal articles or monographs.

It will be apparent from all this that the progress of historical research and the development of historiographical culture does not occur in a vacuum. In every aspect and every relationship institutional pressures are at work (and those already detailed could well be multiplied further) and that these pressures operate in a particular direction. That direction is to affirm a particular model of historiographical practice and to validate the rules through which it functions. It would be possible to conclude as a result (the conclusion which of course the deconstructionists have drawn) that the model is in reality an artificial and arbitrary one and that it is held in place not primarily by scientific logic but by entrenched power and vested interest. Such conclusions however would be far from justified. It is no less compatible with the reality and indeed is far more intuitively convincing to view the institutional pressures as embodying a scientific tradition founded upon a scientific methodology with historiography as a particular domain, one which has been refined continuously through several generations and will go on in this manner indefinitely. Refining may certainly involve dramatic additions and alterations whose validity is tested by the basic principles of scientific methodology, but what is implied here is structured development according to an internal logic, not an epistemological free-for-all. As a comparison, the physics of the late seventeenth century is very different from that of the early twenty-first, but it is nevertheless recognisably in the same tradition in a manner which Aristotelian physics is not.[28] In other words the historiographical institutions, however imperfect and however divergent in particular instances from the model of scientific objectivity and detachment, nevertheless embody a social/intellectual mechanism designed to establish truths and filter out error. What is meant by truth in history is the subject of our next chapter.

5
Reality, Representation, Truth and Narrative

We now turn to consider the theoretical underpinnings of postmodern or deconstructionist approaches to historiography; not a question of a consistent doctrine but rather a loosely articulated set of concerns and presuppositions which give rise to an identifiable formation of thought, containing many inconsistencies, contradictions and contrary pronouncements – equal no doubt to the contradictions, etc. to be found in the assumptions of traditional historiography and *its* proponents, but, like its antagonist, maintaining nonetheless an identifiable strand of internal coherence. Previous chapters have tried to sketch the developments in historiographical consciousness which have made this form of thought something that historians are obliged to take serious account of whether their response is one of enthusiastic acceptance, indignant rejection or cautious evaluation. I have suggested that the postmodern sensibility was the product of a particular political conjuncture – but whether its origins were praiseworthy or discreditable is irrelevant to deciding whether or not it constitutes a valid approach, for that can only be judged on the effectiveness of the arguments deployed.

Being and seeing

When I was an undergraduate student there used to be active among the student milieux a rather spooky right-wing organisation called Moral Rearmament, which proclaimed four Absolutes, one of which was Absolute Truth (another was Absolute Purity). We lefties were thus able to mock its missionaries relentlessly, for philosophically naive though we were, we well understood that the notion of absolute truth was an absurdity anywhere outside mathematics (where the conclusions are implicit in the premises) – and even that can be questioned.

To acknowledge, however, that no foundation of absolute and undeniable truth exists is not the same thing as saying that the concept of truth is meaningless. To explore this it is necessary to consider briefly the notion of truth in general[1] before considering at greater length the question of historical truth in particular.

The first point to be made is that truth, assuming it exists, can only be known through complex cognitive operations – it cannot be experienced directly like anger or happiness, heat or pain or vision, for it is clearly not the same thing as a bare awareness of surroundings or internal states – the concept implies the ability to recognise truth in distinction from non-truth. For a particular individual it is a relationship between their consciousness and what is not that consciousness. The most banal and insignificant material object is the container for a potentially infinite number of truths,[2] any reality is literally inexhaustible. For human beings any reality exists in the series of appearances (not necessarily visual ones) which manifest it, and this series is an infinite one. It is exactly that infinity which distinguishes reality from dream or imagination. It follows that no particular description or element in the series can comprehend the entire reality – it can never be exhaustively described. There is always something further that could be established, other causal connections capable of being made. In principle, a description equal in length to the contents of the *Encyclopaedia Britannica* could be made of a glass of water – and there would still be limitlessly more to be said – and how much more the case for the most complex object in the known universe – the human brain? No description can be more than a cognitive cross-section of whatever is being described. Doubtless to an insect the appearance of reality looks very different than it does to a human, and if microbes or atoms possessed sensory organs it would look very different to those again. As to what is *meant* by reality, I will propose a working definition – reality is what can kill you if you disregard its attributes (and of course may do so in any case).

Nonetheless, if there are an infinite number of truths to be revealed about any segment of reality, that by no means implies that its character is structureless and formless and can be filled with any content whatsoever. Any object, concept, relationship, is distinguished by what is *not* true in relation to it as much as by what *is*. These considerations omit of course the question of whether, out of the infinitude of truths in relation to any reality, a hierarchy can be deemed to exist – are some of them more significant than others? The question may indeed be posed as to why there should be any principle behind a series of appearances (the surrealists achieved fame and recognition by producing artworks which denied that there was) and why there should be hierarchies of importance. The question is not necessarily illegitimate, but it is in the same league as Martin Heidegger's query as to why there should be *something* rather than *nothing*. What is regarded as important in any culture, whether of historians or their audiences, may indeed change over time, but these changes are not arbitrary.

The human brain and sense organs did not appear out of nowhere, but are the products of millions of years of evolutionary development. They do not just happen to exist but exist to serve a purpose, namely survival for a particular type of creature in a dangerous environment. If you judge wrongly and your assessment is out of line with reality you may well finish up as a sabre-tooth tiger's lunch rather than the bison ending up as yours. Clearly the human perceptual and cognitive apparatus, like that of any animal, is adapted to specific purposes; only certain aspects of reality will make an impress – others will remain outside the frame. We do not have eyes that can experience ultra-violet light nor ears that can detect the same range of pitch as dogs. One fact that appears to be well established regarding *homo sapiens* as a species is that humans automatically seek for patterns in their perceptual field and beyond that, explanations for what is perceived and experienced. Since these are evolutionary attributes it is a not unreasonable conclusion that reality is both patterned and explicable though it can never be exhaustively explained, nor even a small part of it.

Science

Such considerations introduce the question of science and the scientific tradition. The word derives from a latin root which means 'to know', and points to a cognitive instrument of extraordinary power, socially organised, which generates knowledge, not available to routine observation, of the patterning and structure of reality. As Marx once put it, if immediate sensation told the whole story, there would be no need for science. Whether the emergence of the tradition which embodies it was a historical accident, or whether it was something that the development of human society irresistibly led up to is a very interesting question, but need not detain us for long. It is only necessary to note that whatever the character of its origins, abstract thought inevitably becomes detached from the urgent necessities of existence, and speculation takes wing.[3] In due course the perfectly accurate observation that reality and its perception are not the same thing all too easily gives rise to the postulate that perceived reality is an illusion. If perception is taken to be illusion then reality and truth might be sought in mystical enlightenment, as tended to be the response in the great Asiatic civilisations, or in the perfection of mathematics, as was the case in the Greek world of the late centuries BCE. In this latter can be found the seeds of the cognitive technique which was to be established and flourish in Europe two millennia later – the scientific method of the modern era.

However complex science may be in its practices, the basic principles of its method are simple and readily stated. They are in the first place that there are no privileged revelations – any claim about anything is open to investigation and enquiry and by that token also open to refutation; a procedure which is particularly applicable to mathematics, which therefore provides the model for scientific discourse. The second is that the simplest explanation consistent with the evidence (leaving aside for the moment the question of what counts as an explanation) is always to be preferred until and unless more evidence comes to light or internal inconsistencies are revealed. As it happens, the paradigm science of physics finds that these explanations are more readily expressed in the language of mathematics than that of words, but that is by no means a defining characteristic of scientific methodology. What any science endeavours to do, whether using highly complex technological instrumentation like physics or molecular biology, or, as with history, largely doing without these extensions of the senses, is to establish the principle linking the series of appearances in a manner beyond what is available to unreflecting observation.

Naturally nobody (and no collective) can simply decide to apply scientific method and then begin discovering things at random. Science is a cumulative enterprise and any new departure begins from the body of knowledge and understanding that has already been accumulated, which is to be further tested, probed, extended and always open to radical reformulation. At this point it is appropriate to address the arguments – or more pointedly the red herrings – which have been generated by the writings of Thomas Kuhn.

Kuhn's seminal text on the structure of scientific revolutions is, whatever its weaknesses, of permanent value.[4] Kuhn himself, it should be noted, unlike most philosophers of science, was a practising scientist. Briefly, he draws attention to the fact that science, whether defined generally or in relation to particular branches of science, does not proceed smoothly and continuously according to prescribed formulae, but discontinuously and spasmodically – perhaps a useful analogy would be the geological stresses which are released in major earthquakes and volcanic eruptions. Under 'normal' conditions knowledge is generated within particular 'paradigms' – for example the laws of celestial mechanics propounded by Isaac Newton in the seventeenth century, or – appropriate to our analogy – geological science which rested on the presumption of geographically fixed continents.

However within any paradigm it is not only knowledge which accumulates, but also anomalies and contradictions – observations which do not fit in with the paradigm's preconceptions, such as for example the suggestive shape of Africa in relation to South America – and whose possible significance is therefore ignored or dismissed. Eventually, however, the accumulation of anomalies reaches the point where the ruling paradigm can no longer accommodate the strain and there then occurs a scientific revolution or shift to a new explanatory paradigm, such as Einsteinian relativity theory or, to continue with our analogy, the theory of continental drift. Nor should one forget, in examining how these paradigm shifts occur, the institutional inertia of established scientific bodies and networks with their intellectual and material investments in the existing paradigm, nor even the personal attitudes, ambitions and jealousies of individual scientists, who have their own agendas and are not detached, impersonal Spockean-type figures – especially those in influential positions.

It might therefore be surmised that the product of science is not an insight and revelation into the actual nature of whatever is being investigated but a specific form of discourse engaged in by the community of the faithful who adhere to this particular system of assumptions and procedures. It has indeed been so surmised by an audience ready to conclude that Kuhn's work pulverises the foundations of the scientific enterprise (Paul Feyerabend is an outstanding example[5] and Kuhn himself seemed to suggest that scientific knowledge in the end is opinion of those competent to pronounce, which did not really do anything to discourage such interpretations); but the surmise is quite mistaken, or at least it has no support in Kuhn's thesis, for all that he appears to believe he is demonstrating is something other than what he is in fact demonstrating. To interpret the thesis as a licence for cognitive relativism is to commit an elementary logical error – for what Kuhn is describing is the sociology of the scientific enterprise, the manner in which its results are arrived at, not the ontology, the question of the status and validity of these same results.

Nor are all paradigms equal, although each in its own way provides access to (incomplete) truth. Once a new one is established there can never be regression to the old, only further advance. Paradigms, like science as a whole, are cumulative, they do not evolve backwards, whatever Foucault's opinion (see Chapter 6). Any new paradigm, since the emergence of scientific method, very seldom displaces and discredits its predecessor in any simple sense (continental drift would be a rare exception), rather it subsumes and incorporates, or to use Hegelian terminology, sublates it. The Newtonian paradigm is perfectly good for limited purposes (relatively speaking – for these purposes include calculation of planetary orbits); what the Einsteinian paradigm does is to explain (among other things) why the Newtonian paradigm works and what the limits of its applicability are. A new paradigm enables a more detailed cross-section of reality to be appreciated than was possible prior to its introduction; the difference is analogous to the advance represented by electron microscopes over optical ones. And finally, the process never ends. If one wants a concrete image for science it would be of an infinite set of Chinese boxes or Russian wooden dolls – every problem solved opens the lid on further questions: reality is inexhaustible.

Language

Human speech, as much as human perception and cognition, is an evolutionary development and like most if not all evolutionary developments was an adaptation to promote survival. The capacity for language both enormously expands the range of available experience and at the same time limits it, for its symbolic character interposes a medium through which the reality to which it refers must be experienced vicariously rather than at first hand. Speech, by enabling representation, also enables experience to be transmitted, potential dangers to be intuited before being experienced in actuality – 'our hypotheses die in our places', as someone once said; but it also establishes the possibility for misrepresentation, whether by accident or deliberate deception.

However the knowledge and understanding of reality is indubitably a social affair, a social construction within the limits which reality imposes, and this raises the question of how far language is capable of producing 'true' representations in any sense of the term, and puts into question all the terminology we have been using so far, including words like explanation, interpretation and representation. What does it actually mean to say that we gain knowledge? Since the latter, even in its scientific versions, is embedded in language (unless it is mathematical, and mathematics may be regarded as language of a sort) can it not therefore be argued that all truths are necessarily linguistic ones: does the signifier (vulgarily, the word) have anything more than an arbitrary relationship to the signified (vulgarily, the concept of the thing, whether vegetable, mineral or abstract)? Does language determine the content of knowledge and understanding as well as convey it?

Philosophers, at least Western ones, have been going around these houses since the time of Plato, but Jacques Derrida claimed to be overthrowing the entire corpus of existing Western philosophy by demonstrating the meaninglessness of Plato's puzzles. His notorious pronouncement that 'there is nothing outside the text' is perhaps not intended to be taken literally (if 'taken literally' in this context has any meaning) but suggests at least that all knowledge is ultimately and only textual, to which is added the proposition that no text has any fixed or determinate meaning – meaning is subverted in the very act of writing – and that it is open to an infinite number of interpretations, none of which, even when contradictory, can be considered intrinsically more valid than another.[6] For Derrida and his co-thinkers 'The paradigm of language ... is not speaking but writing, with its absent author, its unknown audience, its unruly text spewing out its manifold significations, connotations and implications.'[7] Language here tends to be viewed as some sort of metaphysical demon which both constitutes reality and at the same time imposes an impenetrable barrier against it. Somebody has suggested that the image is of humankind as a Gulliver tied down helplessly with linguistic ropes – or perhaps more aptly, indulging in the kind of pun that postmodernists favour, linguistic tropes.

For all postmodernists, whatever their other differences may be, language and representation are the central realities of understanding. Clearly we cannot understand except through language, but the claim is much more radical than that – it is that our identities are formed primarily by language and discourse and that since all reality is mediated through texts there is no reality against which the truth or accuracy of language can be measured – texts can only be compared with other texts, not any outside referent.[8] Representation, in other words, cannot be distinguished from what it claims to refer to. As Alex Callinicos expresses it, '... the practice of deconstruction denies theoretical texts their apparent cognitive content, reducing them to an array of rhetorical devices and thereby effacing any difference between them and explicitly literary texts'.[9]

A number of implications follow. One is that allegedly 'scientific' discourses are, in reality (it is hard to avoid that terminology), no more worthy of credibility than others which are based upon different presuppositions. Alchemy may be as valid as chemistry (as indeed it was for its practitioners), witchcraft as good as physics and astrology no less appropriate than astronomy. The most energetic propagator of this kind of cognitive relativism was Paul Feyerabend, though his intentions were undoubtedly more Dadaesque than seriously intended and even he recoiled somewhat before the end of his life. Michel Foucault never pronounced on physical science and always objected to being designated a postmodernist (though alone of the major postmodern prophets he had pretensions to being a historian) but his phrase 'regimes of truth' perfectly catches the conception being advanced – truth is not 'out there', it is what is imposed by cognitive or linguistic coercion.

Historiographical implications

Relativism

The implications for historical understanding are both immediately obvious and enormous. The belief that the twenty-first century has superior insight into physical reality, let alone human relations, is on this account shown to be fallacious, and the understanding of past generations of their own historical situation is no worse than that of historians now. For example, the radical pioneers of Thompson's *The Making* believed that the political problems of the 1790s had their origin in the 'Norman Yoke' persisting in English political and social relations since the time of the Conquest. No historian of the present would take that at face value, but, appreciating its importance, would attempt to explain why the myth had such a strong grip on the popular imagination. From a perspective of cognitive relativism however, this is illegitimate – the historical understanding of the London Corresponding Society cannot be judged to be mistaken or erroneous, since such concepts have no determinate meaning – if it was true for the LCS then it was true in its fashion.

Nor is this the end of the matter. The cognitive relativism described above shades into a no less controversial form of relativism, which is by no means new to historical enquiry, but receives enormous reinforcement from the postmodern climate, namely ethical relativism. It is stressed often enough, and appropriately, that the historian's function is to explain, not to judge, but the issue goes rather further than this. Central to the thrust of postmodern argument has been an attack on the rational and humane perspectives of the eighteenth-century Enlightenment, for they have been represented on this interpretation as providing the ideological root of Eurocentric imperialism. Such an ancestry, if established, is surely to be deplored (though for relativists it is hard to see why that should be so, since the view that imperialism is wrong itself represents a particularist ethical position) but if it is accepted then it ethically damns all the sciences, both natural and social, which have their origins in the Enlightenment – not only do they lack any claim to cognitive superiority, they are also to be regarded as morally culpable. The Rankean tradition of historiography is to be included among their number.

History and truth

In dealing with history an additional consideration to that of physical or other social sciences has to be kept in mind, namely that by definition the investigation is into a reality that no longer exists; strictly speaking the historian is examining an absence rather than a presence – no one can directly experience the past. What is being dealt with instead is the evidence surviving from the past, generally in the form of written communication[10] which the writer may occasionally have addressed to the future (such communications being doubly suspect) but more usually not. On the basis of such evidence a cross-section of the past is reconstructed – it is presented and explained, always incompletely of course. In this enterprise the basic principles of scientific method are adhered to as much as they would be in astrophysics, though if one accepts a poststructuralist metaphysic, this does not amount to much. According to Hayden White, '... the human sciences [for Foucault] as they have developed in the modern period are little more than games played with the languages in which their basic concepts have been formulated',[11] and though White is at pains to insist that Foucault confines his critique to the *human* sciences, other writers such as Feyerabend have not hesitated to extend it to science in general.

Comparably with any sort of investigation in physical science, no historian selects a theme at random or from caprice, gathers together a manageable corpus of evidence and proceeds to investigate it in a cognitive vacuum. What he/she does instead is pose a problem seeking an answer, even if that problem is no more than the establishment of a chronology. As any basic textbook of historical method, such as Marwick's *The Nature of History*, or Ludmilla Jordanova's *History in Practice*, will point out, before they even begin to address the contemporary evidence according to Rankean procedures, historians will so far as possible study everything relevant (monographs, articles and so forth) that has been written in the area by previous historians dead or alive. In other words they will be building on the work done by their predecessors, absorbing their understanding (even when they violently dissent from it) and entering into dialogue with them. They will in any case probably have selected the particular theme of their investigation because of longstanding interest in the general area to which that theme belongs and with which they will already have considerable, perhaps intimate, familiarity. Previous deep knowledge and understanding of the framework and context of what is about to be examined is the prerequisite for any significant piece of historiographical production.

The point may be examined through an example which initially appears to contradict it. What for example of the opening of a new and previously neglected historiographical field, such as, in the late 1960s and early 1970s, women's history, where the guides and signposts existing in well-established historiographical fields are absent? These pioneers however were not setting off from nowhere, for they were of course perfectly familiar through previous work they had done with the historical society which had excluded women and hidden them from history. They had to be in order even to know where to look for the primary evidence which would enable the history of women's subordination and their resistance to it to be reconstructed.

As was noted earlier, the sources relevant to any theme (assuming for our purposes that the historian is working on something comparatively limited and that has not previously been enquired into) do not arrange themselves to provide the historical reconstruction. If among the sources is a contemporary or near-contemporary narrative then that will indeed provide a convenient starting-point to which the other evidence being handled can be related (and for the last two centuries or so newspapers may serve this purpose, depending on the theme), but for earlier eras the narrative, if one is required, has to be put together from the discontinuous information provided by letters, memoranda, written agreements, reports, lists and so forth. Principles of selection have to be applied (whether or not a narrative is being compiled) as do ones of arrangement and organisation, and judgement – which may in any individual case prove mistaken – as to the significance of individual pieces of evidence or the connections between them. It can be imagined, in part, as doing a jigsaw puzzle where not only are a large number of the pieces missing but many of the available ones are redundant.

A large part of the judgement lies in evaluating the reliability of any of the sources (we are assuming that the sources are written ones). This does not necessarily mean that whoever created the source was lying or deliberately aiming to mislead, although certainly that possibility has to be taken account of.[12] For example, minutes of meetings tend to be an important source for a very wide range of historical investigations, from Cabinets to local sports societies, but minute-keeping is a fairly modern phenomenon. All historians, especially those who have a more than passing acquaintance with committees are fully aware that minutes hardly ever reflect what actually transpired at a meeting – they are a highly artificial art form. Worse, they may even reflect the precise opposite, and be rewritten to record what a subsequent meeting decides ought to have happened in place of what actually did.[13]

Regardless of the complexity, the accuracy, the expertise with which the historian reconstructs and interprets the past reality being addressed, the resulting product will never amount to more than the merest fragment of a representation of a limited number of its aspects. Such is the inherent nature of the epistemological relation between knowledge and the objects of knowledge. If the description in a historical account can be compared to a map, then this is not a matter for regret – there would be no point in a map which was co-extensive with the geographical area that it was intended to represent. The essential function of symbols is to abstract from whatever it is they refer to and through that abstraction to make their referents comprehensible to consciousness and in many instances (such as a map) to make them manipulatable for human purposes.

What is meant by 'comprehensible'? Intuitively this is easy enough to grasp. To put it more formally, and referring back to the point made earlier, we may say that it means that the principle behind the series of appearances is recognised. This implies the separation out of what is intrinsic to the reality under consideration and what is contingent, in other words the recognition of what is important and what is not; the attribution of hierarchies of importance and indeed the application of scientific method over the course of centuries establishes which principles connecting appearances can be relied on and which cannot. To take an example which is imaginary but by no means fanciful: a historian may have before him or her a monastic chronicle from the tenth century which records plagues, crop failures, famines and Viking raids, and also notes that 'on Michelmas night the monastery was troubled by an invasion of ghosts, vampires, demons and other diabolical entities'.[14] The historian will take the chronicle as serious evidence (though definitely not the final word) for the plagues, hunger and invading Norsemen, but will certainly dismiss the record of supernatural manifestations, though these were no less important for the culture of the time.

In any case a historical account will possess greater or lesser accuracy and comprehensiveness depending on how well or badly the evidence available for its reconstruction is handled and how effectively connections are established. It will of course be partial, and equally be subject to the necessity of fitting the evidential jigsaw together: it will have a beginning, a middle and an end (but phenomena such as wars, reigns, plagues and revolutions do in actuality possess these characteristics) and employ a variety of rhetorical tropes. It will certainly never be the last word and will always be subject to modification and further development. However, if the historian has done his or her job effectively these modifications will (as with paradigms in physical science) subsume the previous account or interpretation, not overthrow it. *The Making* is an incomplete examination of its theme because (among other reasons) it lacks the dimension of women's history but it nonetheless adds enormously to our understanding of the political evolution of the radical and working-class movement between the 1790s and 1830s. In the technological world when a mechanism is rendered obsolete it does not follow that the designers of the previous model were wasting their time – the advances they made initially are incorporated into the new version:

> ... even if knowledge is not, in any simple sense, cumulative (the present is continually subverting our understanding of the past), the gains of previous generations do provide us with the invisible premises from which present-day enquiry starts, and the hinterland of thought in which we move.[15]

The events, productive relations, institutions and cultural climates of past eras are not unreachable in the present, their reconstruction by historical method – i.e., Rankean techniques – are not a matter of arbitrary rhetorical composition, or at least the arguments to the contrary advanced so far give no reason for believing that to be the case. A reconstruction (of Victorian electoral practices; of the diplomacy of medieval popes; of the court rituals of the Ming emperors; of the mechanisms of the Soviet purge trials, or whatever else) is placed in the public domain to be interrogated, criticised, debated and subjected to the tests of evidence and cohesion. The procedure is in principle no different from that employed in the natural sciences, although the language used is different. The rhetorical mode of Trotsky or Isaac Deutscher enormously enhances their work (and is a legitimate subject for historical analysis in its own right) but that work is not dependent upon it, nor does it affect the validity of their conclusions one way or the other except insofar as it might be shown to have distorted their judgement.[16] We have noted that the necessarily limited nature of any reconstruction or interpretation in itself suggests no reason for regarding them as no more than a game played with words. Nor does the necessarily fragmentary nature of any historical construction or the evidence used to construct it provide a reason for not treating the former as a cross-section of a reality, presented with more or less complexity, present through its representations though not directly present to the historian's consciousness.

> If theory persuaded socialist historians to give up the ambition to comprehend the real world on the ground that the effort was epistemologically disreputable, the only effect would be to leave the terrain to the undisputed possession of those with no such qualms, and allow 'just ordinary sound history' to regain its former mastery.[17]

If history is to be distinguished ontologically from myth or fiction certain presumptions are necessary, the main one being that it is possible in principle to reconstruct, via representation, a no-longer-present reality so that it can be understood in terms not essentially different from the understanding of any segment of contemporary reality, physical or human. If the very possibility of such understanding is denied, no further discussion is really possible. The denial, however, has to be reckoned as being an arbitrary dogma unsupported by coherent reasoning – neither the fragmentary character of evidence nor the incomplete nature of understanding provides adequate grounds for the denial. That said, it remains necessary to approach seriously the arguments advanced by the partisans of what may be termed the postmodern turn in historiography, to establish what if any kernel of validity may be concealed amidst the chaff of obfuscation. The forms of the argument are in the first place conceptual and in the second moral or ethical. The former in turn address a range of different though related themes.

Evidence and representation

In the first place there is the question of experience and its relation to representation. The discovery that raw experience is amorphous and protean, that interpretations are (at least very frequently) imposed after the event, is not new – it forms one of the themes of *War and Peace* – the nature of the battle they are engaged in is incomprehensible to its participants. The point is likewise dwelt upon at length and in more philosophic terms in Sartre's novel *Nausea*. Only after the fact does it become possible to understand what has been taking place, to put it in order mentally, especially if the experience occurs outside the grooves of routine. 'We tell ourselves stories', the observation of Sartre's protagonist, can be regarded as one of postmodernism's central slogans. The force of this observation cannot be denied – the application in relation to the written records of institutional meetings has been noted, and it is of course of general applicability. No matter how scrupulously an observer may try to recount an occurrence the account will differ, probably significantly, from those of other observers – or from the event recorded visually by a video camera or aurally by a tape recorder. The longer the distance from the event in question the more unreliable memory becomes.

Nor do the apparently most neutral forms of record escape. A statistical series – say of price movements – distils the experience of myriads of individual transactions – and statisticians are well aware how notoriously difficult it is to construct a statistical series that will be accurate and avoid misleading implications even for the present day, in such records as the cost-of-living index or inflation figures. How formidably these difficulties are multiplied when it is a question of dealing with the past. Similar ambiguities are equally applicable to areas such as demography or social trends in general. Grounds are therefore given for arguing that it is not just a technical difficulty which is involved but that experience is intrinsically too complex to be forced into the procrustian bed of the figures which statisticians gather and historians use.

Other forms of supposedly neutral record are no less subject to blurring and ambiguity. In denouncing E.H. Carr, who suggested that a document conveyed only what its author thought, wanted other people to think or perhaps even what the author thought he wanted to think, Arthur Marwick scornfully drew attention to documents like charters, acts of parliament and diplomatic treaties. Unhappily these too come subjected to a gap between intention and record, surrounded by an aura of ambiguity. Treaties and acts of legislatures are both notoriously subject to interpretation and the latter provide many welcome income opportunities for lawyers. The problems go beyond even that. Documents such as these cannot reveal altogether their meaning on internal evidence alone. Their clauses and stipulations may be meant to be taken seriously and put into effect – or they may not, they may simply exist for the record. Or they may be seriously intended and meaningful on the one hand or seriously intended but hopelessly utopian on the other. The charter by which monarch X confers a fief on baron Y may indeed record a simple allocation of territory, or it may be no more than a gesture, because the fief is in the actual possession of lord Z who has sufficient armed force to keep hold of it regardless. The Catholic Church used to have (it may still do for all I know) a system of bishoprics *in infidelibus* – dioceses to which an incumbent might be appointed but where the church could exert no authority. Different episcopal appointments in other words might have the same formal character, but take on totally different meanings. Marwick's records in other words, as much as the personal letter or diary, come saturated with the intentions of their authors.

Sufficient has been said to demonstrate that the gap between experience and record is a real one with real consequences for historians. The only point to be made is that postmoderninsts were not the first to reveal it, nor are more orthodox historians, in the main, unconscious of it or inattentive to its implications. The first rule of historiography is that written or figurative sources are never to be taken at their face value, but always and watchfully subjected to critical interrogation. Sixteenth-century individual or group portraits are on the face of things a realistic genre of painting, but once it is realised how heavily loaded they are with symbolism they take on quite a different level of meaning (often disputed) once the symbolism can be interpreted.

A further, and particularly notorious, instance concerns the celebrated 'standard of living' controversy in relation to early nineteenth-century Britain (England for the most part). Did living standards for the masses improve or deteriorate between 1800 and 1850? Passionate debate raged in historical journals and monographs between 'optimists' and 'pessimists'. This example is particularly revealing, for here the main (though not the only) evidence in question was indeed statistical, and the argument turned upon its reliability and proper interpretation. Political issues were also at stake, for if it could be demonstrated that early Victorian capitalism was good for the working class, how much more so must the same be true for more advanced variants. The issue was never finally resolved one way or the other; the only conclusion which could be appropriately drawn was that it depended on what was meant by standards of living. The effort was not wasted however, for that at least was a conceptual clarification. The essential point is that historians on both sides of the debate were sensitive to the need imaginatively to penetrate the gap between the experience of the individuals who lived through this phase of industrialisation and the statistical series which purported to represent it. Again one could go on. The Fogel and Engerman volume *Time on the Cross* brought its authors much obloquy for attempting a statistical analysis of the economics of North American slavery while leaving out an account of the experience behind it – setting aside the fact that their statistical technique was also seriously flawed.

How then, in epistemological terms, to cope with the inescapable subjectivity of the written record and the ambiguities of other sorts of artefacts which form sources of evidence regarding the past? Briefly, by careful interpretations, criticisms and comparisons and recognition in every case of where the boundaries of evidence permit no reliable conclusions to be drawn. The process in principle is an endless one, which is not the same thing as saying that no true historical knowledge is possible. Out of such materials a narrative is constructed. Even the most synchronic piece of historical analysis obeys an implicit narrative structure, for the dimension of time is inescapable and every element in such an analysis, whether it be a material object, an institution or an ideological construct has been formed in the processes of time. Every narrative has to be plotted, but not all emplotments – a term we will shortly explore – are equal in the sight of God or science – some will have emphatically better explanatory force than others, and history is a progressive science because it builds upon and amplifies the most effective and encompassing explanations – those which most adequately grasp the principle covering the series of appearances.[18]

Hayden White and others

'There is an inexpungable relativity in every representation of historical phenomena.' This statement is in no way controversial and could have been deduced by any reader of Carr. It comes however from a piece by Hayden White entitled 'Historical Emplotment and the Problem of Truth', and White may be reasonably regarded as the pioneer of the application of deconstructionist concepts to historiography. Cognitive relativism and linguistic considerations are central to the approach which he developed and upon which subsequent writers in this newly-established tradition have continued to build.

White introduced the concept of 'emplotment' as central to the understanding of historical narrative or description – and it applies as much to cliometricians using statistical analysis upon which to base their conclusions as to the traditional form of relation of historical events. What it means simply is that historians have to cast their analyses/accounts in the form of narratives or descriptive quasi-narratives, and that to do so they have not merely to select from the mass of evidence available (with all the subjective implications which this entails) but to construct by means of literary techniques the accounts which they subsequently produce – otherwise it will make little sense to the readers (or viewers if a different medium is being used). Like any novel the historical narrative has to be plotted and the words so arranged as to make it intelligible for the reader: moreover the historian will be striving to convince as well as inform (if indeed the two concepts can be separated) and implicitly appealing to the reader to accept the product as a true account embodying appropriate and well-substantiated judgements. 'Emplotment is the way by which a sequence of events fashioned into a story is gradually revealed to be a story of a particular kind.'[19]

Standing behind White is the figure of Northrop Frye. Frye is not a historian nor a theorist of historiography, but very much a literary theorist, whose seminal text, *Anatomy of Criticism*, appeared as long ago as 1957 (Novick termed it 'proto-structuralism').[20] He analysed the structure and the mode of literary productions around the core concepts of metaphor, synecdoche, metonymy and irony. The approach is formalistic and one which certainly calls into question the possibility of any substantative information being conveyed (other than incidentally) via the forms of emplotment which historians habitually use. What Frye is analysing, in essence, is the practice of rhetoric, of securing verisimilitude and conviction in the reader by the employment of linguistic strategies. The implication of White's position, having modelled his reading of historiography along similar lines, is that the latter is essentially a branch of rhetoric and that no ontological distinction can be drawn between the presentation of a narrative or argument and its content.

It has to be conceded that White is drawing attention to a real and significant dimension of what it is that historians do. In some degree Carr was there before him, when he observed that when engaging with a historian a reader should always 'listen for the bees buzzing, if you cannot hear any either you are tone deaf or your historian is a very dull dog'. What White does is to analyse and explain how the thing is actually done and the rhetorical strategies the historian uses to achieve the semblance of truth. It follows that when evaluating any piece of historiography it is necessary to be attentive to how emplotment is handled and to be aware that rhetoric is implicit in any piece of historical prose.

Metahistory

White, an American theorist, has written extensively, mostly in the form of articles and short pieces. His foundational work is *Metahistory: The Historical Imagination in Nineteenth Century Europe*, published in 1973, and though he has in some respects developed and even shifted his positions it remains central to White's evaluation, forming an original and pathbreaking historiographical initiative and developing the themes with which White is identified and which he has continued to expound in his subsequent writings.

In order to illustrate his thesis White takes as examples eight nineteenth-century writers, four historians (whom he refers to as 'master historians') and four historical theorists. The former are Ranke, Michelet, Tocqueville and Burckhardt; the latter Hegel, Marx, Nietzsche and Croce (specifically saying that he does not regard their differing theoretical positions as being of first importance). In principle though, his argument and concepts should be applicable to any form of historical writing and White contends that – with one very significant exception – they most certainly are. 'I maintain that they contain a deep structural content which is generally poetic, and specifically linguistic, in nature and which serves as the precritically accepted paradigm of what a distinctively "historical" explanation should be.'[21] And, 'In this theory I treat the historical work as what it most manifestly is: a verbal structure in the form of a narrative prose discourse.'[22] The exception is 'the monograph or archival report';[23] though these after all tend to comprise the bulk of historians' output.

White might be thought to have thereby knocked a large hole in his own thesis before he has got properly started, but perhaps he does himself an injustice and the concept can cover monographs as well. The evidences upon which *any* historical narratives are based do not arrange themselves of their own volition into a coherent picture; on the contrary, they have to be put into order by the historian's imagination, and have to be plotted in a manner analogous to the way in which a novelist plots the imaginary events and situations that make up the content of the novel. Historians generally prefer to work within the conventional framework of beginning, middle and end – but there is nothing sacred or necessary about that, and all kinds of modifications or variations are imaginable. The manner in which, within such basic structures, the individual elements of the narrative or analysis are arranged have further scope for infinite adaptability, and the particular forms that are used will have implications for the overall meaning of the completed historical account.

This is a most valuable insight and White deserves all credit for emphasising it. Once stated it appears self-evident and can be read as an implication of Carr's analysis but had previously never received the attention it merited. Once foregrounded, it promises all sorts of interesting lines of investigation in historiographical studies.

White, however, discounts the notion that there exist an indefinite number of potential emplotments. Instead he insists that the possibilities are limited to four in number: 'For emplotments there are the archetypes of Romance, Comedy, Tragedy and Satire'[24] – which might appear somewhat restrictive (though White does not deny that they can be mixed in the same work). Moreover, for White, these emplotments represent only the surface structure of a historical work – beneath them there lies a deep structure, that of the tropes, with which historians choose conceptual strategies. 'On this level, I believe, the historian performs an essentially *poetic* act'[25] (original emphasis). Again, the tropes are four in number (White appears to hold something of an obsession with the number four – it appears in other contexts as well, including the number of available political standpoints – one almost expects to encounter the four humours and the four elements). The tropes are purely linguistic in character, Northrop Frye's metaphor, metonymy, synecdoche and irony, and, 'it is my view that the dominant tropological mode and its attendant linguistic protocol comprise the irreducibly "metahistorical" basis of every historical work'.[26]

We will avoid spending time on examining the normal meanings attached to these terms and their usage in speech and writing, but concentrate instead on what they mean in White's discourse – which, it has to be said, seems to bear little relation to their ordinary definitions. Roughly, metaphor is the trope defining historical writing prior to the nineteenth century in which an account proceeds (allegedly) without awareness of deep-seated historical contradictions or a defining conception of the forces which produce historical development or perspective on ultimate outcomes – the most simplistic of the four available. Metonymy means a conception of history driven by mechanical forces and torn with conflict; synecdoche one of organic relations and ultimate harmonious outcomes; irony a disabused perception of the inadequacies of the other three accompanying a disillusioned and pessimistic perspective on human hopes. It can be seen how these correspond respectively to romance, tragedy, comedy and satire, but whether the latter can be regarded as surface structures and the former as deep ones is a different question.

It will also be recognised without difficulty that the four tropes and the four accredited emplotments are literary concepts and conventions. White is indeed primarily a literary theorist rather than a historiographer and he acknowledges his heavy debt to Frye and Kenneth Burke.[27] At bottom, White is convinced that although 'Historical works are made up of events that exist outside the consciousness of the writer'[28] no form of emplotment can be regarded in relation to those events as intrinsically superior to another – in his view the series is not connected by any principle which *also* 'exists outside the consciousness of the writer'. Hence for instance Marx (but it could be any of his other examples) is 'a representative who must be regarded as neither more nor less "true" than the best representatives of other modalities with which it (sic) contended for hegemony ...'.[29]

We will set aside for the moment the question of what relevance tropes or emplotments of these kinds may be thought to have to an investigation of say, demographic trends in eighteenth-century Massachusetts or the management of water resources in eighth-century Byzantium, and concentrate for the moment on discussion of the categories themselves. It will be observed that the master tropes appear to be a fairly arbitrary assemblage and that they are all drawn very much from the Western literary-cultural tradition, and indeed it is unclear from the writings of White himself or his commentators (contradictory statements abound, sometimes on facing pages)[30] whether they are supposed to apply to all historiography everywhere, past, present and imaginable, or only to that formed within that tradition.

White's discussion of his eight examples is both readable and interesting, and apart from the fact that he has something significant and original to say he writes intelligibly (though unintelligibility has proved no barrier to the acceptability of Foucault or Jameson, not to speak of Derrida or Barthes). Some useful insights are gained, particularly on Hegel and Nietzsche,[31] though all of them, true to his initial promise, are treated from the standpoint of a literary critic – the concentration is on form rather than content. The treatment is also extremely abstract, the amount of information accorded on the economic, social and political contexts in which they worked would, when put together, scarcely fill a page. He has most difficulty with Marx. The attempt to assimilate Marx's economic theory (which he misunderstands and where the magic number four once again puts in an appearance) to a model of literary composition is scarcely White's happiest hour, and his analysis of the base/superstructure metaphor, while defensible, is far more contentious than he acknowledges – arguing that relations between the base and superstructure are entirely unidirectional[32] and that Marx is effectively advancing a model of technological determinism. White's overall estimate must be less than convincing to anyone other than a convinced deconstructionist:

> The essence of Marx's thought about history ... consists less in an attempt to combine what he thought was valid in the thought of Hegel, Feurbach, the British Political Economists, and the Utopian Socialists than in his effort to synthesise the tropological strategies of Metonymy and Synecdoche in a comprehensive image of the historical world.[33]

Marx also seems to be treated differently from the other seven in that the analysis in his case appears to rely on volumes of excerpts rather than the full texts of the writings in question.

Since writing *Metahistory* White has continued to develop his analyses in a variety of contexts built on this foundation, and as noted, has been recognised as the pioneer spokesperson of the linguistic turn in historiography. Taken in sum, therefore, how does the text stand up to critical inspection? Unquestionably there are serious problems.

In the first place White is breaking a cardinal rule of historical investigation; he is producing preselected examples to prove his thesis of the development of the nineteenth-century historical consciousness from metaphor to irony, without demonstrating it in more generalised terms. Why these particular eight, apart from the fact that they were outstanding historians and/or writers? As White strings them together they provide a picture of the development of that particular historical consciousness, but it has been pointed out that a different selection of eminences could have been made which would have pointed to quite different conclusions – one including, for example, Droysen, Macaulay, Maitland and Lord Acton.

Another point which might well strike the reader of *Metahistory* is that White's essential insight regarding emplotment would not be damaged in any way – on the contrary it would be improved considerably – if the whole apparatus of tropes and the speculative argumentation based upon them were to be discarded. Despite the fact that they are of course intrinsic to White's conception, they give the reader the appearance of a superfluous fifth wheel arbitrarily nailed on to his analysis. Even within the limitations noted in the last paragraph *Metahistory* would be a better book and the remainder of its argument would read pretty much as before if this surgery were to be carried out,[34] and even his contentious assertion that 'the best grounds for choosing one perspective on history rather than another are ultimately aesthetic and moral rather than epistemological'[35] would remain unaffected.

Narrative

All the way through *Metahistory* and his other writings White appears to assume that historiography is cast in a narrative form and that the degree of narrativity, if one may so express it, remains constant – emplotment is after all essentially about narrative. In reality, although no historical writing escapes entirely from a narrative dimension, in some that element is very weak indeed, so White's claims are empirically dubious even at this basic starting point. Leaving that aside however, and focusing on historical reconstructions where narrative is undeniably prominent, is the structuring of a historical account in this way an (admittedly unavoidable) imposition by the historian, a 'poetic act' to put it at its strongest and not an abstraction from the historical reality unavoidably imposed by the evidence?

There is an argument (which I find convincing) that narrative is not an *arbitrary* construction, a tropism, but something which verbally maps a real dimension of existence and thereby enables consciousness to grasp the succession of events in time. It is, after all, though forms may vary greatly in detail, a cultural universal encountered wherever human collectivities are to be found. The literary critic Barbara Hardy notes, 'for we dream in narrative, daydream in narrative, remember, anticipate, hope, despair, believe, doubt, plan, revise, criticise, construct, gossip, learn, hate and love by narrative'.[36] It is simply not true that 'life has no beginnings, middles or ends'.[37] As someone has remarked, wars (or most of them at any rate), massacres, famines, festivals, political regimes, journeys and ceremonies have fairly clearly identifiable beginnings and ends, even if their preconditions and aftermaths are left out of the picture.

> The real world, White avers, has no beginnings or endings ... [however] the end of something like the First World War, is of course not the end of the world: things of interest to historians continued to happen after 1918. But it can surely be concluded, on grounds that have nothing to do with the deliverances of the aesthetic imagination or the serving of ideological ends, that these further happenings were not further episodes of the war. It can be a matter of simply seeing that the concept of a world war, a concept that is not particularly obscure, was no longer instantiated.[38]

Moreover there exists a universal and very clear-cut model which links narrative to actuality, or if you prefer, *forces* actuality into a narrative structure. We are all born at a specific point of time, mature and age (if we live long enough) according to biological regularity and die, again at a specific point in time. None of that is to ignore the fact that the sections into which historians cut up the past – classical civilisation, late antiquity, Middle Ages, early modern, modern and equivalents for non-Western cultures – are intellectual constructs, devices for thinking with, but it is to insist that they are not arbitrary constructs but abstractions from discontinuities existing within the continuities which actually are revealed in the record.

> It is no exaggeration to say that historians (and many anthropologists) are probably the only people around who think that human societies do not evolve out of each other but are so many entities, to be studied as configurations which have nothing much to do with what came before or came after, each, as Ranke used to put it, equidistant from God.[39]

There is not one true narrative of any sequence of events, there is in fact a potentially limitless number, but this does not mean that these potentially different narratives are arbitrary and can be self-contradictory; if any are self-contradictory it is an indication that there is something wrong with the construction and that one or the other (or both) must be false. A central commitment of historical research is to *exclude* certain interpretations or narratives as inconsistent with the evidence available – such as a narrative of the Second World War that denies the existence of the death camps. What the different narratives, consistent with the evidence, do is point to, elaborate and explain different dimensions and aspects of a single reality that was experienced as such by those who participated in it or lived through it.

Other deconstructionists

The existence of any such single past reality, recoverable to the understanding by evidence, is emphatically denied by deconstructionists and postmodernists. White is explicit that interpretation takes precedence over evidence, and so the question at issue here is whether a rhetorical fabrication of apparent truth is all that can possibly be attained, and represents the limits of the historian's endeavour. To take the matter further – can no difference in principle be recognised between historians and authors of fiction and all the elaborate Rankean procedures be dismissed as tediously unnecessary and irrelevant ritual designed principally to obfuscate and give historians an inflated sense of their intellectual credibility?

There are indeed some who are ready to embrace enthusiastically such conclusions in their full rigour. Most of what has been written by Keith Jenkins, especially his historiographical primers *On 'What is History?'* and *Rethinking History*, is a relentless and sustained assault on the good faith of historians in the Rankean tradition and the intrinsic value of what they produce. If we are to believe Jenkins such historians, assuming they are employed in higher education as most of them happen to be, are motivated, whether consciously or unconsciously, primarily by the desire to exercise pedagogical power over their students as compensation for the anachronistic nullity of their own historical endeavours and their exclusion from the centres of real social and political influence. Jenkins indeed is so splenetic as to be an embarrassment to others in the same camp. Patrick Joyce, perhaps the most notable of the British historiographical postmodernists writes:

> ... living with difference means living with Jenkins. However Jenkins's consistent failure to consider the dialogic aspects of past and present in the writing of history means that his work has limited interest. His is a kind of idealist or subjectivist postmodernism, which is the objectivist position of his opponents stood on its head. As so often in these debates, seeming opposites – Jenkins and Evans for example – mutually constitute one another.[40]

Though the force of the critique is somewhat mitigated by the fact that Jenkins also appears among his acknowledgments.

Hans Kellner, a leading American representative, has commented that *Metahistory* as a text can be considered as an attempt to *avoid* the deconstructionist abyss which is implicit in White's theory, '... the deconstructionists will trope the turns and turn the tropes, unfolding their texts until they have arrived at their nondestination'.[41] Elsewhere he had declared that Derrida's writing 'like Milton's no less difficult prose', is 'a chaotic field of signifiers'.[42] When one has recovered from one's astonishment it might well be to agree with the latter phrase, but to treat the former as no more than a postmodern joke. In the same article Kellner goes on to write that, '"Truth" and "reality" are, of course, the primary authoritarian weapons of our time',[43] to which one might well retort that if truth and reality are such discredited concepts, what possible basis can there be for objecting to authoritarianism?

In Europe, the philosopher F.R. Ankersmit from the Netherlands is undoubtedly the pre-eminent deconstructionist commentator on historiography and a member of the *History and Theory* editorial board. He defines postmodernism as ascientistic rather than antiscientistic – having presented a bizarre picture of science as though, ideally, true information should put an end to debate and interpretation – and then goes on to urge that 'the postmodernists's aim therefore, is to pull the carpet out from under the feet of science'.[44] According to him, '... historiography is really part of the contemporary cultural world and ought to be studied in its relation to contemporary painting, sculpture and literature',[45] and is even ready to declare that '... science and politics do not belong to culture; if something can have a use or a disadvantage or enables us to manipulate the world it is not a part of civilisation'.[46]

Alun Munslow is less immoderate and more measured in his language and for that reason provides perhaps a clearer insight into the general trend of deconstructionist thinking. According to Munslow,

> ... White offers a model of historical narrative in which its form is taken to prefigure the historian's understanding of the meaning of the content of the past ... History at every level, therefore, is a text possessing an imposed or invented meaning.

Munslow expresses the argument forcefully: 'It is White's contention that ... our knowledge of the past is through a poetic act', a 'fictional invention'.[47] These are, as we have seen, dramatic claims, and Munslow goes on to elaborate their implications, though once his text is examined in any depth his postulates turn out to be based upon bad argumentation, elided logic, *non sequiturs* and statements that are manifestly true but also trivial and incapable of bearing the theoretical weight placed upon them. For example, 'the reconstructionist argument that they have discovered *the* reality of the past (original emphasis) is undermined'. The statement is a red herring in that hardly any historian today, and certainly not a 'reconstructionist' one would make such a claim. 'People in the past do not actually live stories [true but banal] (that is they do not impose emplotments of a particular kind on their lives and times in order to make sense of them).' A *non sequitur,* and manifestly false, for people and communities do most certainly impose, in memory, emplotments upon the events of their lives and times immediately they have lived them.[48] Munslow quotes an unexceptionable statement from White that, '... historical facts, originally constituted as data by the historian must be constituted a second time as elements of a verbal structure ...' and then asserts that, 'it follows that ... their meaning is determined by the tropic mode of their narrative construction ...'. Actually it does not follow at all, the assertion is again a *non sequitur* and a highly contestable one.[49]

It is further suggested that 'The historian may well be convincing, plausible, or telling good rather than bad history when the story rendered appeals to the same stock of myths and ideological and methodological preferences shared by the reader.' Perhaps that may be the case, but the readers thus referred to may be suspected of being lazy ones, for good rather than bad history might be more reasonably thought of as history which challenges the readers' unexamined presumptions, etc., and requires critical engagement rather than unthinking assent.

> A theoretically informed approach ought not to be identified with any particular way of writing and it is in no sense dependent upon canonical texts or heraldic verbal devices. The theoretical worth of a project is not to be gauged by its manner of expression, but by the complexity of the relationships it explores.[50]

Munslow goes on to quote with approval Ankersmit's statement that the historical narrative, 'resembles a belvedere: after having climbed the staircase of its individual statements one surveys an area exceeding by far the area on which the staircase was built'.[51] One can of course demonstrate anything by silly analogies. The one which Munslow himself then goes on to use – Ankersmit has also done so – is more meaningful, but nevertheless inappropriate, and its faults reveal some of the intrinsic weaknesses of deconstructionist argument. 'History thus conceived', he suggests, 'is more like a painting than a forensic reconstruction – an aesthetic appreciation of a past world rather than the recovery of its lost reality.'[52] Well, no, actually it isn't. There is an essential and important difference, in that a painting, though it can be critically examined at great length in relation to its employment of space, line, colour, etc., can also be grasped instantaneously (with greater or lesser sophistication) simply by looking at it, while a historical text, good or bad, can only be absorbed over time, serially and through the comprehension of words and concepts in relation to its subject matter. Forensic reconstruction is what it purports to be *about* – though you can argue if you like that forensic reconstruction is impossible, as White and his followers do – but then the analogy is not with painting but with the novel.

The tendency in deconstructive analysis to detect, in a rather Freudian fashion, portentous significance in offhand illustrative remarks is well illustrated in the rather po-faced conjunction Munslow makes between White's interpretation of historiography and Marx's comment at the opening of *The Eighteenth Brumaire of Louis Bonaparte* that historical events repeat themselves, the first time as a tragedy, the second as a farce – which Munslow asserts, 'can only be taken to mean that history is written by human beings ...'[53] and is thus an act of narrative interpretation rather than a valid reconstruction. In actuality Marx did not believe for a moment that historical events repeat themselves and even less was he making a historiographical comment – what he was doing was mocking the would-be revolutionary leaders of 1848–51 for trying to dress themselves in the metaphorical garments of their great predecessors 60 years earlier.[54]

In some respects the argument remains a dialogue of the deaf, for White along with most deconstructionists is not only a literary theorist rather than a historian, but a formalistic one at that, as well as being very weak on logical exposition. It is difficult to avoid the conclusion that White's orientation towards history, like Derrida's towards language, is ultimately a mystical one, a suspicion not allayed by the recurrence of the word 'sublime' in his discourse. Alun Munslow glosses it thus: 'the deconstructive consciousness willingly acknowledges the sublime nature of the past – its literal meaninglessness, its lack of centre, and its consequent lack of truth'.[55] The 'sublime' is referred to also in the following terms, 'By this White means the celebration of the undiscoverable, possibly meaningless, and open-ended nature of the past. Such meaninglessness is the only invitation that potentially oppositional and dissenting groups of historians may get to challenge certaintist (eg fascist) history'[56] – though for unreconstructed evidentialists[57] it is rather difficult to discard the presumption that the best, indeed the only, antidote to fascist historiography is to uncover the truth of events. Munslow further elaborates in interpretation of White, 'When we have decided that we know what it means – then that is what it means' – which must come as joyous news to Holocaust 'revisionists', believers in divine providence and other species of obscurantism.

Historical emplotment

Once the baroque architecture of deconstructionism has been dispensed with, the basic insight regarding emplotment nevertheless remains valid and the way historians handle the issue is worth noting. It has to be kept in mind that historical writing, even the most neutrally composed report, is *in some respects* a literary artefact, and is exceptional among the human sciences in the degree to which aesthetic considerations enter into the evaluation of its products. Even so this remains a secondary issue. It is possible to imagine a piece of historical writing which was an aesthetic disaster and wretchedly composed, yet yielded new knowledge and interpretations of the utmost importance.

All historical accounts are reconstructions which can never reveal the full reality of whatever is being investigated. The evidence is necessarily incomplete, fragmentary, and, if documentary, filtered through[58] the subjectivity of its producers. Moreover, paradoxically, it is in most cases too abundant to be used in its entirety, and the historian is therefore compelled to select. These conditions have been well understood, intellectually as well as implicitly, ever since the publication of Carr's volume.

The artificiality of the reconstruction goes further than that however – much further – for the evidence, once collected and selected, does not arrange itself spontaneously. The historian's finished work, whether that be an article, a volume, a series of volumes or something in non-print media, has to be a product in which the historian has arranged and put in order the evidence as well as provided the links, explanations and interpretations which turn it into a connected and comprehensible communication capable of being understood and evaluated by an audience.

In a very large number of cases that organisation will in its elements follow a narrative structure, though a straightforward narrative re-counting would be rare – there are very few historical productions which do not have a primarily analytical intent, and even the most un-varnished narrative embodies an analytical element to some degree. In any event the historian will be obliged to assemble the evidence in such a way that it makes sense, and to make sense it must follow the lines of an interpretation, an interpretation which will be provided by the historian and which may or may not make the best sense of the evidence under discussion. This of course is where disagreement and contention with other historians is most likely to arise. In addition, the style of writing employed by the historian comes into the equation. To write in wholly flat and neutral tones, in the style of a government communique, avoiding metaphor or any linguistic device to give colour to the narrative or analysis would produce a very flat and virtually unreadable result. An element of rhetoric consequently enters into every historical reconstruction, gives it colour and contributes to the argument. Taken together, these considerations reveal a very important dimension of what historians are doing, and may fairly be summarised under the neologism 'emplotment'.

However, even if there are beginnings, middles and ends in life, nothing compels the historian in constructing the narrative to start at the beginning, proceed through the middle and finish up with the end – though in empirical fact that will be how most historical narratives are constructed. Literary texts by contrast very commonly are not composed in this fashion, particularly in an era of literary experimentation, but employ a range of formal devices to manipulate chronology in order to heighten the effect the author wants to achieve – novelists can very well commence in the middle, or at the end, and then use the narrative to explain how this end was arrived at.[59]

Not many historians consciously indulge in stylistic experiments, or deliberately play with plot structures or the scholarly apparatus which historians use, but it is certainly possible to imagine how it might be done. I could as an experiment, for example, write an article which was conscientiously researched and adhered to Rankean standards but whose main text consisted deliberately of nothing but trivialities and where all the substantive information and discussion was confined to footnotes. It would be unlikely however to find acceptance in any refereed journal. Of course such an idea contains an implicit judgement of what constitutes triviality as compared with substantial matter, and a radical deconstructionist might contend that any such judgement could only be made on arbitrary criteria. To be sure, what one era regards as trivial another might find significant – Joanna Southcott for example – but a rough measure is the degree of consequentiality of the event or situation in question. If we cannot agree, for instance, that Adolf Hitler's dietary preferences were less consequential than his political or military decisions, then historical dialogue breaks down altogether.

Fictional history

As White puts it, if a historical text is treated

> as what it manifestly was, namely a rhetorical composition, one would be able to see not only that historians effectively constructed the subject of their discourse in and by writing, but that ultimately what they actually wrote was less a report of what they had found in their research than of what they had imagined the object of their original interest to consist of.[60]

'Rhetorical' and 'imagined' in conjunction would certainly appear to suggest the elimination of any real distinction between historiography and fictional composition, or as Callinicos expresses it:

> ... textualism wants to place literature at the centre and to treat both science and philosophy as, at best, literary genres ... the practice of deconstruction denies theoretical texts their apparent cognitive content, reducing them to an array of rhetorical devices and thereby effacing any difference between them and explicitly literary texts.[61]

A licence would therefore seem to be issued for any sort of alteration of the documentary evidence, or invention, which the historian might regard as appropriate to his or her purpose and compatible with the aesthetic effect that is being aimed at – while not ceasing to be a legitimate and valid historical text.

Precedents for such a practice certainly exist, though I have not seen them mentioned in any of the deconstructionist literature I have come across. In the forefront is Solzhenitsyn's *Gulag Archipelago*, which in the form of a novel endeavours to recount the history of the Soviet prison-camp system, based on very extensive research among its survivors, but neither equipped with the scholarly apparatus deemed indispensable to historiography nor purporting to be a soberly factual account.[62] From the other side of the Cold War divide can be cited Rigoberta Menchu's *I, Rigoberta Menchú*,[63] which was marketed as a factual memoir, later shown to be largely invention, yet nevertheless defended by its partisans as essentially and symbolically true. There is also the genre of 'faction', avowedly fictional reconstructions of actual events, pioneered by Truman Capote's *In Cold Blood*.[64]

It would not be surprising therefore if experimentalist historians were to proclaim a boundless and unalloyed freedom of invention, totally abolishing the historiography/fiction distinction, but most are, surprisingly, reluctant to take this final step, although a few have in the end been sufficiently bold.[65] However this is exceptional, and the majority, even while denying the possibility of truthful reconstruction, enter a reservation that historiography is in some sense bound by its sources and that this is what characterises the genre.

According to Munslow, 'White does not dispute the fact that the past existed, and he is not anti-referentialist',[66] and he also writes on his own account that, 'What the historian must do is locate the different types of stories *that the evidence will support*'[67] (emphasis added) and 'Deconstructionists do not automatically doubt the truth of individual referential statements, nor do they claim that it is impossible to demonstrate that certain events did or did not happen ....'[68] This caution (or coyness) is well advised, but it appears to me to that it explodes most of their theory and leaves little of their case standing beyond the original insight that historical narratives have to be emplotted and that the techniques of emplotment used by the historian should be identified and will be germane in evaluating their interpretations. Reconstruction on the basis of documentary and other evidence is the court of final appeal. Solzhenitsyn's novel is enormously suggestive and emotionally affecting, but the confirmation of its truth-claims depends on archival research of the standard and established sort, and the novel is not always a reliable guide to every aspect of the Gulag experience – the Trotskyists, for example, as well as other communist oppositionists, are written out of the script.

The most appalling events of the twentieth century, where the questions of truth or falsehood are of the most sharp and urgent relevance, is the area in which deconstructionists/postmodernists appreciate themselves to be most vulnerable. As Richard Evans has put it, 'the Holocaust was not a narrative, it was something that actually happened'. Most deconstructionists make a point of acknowledging the Holocaust's reality, but they nevertheless have a problem arising from the circumstance that since their denial of a necessarily restricted sphere of interpretation cannot, however much they try, effectively be dissociated from denial of a provable fact, their approach can readily be called in aid by elements who wish to deny altogether that this historical event actually occurred. *History and Theory* actually conducted a symposium on this question in 1994. White himself, it has to be said, has tried on more than one occasion to address the issue,[69] but his convoluted argument, which gives a reader the impression of embarrassing even himself, signally fails to convince. He raises the question of whether the history of the Third Reich could be seriously emplotted in a pastoral or comic mode, but altogether fails to answer it, avoiding the issue by demonstrating that it *can*, under very restricted criteria, be emplotted in an ironic one[70] – which doesn't come as any great surprise. It is a point worth noting that in the David Irving libel trial it was no poststructuralist or postmodernist historian or theorist that the defence called upon to deconstruct Irving's lies, but the despised 'empiricist' Richard Evans.

An appreciation of the significance of emplotment and the malleability of narrative – which is implicit though not developed even in E.H. Carr's discussion – is a valuable critical aid in the evaluation of a large range of historiographical products (although not every one of them). To attempt to assimilate historiography to a literary mode, however, is of benefit neither to literature nor to history.

6

Grand Narrative

The phrase itself is one we owe to postmodern thinking, indeed it was first used in the late 1970s (in the form 'metanarrative') as virtually the essence of the postmodern outlook, when Jean Lyotard described that as being 'incredulity towards all metanarratives'. The term may of course be understood in a number of differing senses, although there is no doubt that the metanarrative being targeted then was Marxism, at that time falling out of fashion in French intellectual circles. Soon, however, an 'unremitting hostility towards totality' of any sort became the fashion and:

> all totalizing thought has now tended to become characterized, or rather caricatured, as a surreptitious form of will to power ... "and it is as such that the term has been used to characterise everything from liberal humanist ideals to the aims of historiography".[1]

The questions being addressed are ones of the utmost significance: they relate to the place of *homo sapiens* in the world and people's and cultures' self-identification and recognition of themselves. The questions may be summed up as follows: does history have a meaning? is history going somewhere? is there something which can reasonably be categorised as a 'historical motor'? is it possible to identify a reason why the historical process has taken the shape that it has? can the term 'progress' be legitimately applied to that process? The questions are related, though by no means identical, for it is necessary to distinguish teleology – the assertion that there are forces at work in history propelling it towards a predetermined outcome – from an explanatory principle which makes it possible to understand *after the event* why history has proceeded as it has from the emergence of the species but says nothing about the necessity of it having followed any particular route. Any one of four answers is possible in principle – there may be a teleology in operation or there may not; there may be a universal explanatory principle lacking teleology, or there may not. None of these can be assumed in advance.

It may be reasonably surmised that, even had there been no intellectual or cultural antecedents, the development of science and technology during the last four centuries or so would have in itself generated the notion of history proceeding in a particular direction and given rise to the concept of historical progress. In actuality however antecedent ideas were already available as raw material out of which modern notions of that sort could be formed.

The notion of a secular historical destiny for all humanity and to which the future is heading is a modern invention; like most of those, a site of social and cultural contradictions. Agricultural societies, let alone pre-agricultural ones tend to be conservative (and with good reason) and it is presumed among them that the rules of social *praxis* having been laid down in antiquity, the future will go on repeating the past *ad infinitum* (which need not exclude a recognition of social revolt or political revolution, as in imperial China, only that these things will make no difference to the basic tenor of living – one dynasty will simply replace another). Even in so culturally sophisticated a society as classical Greece, from where the Western tradition of historiography takes its remote origin, the presumption was that the course of history was not linear, rather that it moved in cycles: what occurred in the past would occur again in the future. The ideologists of the Roman Empire assumed that the city and its political system would last for ever.

Teleologies

Divine destiny

The ancient Hebrews (or at least their literate classes) must be credited with the invention of the idea of history as a sacred drama with themselves in the starring role. It represents the first of the great metanarratives and one destined (if such a word is permissible) for a momentous future. There is no hope of explaining precisely why the concept arose in the time and place that it did, though the particular combination of a peculiar national myth together with domination by stronger powers, defeat, exile and return to the sacred territory presumably had a lot to do with it. It was subsequently, with suitable modifications, adopted as the foundation of the Christian church's understanding of its own divine role, placing at the very centre of Christian consciousness a grand narrative of a journey through time from Eden to apocalypse and the final judgement. The medieval Christian culture provided the foundation and supplied many of the elements for the one which was in due course to dominate the globe and it has been argued that all subsequent notions of historical progress are secularised versions of the Judeo/Christian scheme.[2]

It would be an over-precipitate assumption for readers to imagine that the religious version of the grand narrative alluded to above is dead. In areas (both geographical and cultural) dominated by fundamentalist faiths committed to its several variants it continues to enjoy many thousands of adherents. In circumstances where governments, particularly the governments of nuclear superpowers, fall under the influence of individuals who are influenced by it, it could indeed have very serious consequences. Fundamentalist Christianity remains strong in the US and in that culture imminent apocalypse continues to be widely anticipated. These were beliefs shared at least in part by Ronald Reagan during the term of his presidency and might clearly have had consequences for his handling of nuclear strategy. Happily they did not during that period result in nuclear conflict, but there is no telling what the future is likely to bring. However intellectually discredited, it is worth keeping in mind that this particular form of grand narrative remains active upon the political stage. To what extent sincere Christians not of the fundamentalist persuasion continue to believe that the universal Last Judgement will be the final end of the human journey is an interesting question, but not one that I would have any confidence in trying to answer.

Historically, the notion of the Millennium has been important. This is not any stretch of a thousand years counting from the presumed birth of Christ, but the thousand years of divine government abolishing all wrong and oppression and preceding the final struggle with the antichrist. Visionary religious expectations that political and social upheavals portended the commencement of the millennium ushered in the modern world. The Christian sects which embraced these hopes were in a sense reverting to type, for similar expectations of imminent apocalypse had marked the beginning of Christianity and may well have been one of the prime reasons for its success. The renewed vision of the social world about to end prior to holy renewal represented an important aspect of the Lutheran Reformation in the Germany of the early sixteenth century. The same pattern occurred with the English Revolution of the 1640s, perhaps most clearly exemplified as a grand narrative with the Fifth Monarchists, convinced that the monarchy's overthrow marked the end of the age of four secular monarchies (Assyrian, Babylonian, Greek and Roman) and signalled the beginning of the Fifth Monarchy, that of the Saints.

Utopia

Loosely speaking, these visions and expectations can be designated as utopian.[3] More precisely, however, that term should perhaps be reserved for secular versions of the millennium, given its origin in Thomas More's celebrated book, the English translation of whose title is, precisely, 'Nowhere' and which describes a perfect community whose institutions are human rather than divine creations. More's exact intentions in writing the book are unclear (and contrary to postmodernist theory, these intentions are vital in determining its meaning). It can be read as a satire on the oppressive social and cultural characteristics of More's England or as an imagined sketch for what a regime of social harmony would look like. Contrariwise, it may be intended as a demonstration of the kind of commonwealth whose realisation can never be hoped for in view of the ineradicable taint of original sin. Possibly the intention is even darker than that, and More intended to suggest not a perfect but a damnable society which the hubris of perfect institutions would produce – for the Utopians practise suicide and euthanasia, both mortal sins according to Catholic teaching and a standpoint which More, as a Catholic martyr, could not fail to share.

Be that as it may, Utopia came to enjoy a positive connotation, though again, as with the Hebrew grand narrative, the expanding technical possibilities and social visions of the early nineteenth century would almost certainly have given rise to utopian proposals and brought about attempts to institute utopian communities whether or not More had ever written. A whole line of such attempts are recorded, Robert Owen's being the best remembered.

In practical terms it may not make much difference, but conceptually there is an important distinction depending on whether such endeavours are seen by their creators as an act of will by an originator or originators unbeholden to the past, or whether historical development is seen as irresistibly pressing towards the culmination of the good society, whose time has now arrived. In the former case what we have is merely the attempt to create utopia by fiat, in the second a grand narrative.

There can be no question but that Hegel is the author, or at least the inspirer, of utopian perspectives in this second sense, although, with a different emphasis, credit should also be given to Condorcet, as will be discussed below. Hegel viewed the range of historical development as the progress of mind becoming conscious of itself. He did not however prescribe what should follow when that stage of consciousness had been attained, as he believed it had been with his own philosophy. The point about the original utopia and its imaginative successors is that they are static – the ground plan for the perfect society had been laid down, in some cases in even enough detail to include drainage systems, as Marx sarcastically remarked, and it was simply to be followed thereafter. Hegel came to convince himself that the end (in both senses) of history in the material sense had been attained with the Prussian semi-absolute monarchy, but he could scarcely pretend that this result approximated to any sort of utopian imagining – it was simply the appropriate material reflection of the development of Mind in its final stage.

Marx, famously, turned Hegel on his head or rather, as he put it, set him the right way up, finding the key to historical change in the dialectic of forces and relations of production rather than the self-development of Mind. The fundamental concept remains, however, in the perspective of both thinkers, that the development in question is cumulative and progressive, proceeding from a lower stage to a higher and, in Marx's case, culminating in a predetermined sociopolitical outcome – the triumph of the proletariat as a precursor to the classless, unalienated society of abundance, to conclude the epoch of prehistory and introduce that of history proper.

Marx and Engels were at pains to distance themselves from their utopian predecessors (though they did nevertheless express appreciation of their imaginative achievement) turning the term into one of political dismissiveness. They insisted instead that by contrast to the utopians they were 'scientific socialists' – i.e., that socialist society was not a scheme issuing from the brain of this or that thinker (least of all not themselves) but implicit in the course that history was following, and that their own achievement was to have recognised and explained this reality. They said this repeatedly and emphatically, all their writing confirms it and it seems to me that, for better or worse, it is the inescapable meaning of their entire *oeuvre*, both in theory and practice.

Marxist utopia?

An essential characteristic of the distinction that Marx drew between himself and the utopian socialists was the refusal to stipulate, beyond the most apparently evident outline, what the dictatorship of the proletariat or the socialist society would actually be like.[4] That, he stressed, was a matter for the proletarians dealing with the actual historical contingencies when the time came, to settle for themselves. The distinction is genuine and important, for, contrary to the fixities of utopia, it acknowledges the openness of history and the indefinite range of choices available to historical actors, even within the scheme of a grand narrative. Freedom, Engels remarked, is the recognition of necessity. This was not intended to mean, as it is frequently misrepresented, that we ought to recognise the inevitable and that we'll then feel reconciled to it, but that by understanding necessity we learn how it can be manipulated so that freedom can be exercised – in order to fly, it is essential to recognise the necessities of aerodynamics. Their contention was that because the laws governing the course of historical development had not been understood in the past, humanity was blindly a slave to them and so projects of freedom inevitably turned into their opposites. By contrast, the historical dialectic which had in the nineteenth century produced the material instruments for human liberation had also produced the understanding that would enable them to be used.

Undoubtedly Marxism was a teleology. It did not of course postulate a divine purpose to be worked out in and through the course of history, nor a universal Mind to be identified with History, in the style of Hegel. Nevertheless the final outcome of communist society and the initiation of history proper as distinct from prehistory were, on this argument, implicit in the very character of human society as collective consciousness engaging with the material world to produce the necessities and luxuries of life – a web of reciprocal labour. All the stages through which social evolution had passed, from primitive communism through every form of class society were moments, in the Hegelian sense, of the process. The Marxist reading of human history (which they polemically termed 'prehistory') led towards a predetermined result.

The vision was one which enthused and inspired several generations of activists around the globe and altered the direction of history in the twentieth century. It was certainly understandable that the attack which developed in France during the 1970s on the philosophical basis of Marxism should have concentrated upon this grand narrative. Clearly, in anything like its original and unrefined form it is untenable, and was evidently so even well before the events which terminated 'the short twentieth century', the collapse of the Soviet bloc and the USSR. Whether it nevertheless contains any elements that might still be valuable for historical understanding is something we will return to later on.

Liberal versions

There are other secular grand narratives, however, apart from the Marxian one and that have no relationship to Hegel. The oldest of these has its origins as far back as the eighteenth century and is the original form of what came to be termed 'The Whig Interpretation of History'. This was a peculiarly British, or more correctly, English, product and was at its most influential during the late nineteenth century, the era of high imperialism. It represented a climate of thought (as the word 'interpretation' implies) rather than a fully-developed ideological discourse like the Hegelian or Marxian.

It is a perspective on political development which sees the course of events since the Norman Conquest – or even since the Anglo-Saxon settlements – as leading, not accidentally or fortuitously, but ineluctably, to the climax of the Westminster constitution: the presumption that the Saxon Witanagemot, Magna Charta, the Bill of Rights, were preparatory stages for the fully developed system of two-party cabinet government, state institutions and common law characteristic of the Gladstonian era. It can be expressed in the terminology of writers who had unthinkingly internalised its assumptions – 'liberty broadening down from precedent to precedent'.

It can be seen sketchily at work in the official self-satisfaction with English political institutions (including the system of 'Old Corruption') manifested during the late eighteenth century in opposition to radical challenge. Half a century on, when that challenge had been absorbed and neutralised, the most significant and effective propagandist of the Whig interpretation, which was constructed to celebrate the outcome in the political and social stability of the 1850s, was Thomas Babington Macaulay whose (very readable) volumes are filled with asides as to how Britain owes her happy state of freedom at that time as much to the mistakes and frustrated bad intentions of tyrannical kings as to the good ones of Macaulay's heroes. However the technically much more sophisticated historians of the succeeding generation, Bury, Freeman, Acton and above all the great constitutional historian Bishop Stubbs, were scarcely less important in establishing this historiographical and popular climate, for whatever their technical merits they wrote within the framework that Macaulay had constructed and the presumption of the past as having been designed to lead to their present. As for the mechanisms through which this fortunate historical process was said to have been produced, it was no more than the endemic political good sense of the English or the British race, whereby even errors such as the dispute with and severance from the American colonies were providentially corrected and turned into assets.

Although English constitutional history was the normal theatre for this version of the Whig Interpretation, it could well be, and was, applied to other historical lines of development. The history of the British labour movement is a good example. Its institutional histories in the middle of the twentieth century, such as Francis Williams's *Fifty Years' March*[5] or Cole and Postgate's *The Common People*[6] interpreted the story from the eighteenth century through the struggles of the nineteenth century and the traumas of the early twentieth century as working in some sense to produce the perfection of the trade union and Party structures that existed at the time of Attlee's leadership. A much more sinister caricature (the term Whig scarcely seems appropriate but the formal aspect is the same) can be seen with the notorious *History of the Communist Party of the Soviet Union (B)* (published anonymously in 1938 under the auspices of the Soviet CP, edited by Stalin), designed to demonstrate that the course of the Russian revolutionary movement and the development of the Soviet state had found their natural and appropriate culmination in the glories of the Stalin regime of the late 1930s.

Once pointed out, it is immediately apparent that what is at issue here is an ideological construction – the plausibility of any Whig interpretation resides in its not being too closely inspected. In the case of the original version, it was named and attacked by Herbert Butterfield in the 1930s, significantly a decade when the notion of a providential happy outcome to the course of English history could self-evidently no longer be taken for granted – though, interestingly, he was to retract somewhat during the Second World War at a time when the historical validation of British institutions and culture appeared to be an urgent political necessity. The last flaring ember of this Whig interpretation can be seen in Winston Churchill's postwar *History of the English-Speaking Peoples*,[7] which was treated seriously only because of its author's reputation in other spheres – for Churchill in his politics and temperament was nothing if not a Whig of the old school.

There is, however, a much broader and a more effectively defensible version of the secular grand narrative in a liberal framework, also having its origins in the eighteenth century, intimately linked to the notion of progress – and the one which, it has to be said, despite all recent hesitations and challenges, continues to dominate the Western historical consciousness, not surprisingly in view of its apparently obvious character. In this light history is viewed as driven by two linked forces. The first of these is that of scientific and technological development, apparent throughout the span of history since the neolithic revolution and the introduction of agriculture (or possibly even earlier) culminating in the continuous and indefinite advance of the past two centuries and projected into the indefinite future. The presumption is that this process will go on generating endless economic growth and enhanced material welfare. Associated with it is the presumption that of necessity material affluence and security will bring in its train pressure for growing social freedoms, individual political rights and representative government.

It is a vision which originates in the Enlightenment and is given its first historical expression especially in the writings of the Scottish historians of the mid-eighteenth century, such as Ferguson. However the figure of that period who embodies and sums up such an outlook and whose linking of science and liberal political principles is explicit is the Marquis de Condorcet. Condorcet died during the French Revolution under the shadow of the guillotine – he committed suicide to avoid a certain death sentence and, impressively, wrote the *Sketch for a Historical Picture of the Progress of the Human Mind*[8] while in hiding, his interpretation of past and future history and his political testament. The Marquis was a liberal and an active participant in the early stages of the Revolution, but not a radical or democrat – he was being hunted because of his moderationism. His opposition to democracy was based upon the belief that the masses, in view of their circumstances and inferior education, lacked the capacity for rational analysis and judgement necessary for representative government.

Condorcet observed that science proceeded by open and uninhibited argument, unconstrained either by dogma or by force – the concepts and assertions of its practitioners were to be judged in the court of reason according to the evidence, and at no other tribunal. This was the secret of the scientific advances which had occurred in the course of the previous century. Political debate and decision ought to be conducted according to the same criteria. The marquis was not overwhelmed nor disillusioned by the turn of events in the Revolution and the situation in which it had landed him. Instead he expressed a serene confidence in the future in which the irresistible principles that he was enunciating must prevail, bringing with them universal harmony and happiness.[9]

Although not often expressed in such uncompromising terms, this in essence was the theme which underlay the liberal social and political thought of the nineteenth century and has descended to our own times, substantially reinforced now that its great rival, the Marxist tradition, has met with disaster. Presented with a Hegelian gloss it forms the underpinning of Francis Fukuyama's provocatively titled *The End of History and the Last Man*, which argues that history has indeed reached its conclusion with the triumph of liberal democracy and the defeat of all its challengers:

> A similar linkage between economic development and liberal democracy can be seen in Asia. Japan, the first East Asian state to modernise was the first to achieve a stable liberal democracy ... it is the younger, better educated members of Taiwan's parliament that have pushed most strongly to make it a representative institution ... In South Africa ... [by] the time of F. W. de Klerk's opening to the African National Congress in February 1990, the government was in many ways simply following the opinion of its white electorate, now little different in educational and occupational achievement from its counterparts in Europe and America.[10]

According to this interpretation Hegel was right in essence – he merely judged the culmination of history to have arrived too soon. Liberal capitalist democracy represents the optimum political arrangement for society, the one to which it 'naturally' and historically tends, and now globally triumphant it will in due course absorb the remaining pockets of backward social structure and reign for evermore. The idea has its attractions, and certainly the course of developments, looked at superficially (and Fukuyama's text is very superficial) can appear to justify it. It is not so much a question of liberty broadening down from precedent to precedent as prosperity and liberalism broadening down from technical advance to technical advance. The snake in this garden, increasingly intruding itself upon popular consciousness, is the realisation that technological advance has its costs, both human and more frightening still in the long term, environmental. Even so, as long as major catastrophe is averted, so great are the advantages of expanding technological capability that the general presumption that all is for the technological best is very difficult to dislodge.

This survey of grand narratives is of course necessarily incomplete – it would be possible to list numerous others, for example the global triumph of the Anglo-Saxon (or Teutonic, or Japanese) races, now totally discredited. Nonetheless, enough has been said to provide an indication of what the concept means and where, historically, it has been mainly influential. In one dimension all the grand narratives considered so far are teleologies, no less in the cases where the *telos* is projected into the future than in those where it is supposed to have already been attained, and as much where the driving force bringing history to its predetermined conclusion is regarded as internal to history as where it is supposed to be an outside agency. The recognition that *all* historical teleologies have to be rejected marks an important advance in historiography and in culture more generally. The postmodernists can take a measure of credit for that. Fukuyama's teleology is now the only serious one left in contention, but few serious thinkers would take it very seriously. It was none too convincing when it was first advanced and subsequent events have made it even less so. The mood which it expresses nevertheless does retain a strong hold on the popular consciousness and it is among the business of historians, so far as it lies in their power, to neutralise that form of mythology.

Evolution and culture

But are all conceivable grand narratives *necessarily* teleologies? That is a different matter. Here we have to return to the distinction between the identification of a goal predetermined in advance and a principle of explanation which can be applied after the fact. The difference is readily illustrated with reference to biological evolutionary theory. For long after Darwin's concepts captured the public imagination it was assumed as a matter of course that the purpose of evolutionary change through the aeons of half a billion years or so since multi-cellular life appeared on earth was to produce *homo sapiens* as its highest expression. That was a concept imbricated even in the standard diagram used to illustrate the process of biological evolution, the tree of life, with *homo sapiens* standing on its highest twig, the trilobites and other creatures of the Cambrian era forming the base.[11]

This is an entirely mistaken perception. It is now clear that without the recurrent mass extinctions, most likely as a result of cosmic accidents involving collision with large interplanetary objects, the shape of the earth's fauna would be very different from what it actually is and our own species would never have taken its bow on the biological stage. Even if the interplanetary cataclysm is discounted, any probability that evolution would result in ourselves is not very great. The probable ancestor of the vertebrates was a rather insignificant creature in the Cambrian seas and its chances of survival no greater than those of many which did not enjoy a future. As Stephen Jay Gould famously puts it, if we could rerun the film of life from the beginning there is no reason to expect that the outcome next time would be anything like what it turned out to be in actuality (this is disputed, but the weight of probability appears to favour Gould) – and certainly no reason to expect the arrival of a species equipped with an immense brain and the reasoning power to accompany that.[12] In other words humanity's current presence on earth (and equally that of any other species) is the result of an immense chain of contingencies, any of which may equally well have gone the other way.

None of these considerations however affects in the slightest the power of Darwin's concept of natural selection as an explanatory mechanism.[13] It reduces the mass of evolutionary phenomena, the series of appearances, to a single salient principle which enables the process to be understood. The question is – does something comparable apply in social evolution and in human affairs generally?

It would be pleasing to be able to answer this question with an unequivocal 'yes', but caution and hesitation is in order. The most that can be said with any confidence is that the jury is still out on this one, indeed it is scarcely starting its deliberations. There are two major immediate issues that have to be dealt with: first, the immense confusion introduced in the past by treating possible explanatory principles as teleologies, and the necessity now of sharply distinguishing the two approaches that superficially appear so alike. Second, there is the basic difference between social and biological evolution in that the latter occurs blindly and without any conscious intent, whereas in the former it is conscious actors who are under consideration – whether their conscious action determines the eventual historical outcome is another important question, but the fact that they *are* conscious beings is not an irrelevance.

Cultural progress

In a certain sense a direction to history, identifiable trends, progress if one wants to use that term, is plain and undeniable. Over the millennia the number of human beings inhabiting the earth has grown unceasingly, and in recent centuries exponentially. So has the proportion living in urban locations. So has the mass of material wealth, literacy, understanding of nature and the power to shape and control the physical environment. Of course it may very well all end in tears, and indeed looks all too likely to do so, but that is a separate issue. Of course too it has not been a steady and uninterrupted process, but one riven by contradictions and arrived at via the most appalling and atrocious events and processes. 'Every document of civilisation', as Walter Benjamin asserted, 'is also a document of barbarism.' In addition, the outcome so far has scarcely been one to evoke unequivocal applause, resulting in a world with an obscene maldistribution of resources and life opportunities. For the majority of the world's population who have lived and died during its course, the twentieth century may well figure as the worst of all centuries – though for the lucky minority it has unquestionably been the best. Mark Poster puts it thus, with reference to the Frankfurt School, 'No perspective on modern history could be adequate after Auschwitz if it portrays the past centuries as the march of reason.'[14] That seems unquestionable at first glance, but unfortunately for this argument it confuses two different meanings of reason – moral reason and technological, and reason in the sense of command over nature is no less reason when it is put to humanly perverted purposes – 'pathological modernity' in Detlev Peukert's phrase.[15]

Whether it is to be regarded in a morally positive light, viewed with suspended judgement or deplored, it is impossible to argue seriously that 'progress' in the tightly defined sense noted above has not characterised social evolution. For historians who are not content merely to concentrate on the areas of their expertise but who are exercised for whatever reason about the course of human development considered as a whole, the question is whether this trend is written into the character of human society from its paleolithic beginnings. The invention/discovery of agriculture (with all the implications for what follows) may have been an accident, but (given appropriate climatic conditions and suitable plant species) was it an accident waiting to happen? The answer to this question at least can be suggested with some confidence – it is almost certainly yes, in view of the fact that the discovery was made separately in several different and unconnected locations.

Reasonable certainty probably stops at that point. It is simply not possible to say whether within the techniques common to agriculturalists – sedentary settlement, pottery, woven fabric, domesticated animals – there is implicit the further developments of urbanisation, metal-working, written script and the sort of cultures generically known as 'civilized',[16] let alone the techniques of cognitive abstraction termed 'science'. There is no suggestion in any case that human culture considered as a whole *had* to develop in the manner it did – that would be a teleology – but simply a question of whether, assuming the likely appearance of agriculture, in the social interaction of human beings with their environment and with each other a general tendency exists for development along the lines of multiplication, urbanisation and growing command of nature. My own guess, for what it is worth, is that there is indeed a tendency in this direction, but that it is a relatively weak one – that social evolution in some region or other of the world to the level of the classical Roman or Chinese civilisations (which were both, especially the latter, enormously sophisticated and technically knowledgeable) was a reasonable probability, but the probability is also that it will not go beyond that point.

The cognitive revolution associated with scientific method, which has transformed the understanding of nature, was something which, although it has very long roots – roots stretching from classical Greece to the seventeenth century in Western Europe and which might very well have been cut on more than one occasion – has emerged only once, and most likely was a historical contingency which might as easily have never taken place. Moreover, all the efforts of physical scientists, developing throughout the eighteenth and early nineteenth centuries, would have remained intrinsically limited without the concurrent emergence of unprecedented technologies. It is easy to see that so long as societies were confined to natural power sources – human and animal muscle, wind and water – the level of technological development was intrinsically limited; roughly to that achieved in classical Chinese culture.[17] To pass beyond that stage requires the development of an artificial power source, in the first place that of steam; and that in turn was dependent upon natural endowments, especially coal, in the right place – and above all the existence of a sufficient market making it worth undertaking the necessary investment to make the widespread use of this engine a practicable possibility.

Throughout the millennia human society, considered globally, had been accumulating social and cultural capital and had effectively become a global system well before the technological breakthrough,[18] yet the chances are that only an unpredictable and unlikely chain of circumstances (analogous perhaps in the biological evolutionary scheme to asteroid collision which produced the mass extinction of 65 million years ago) enabled that capital to be exploited to bring to reality the world which we now enjoy or endure.

What implications does all this hold for historical grand narrative or metanarrative? It is highly unlikely that any single dominant process equivalent to natural selection in biological evolution will be identified for the course of human development from the paleolithic to the era of advanced technology. If however certain tendencies or probable lines of development can be empirically identified and the reality appreciated that particular levels of development determine the range of possibilities open to those who inhabit them, then conclusions about social evolution can be sustained. It is not simply a case of one damned thing after another and even less one damned narrative after another. The generalisations are sketchy to be sure, but they do provide a framework. Moreover, it can be empirically observed that during the past five millennia literate agriculturally-based cultures on the Eurasian landmass have tended towards certain recurrent patterns of state centralisation and dissolution, a very useful framework for understanding and interpreting certain broad areas of past history. With the breakthrough to industrial technology, however, all previous bets are off, though of course industrialised market society (and the non-industrialised spaces within its orbit) exhibits a developmental logic of its own, though of a very different sort.

Marxism

Lurking behind every endeavour to interpret long stretches of historical development is the spectre of Karl Marx, and as noted above, the assault on grand narrative was initially directed at Marxism as a specific ideological enemy. Quite apart from the postmodernist assault, however, in the past half-century there have been a number of very interesting attempts to advance plausible interpretations of long-term historical evolution, such as those of Gellner, Runciman or Mann,[19] and all have been presented explicitly as alternatives to Marxism. That this should be the case suggests that the Marxian perspective on history or historical materialism, being still felt to be worth refuting and replaced, remains more than a mere historical curiosity, but if so, what status does it have and what does it have to offer to the historians and their audiences in the twenty-first century?

First it is necessary, as we might say, to deconstruct Marx's idea of history. Neither Marx nor Engels published any text that was specifically a work of history in the normal meaning of the term, although everything they wrote is saturated with a profound historical consciousness. Their concept of history is implicit in what they wrote regarding economics, politics, social theory and current affairs. The essence of historical materialism is regarded as being contained in the fragment 'A Preface to the Critique of Political Economy', with its phrase regarding the precedence of social being over social consciousness. The vision of human development associated with Marxism is sketched in the early sections of *The Communist Manifesto,* where the assertion that all hitherto recorded history is the history of class struggle occurs and the span of human history is outlined – though as a preliminary to what the main business of the pamphlet is about. A more developed examination of historical development is contained in *The German Ideology*, but this was never published in their lifetimes, nor, after its initial intended publication failed, did they consider it worth resurrecting. The central endeavour of Marx's life however, was the critique of the dominant political economy of his era (which he of course regarded as a historical concept as well as a historical reality) and it is not an accident that his masterpiece was entitled *Capital* rather than *Capitalism*.

Any reading of Marx's and Engels's argument must unavoidably conclude that their historical outlook, with its Hegelian antecedents, did constitute a teleology – though Frederic Jameson denies that the sequence of modes of production is actually a master narrative.[20] However, it is difficult to read in any other light their contention that class struggle was the central fact of all history and would culminate in the victory of the proletariat once the bourgeoisie had created the necessary preconditions. For Marx historical evolution was driven by the contradiction between developing means of production and relations of production unable to facilitate their full development – when the contradiction became unsustainable then the mode of production underwent revolutionary change. The contradictions inherent in the capitalist mode necessitated its replacement by socialised production which would realise the potential, implicit but unrealisable under the capitalist mode, for full human development. The proletariat was the only social force capable of bringing this to fruition and would not fail to bring it about.[21] Past history was interpreted in the light of a predetermined outcome which they believed that their scientific approach had identified. Not that they thought of themselves as demiurges of history or even as geniuses who had been gifted with insights denied to their contemporaries – from their point of view (and they explicitly said as much) the same conditions which were producing the impending proletarian revolution would necessarily produce its intellectual foreshadowing – that just happened to have been embodied in themselves.

Marx was easily the most perceptive social thinker of his generation or his century, in some ways his insight into developing tendencies was far ahead of anybody else's, and his unique forecast of how the nature of capital would tend to develop towards monopoly concentration in the absence of a socialist revolution has turned out pretty much as predicted. Capital, but not capitalism. Although the present division of the world between the affluent and the destitute might be suggested to vindicate the notion he projected of increasing wealth at one pole and concentrated destitution at the other, in fact the adaptability and flexibility of capitalism in securing both economic and social strategies for its own survival and the total failure of the proletariat to combine against it have conclusively refuted Marx in empirical terms.[22]

The teleological form in which historical materialism was cast therefore has to be rejected along with all teleologies. Is there however – to use Marx's own terminology – a valid kernel within the historically discredited husk? The question of class struggle is worth considering initially. Marx said that he claimed no credit for this discovery – it had been enunciated by earlier thinkers. Much of course depends on what is to be understood by 'class'. It seems to me that the concept becomes incoherent if one accepts E.P. Thompson's insistence that class consciousness is an intrinsic part of the meaning of social class (though there is some warrant in Marx for such an interpretation), and even more so if it is presumed that the individuals and collectives of the past have to be taken at their own social valuation – that their primary social identity was whatever they themselves considered it to be. My starting point in this regard is therefore the one that it is legitimate for historians to recognise things about the inhabitants of that foreign country, the past, that they could not recognise about themselves and that they occupied a class position whether they knew it or not.

This said, it appears evident that individuals either produce the necessities (and the luxuries) of life for themselves – co-operatively of course and including a system of roughly equal exchange – or else they do not. If they do not, then the obligation has to be undertaken by somebody else and if a significant social group achieves a position to enforce that obligation on the remainder of the populace whether by economic or extra-economic coercion then they are constituted as an exploiting class, regardless of whether the parties involved recognise themselves in those terms.[23] Historically that has been the reality over the span of written history since the emergence of the early riverain civilisations of the Middle East. In general terms the standard form of the relationship has been the compulsory extraction of a surplus – whether under religious persuasion, legal obligation embodied in systems of law, or sheer terror (or indeed an amalgam of all three) – from subordinated cultivators. Chattel slavery has been important in certain ancient cultures, but never central.[24]

There exists, however, another method of extracting a surplus apart from the three noted above, and that, in the most general terms, is through systems of unequal exchange, which may in some instances embody an openly coercive element, or on the other hand conceal any coercive character and have the appearance of forming an entirely voluntary relationship. These too are of great antiquity, but prior to the era of industrialisation and capitalist economic structures they formed a peripheral aspect of social relationships, existed so to speak on the margins of the pre-capitalist economies. The modern era however sees them develop as the primary mode of profit and accumulation through the creation of workforces which have access to the means of subsistence (or at least socially acceptable means of subsistence) only by labouring for the profit of an employer – whether individual, small firms, transnational corporations or the state-supported organisations that exist in the last instance to perpetuate the relations which keep the system operational. As Bertold Brecht expressed it, 'What's robbing a bank compared to opening one?'

That of course is a very oversimplified outline and ignores whatever role may be played by the state in allocating the surplus between classes apart from deploying instruments of repression. Moreover, the components of the social groups in question interpenetrate, are fuzzy at the edges and give rise to any number of problems of definition. Nonetheless it seems clear enough and hard to deny, except from motives of deliberate or unintentional obfuscation, that any twenty-first century society, and global society as a whole, is made up of class groupings which exist in conditions of exploitative relations to each other and that these are overwhelmingly relations of unequal exchange mediated through the labour market.

Class

Relationships of exploitation are inherently and intrinsically antagonistic in character, a theatre of perpetually renewed conflict and negotiation as the parties concerned endeavour to define and redefine the terms of the relationship to their respective better advantage – a character even of slave societies where the degree of scope for the exploited party to extract concessions is at its most minimal. The Roman Censor Cato once boasted that he made sure that his slaves never did anything other than work or sleep, but this was unusual – and the fact that the comment was noted as exceptional speaks for itself.

It is of course very much to the advantage of the dominating class to define if possible the relationship as non-antagonistic (hardly possible in the case of slavery but feasible in nearly every other), and various ideological formulations have been used throughout history as instruments to this purpose. The culture of Hindu society concealed economic exploitation through an elaborate and religiously-justified system of hereditary castes, well designed to confuse and segregate the division of labour and conceal the extraction of surplus. The medieval era developed the concept of three harmonious and divinely ordained orders of society, men who pray, who fight and who work and thus the knight and the clerk need have no qualms about taking from the peasant or the artisan what after all was no more than their rightful due.

The exploitative character of the wage contract is in different ways both easier and more difficult to conceal. In the early decades of industrialisation in Britain, when an officially religious culture still predominated, efforts were made to instil into wage labourers the idea of a divine obligation to serve their masters faithfully and uncomplainingly. Edmund Burke spoke of 'the laws of commerce, which are the laws of nature and therefore the laws of God'. In the course of the nineteenth century religiously-influenced labour leaders carried on the same tradition. On the Continent at a later date confessional trade unions organised by the Catholic Church strove to counter revolutionary influences by asserting the essential equity of the wage contract and non-antagonistic relations between employers and workers. In all cases conflict nevertheless was constantly breaking out – over the price of labour-time, over hours of work, over conditions of employment – and to the duty of docility in an essentially harmonious system the workforce would pose the counter-demand of a 'fair deal' – which did not dispute the essence of potential harmony in the future but certainly asserted its non-existence in the present. Of course, as Ralph Miliband has pointed out, these conflicts did not engage all the members of the respective classes at the same time, but only a limited number of individuals in isolated episodes, so class conflict in this sense is a shorthand term for disputes which erupt and are settled, with or without overt interruption of the work process, at countless different times and in vast numbers of localities, an ongoing and perpetual struggle with definite purposes certainly, but only in exceptional instances with any strategic intention of shifting class relationships as such in a drastic or fundamental manner.

In any event it became clear that though religion might provide a useful antidote to revolutionary ideologies it would not effectively discourage workers disputing with their employers over the allocation of their product. The wage contract however has two distinctive and connected attributes. In the first place it has a voluntary appearance (on the assumption that property relations are taken for granted and not to be questioned). However it shares that particular characteristic with relationships of rent or hire and it is not too difficult for the working tenant or leasee to come to view the landowner or equivalent as a parasite abstracting part of the tenant's earnings and whose ownership privileges therefore lack legitimacy. The wage contract is different however – it possesses the unique quality that although the worker may appreciate on an abstract level that he or she is working for the boss's profits and therefore part of his/her worktime is being abstracted, the payment of wages, however miserably inadequate, unlike all other economically exploitative relationships, does not have the overt appearance of *taking something away from* the employee. A sense of exploitation and grievance may certainly be there, but the mechanism by which it operates does not strike on the nerves as it would for a serf or a sharecropper.

Therefore the impression of a potentially fair bargain remains if only employers can be induced to it by trade union or legislative pressure and this is not the least of the reasons (there are plenty of others, including potential social mobility and the reality that workers do indeed have a lot more to lose than their chains) why Marx's expectations of a revolutionary class united in a revolutionary project by general understanding of the inherently exploitative character of wage labour have been confounded – class consciousness may very well be powerful and even militant but it still regards the overall social order as acceptable in actuality or at least potentiality. Indeed in societies of strong labour movements that is the normal reality. There has only been one successful working-class revolution in history, namely that in Russia in 1917 and in that case the workforce did not overthrow the state primarily out of fury at the nature of the wages system.

The Marxian concept of social class remains invaluable for analysing exploitation in its economic dimension throughout history, but there is no simple relationship (a relationship may exist but it is a weak one) between that and the social identities formed by the various collectives involved. Other multiple identities, sexual, cultural, political and national, come into the equation. Occasionally the relationship looks obvious. The political and cultural attitudes of the traditional German lower middle class between 1870 and 1914 appear a fairly clear projection of their economic situation in the Germany of the period. Yet across the border the majority of their French counterparts, similarly situated in economic terms, adhered to a totally different political-cultural outlook. To be sure intense nationalism was manifested in both cases, but nationalism in the two cases took on wholly different meanings.[25]

Class mobilisations are fairly uncommon and very seldom indeed do they occur under the banner of class. The most frequent examples of such mobilisations are those of exploiting classes uniting to protect their privileges and property against threats from below, as observed more often in the twentieth century than most previous ones, from Italy to Chile. This is accounted for without any doubt by the fact that in the twentieth century, the 'age of extremes', attempts to overturn the class order have been exceptionally persistent and frequent. However, the rhetoric surrounding such counter-mobilisations has seldom if ever presented them in terms of defending privileges of exploitation, but in the name of religion, family, property, order against anarchy, culture or even civilisation. Nor for that matter on the rare occasions when industrial working classes have mobilised as a class (Russia always excepted) has it been under uncompromising class slogans – but generally by reference to such concepts as 'fairness' (Britain 1926), 'the people' (Spain 1936), or 'democracy' (Germany 1918–20).

Where does this leave the grand narrative of class, understood in the Marxian sense of systemic exploitative relationships? Such relationships have unquestionably been a pervasive feature of social existence throughout recorded history and have produced a level of ongoing and constant conflict, sometimes less intense, sometimes more so, but only very occasionally erupting into violent armed struggle and on those occasions almost always culminating in the total defeat and exemplary punishment of the insurgent subordinate classes, from the slave revolts of Roman times to the repression of peasant guerrillas in Latin America during recent decades. However, the record does not support the scenario sketched at the beginning of *The Communist Manifesto* of the struggle between classes as the driving force behind historical development, with new forms of production relations embodied in subordinate classes bursting through to replace the rule of historically superannuated classes and instituting new modes of production. Closer historical analysis of ruling-classes-in-waiting, whether feudalists at the fag-end of the Roman Empire, the seventeenth-century English bourgeoisie or the eighteenth-century French one shows them to have been not at all revolutionary classes and indeed quite at ease with the decadent rulers they were about to replace – or indeed even well integrated into the latter's society. Although these classes may well have been the beneficiaries of the upheavals and the social reconstitutions which followed the revolutionary storms, and though their specific class ideologies may have pervaded the cultural atmosphere (and these realities are undoubtedly of central importance), they neither initiated nor directed the revolutions which elevated their representatives into the seats of power nor intended the overall social transformation which consolidated the mode of production with which they are identified.

Nietzsche and Foucault

It has to be conceded that Frederick Nietzsche was more than a madman with a dubious ideology and a preposterous moustache; he was unquestionably a thinker of genius, even if misapplied. Even so it is difficult to understand why he has taken on such iconic status for a generation of reputedly left-wing writers and theorists over the past three decades or so. He was a vociferous elitist and an embittered misogynist, a celebrant of slavery and relentless enemy of all the emancipatory movements at the end of the nineteenth century – rationalism, feminism and above all socialism.[26]

Perhaps part of the answer is that in addition he possessed an acute insight into the dark side of modernity, repudiated it with all his considerable energies and foresaw its disintegration, albeit from an individualist position on the extreme right rather than the left. He influenced many of the leading European minds of the earlier twentieth century and was admired by the Nazis – Hitler once presented Mussolini with a set of his complete works – though it is unfair to see him as a progenitor of National Socialism; had he lived into the 1920s or 1930s he would almost certainly have despised it and he was relatively free from the rabid antisemitism which characterised the German right of his own time. He foreshadowed more the German 'conservative revolutionaries' of the Weimar era, such as Ernest Junger, who naturally viewed him as their theoretical inspiration.[27]

Be that as it may, Nietzsche may be reckoned to be, more than any other thinker, the patron saint of postmodernism – he himself commented, 'I have a terrible fear that some day one will pronounce me *holy*'[28] – the twentieth-century critique of modernity springs directly from his attack, his insistence that 'the apparent world is the only: the "real world" is merely a lie' and:

> We have arranged for ourselves a world in which we can live – with the acceptance of bodies, lines, surfaces, causes and effects, motion and rest, form and content. Without these articles of faith no one would now be able to live. But this by no means constitutes a proof.

> Life is no argument. Amongst the conditions of life error might be one.[29]

It can be viewed under one aspect as an extension of the earlier Romantic recoil from a world increasingly being remade by science, technology and mass institutions. For Nietzsche modernity (and certainly too the Christian era which had preceded it) represented a decline, a falling away from a classical era of greater authenticity and the aristocratic values said to underpin it.

If one takes Nietzsche seriously then clearly history, in the sense of historical beliefs, has to fall into the category of useful fictions rather than being regarded as in any sense a true record of the past. Knowledge, in the words of Peter Dews, was whatever was taken for knowledge in a particular era.

Michel Foucault

For Michel Foucault as much as Nietzsche, the idea of progress was anathema. Foucault claimed that his reading of Nietzsche was central to the formation of his mature thought, in his shift between the 1960s and the 1970s from a structuralist to a poststructuralist mode – though he himself did not employ that terminology. The influence can be seen in several dimensions of Foucault's later work. It is a reasonable inference from his writings that, like his mentor, Foucault regarded modernity as a derogation, a degeneration from an earlier more authentic state of social being, despite the fact that no such proposition is ever explicitly articulated. Foucault's intellectual trademark, so to speak, again paralleling Nietzsche, is his focus on (it might be fair to say obsession with) power as the constitutive force of intersubjective reality, and in particular constitutive of knowledge and its discourses. Here however there is an important difference. Whereas Nietzsche viewed power in this sense in a positive light – the superior individuals were those who imposed their order upon the chaotic flux of reality, achievement reaching its highest expression in artistic creation – Foucault interpreted power-knowledge in negative terms, as the expression of relations of domination and subordination to which he was politically opposed.

Hayden White, before Foucault had fully developed his standpoint, had some interesting observations to make.[30] He refers to Foucault as an 'anti-historical historian' and suggests that, striving for 'the dis-remembrance of things past ... he writes "history" in order to destroy it as a discipline, as a mode of consciousness, and as a mode of (social) existence',[31] adding that 'To transfer prose into poetry is Foucault's purpose.'[32] White also notes a bifurcation in structuralism, between what he terms its 'positivist' branch with scientific pretensions, represented by figures like Lévi-Strauss or Althusser, and the 'perversely obscurantist', 'eschatological' fork who 'take seriously Mallarmé's conviction that things exist in order to live in books. For them the whole of human life is to be treated as a "text" the meaning of which is nothing but what it is',[33] who it might be said, proceed by assertion, rhetoric and metaphor in place of argument and demonstration. As a designation of what was to develop into poststructuralism, White's comment undoubtedly represents an acute early insight.

The principal targets of Foucault's critique were what may be termed the applied social sciences[34] of the epoch of modernity – medicine, penology, criminology, psychology and psychiatry – and it must be conceded that all of them have murky pasts and have been complicit to greater or lesser degrees with the malign operations of authoritarian power holders[35] (the same point could doubtless be made about historiography). Foucault however means something more and different from this: he does not for an instant accept that these were neutral techniques which unfortunately got into the wrong hands. Instead he argues, and here he is drawing on his structuralist past, that they were constituted in discourse. By discourse is meant 'a collection of ideas and practices with a common object and mode of discussion' – and discourse is inevitably and invariably about power, power constitutes it and the knowledge it produces, hence the striking phrase, 'regimes of truth'. It is not simply that the discourses of power/knowledge are coercively imposed: the worst aspect is that the patient/prisoner/citizen is induced to internalise them – like Winston Smith at the conclusion of *Nineteen Eighty-Four*, though without requiring the apparatus of Room 101.

Why should it be that the human sciences have these sinister characteristics? As Peter Dews perceptively notes, Foucault is echoing a central concern of the Frankfurt School, itself echoing Max Weber – the fear that the development of instrumental reason was a Frankenstein process running out of control which threatened to suck identity and personality out of the individual, inaugurate the servile state and reduce the populace to a homogenised mass of tabulated, categorised, regimented, controlled and contented ciphers.[36] All this quite irrespective of the intentions of the individuals directing the process, they need be neither Nazis nor Stalinists, their intentions might well be the most humane and worthy imaginable but instrumental reason enforced its own requirements and the outcome was the same in any case, with the controllers being as much prisoners of the process as the controlled. In

Foucault's universe power does not belong to individuals, groups or institutions, it is impersonal, pervasive.

The question remains as to why instrumental reason should take this form rather than a benign one. Both the Frankfurt School and Foucault were strongly influenced by psychoanalysis or psychoanalytically-derived concepts, and so to that extent the answer might be sought in the constitution of the human psyche; but the adherents of Critical Theory were Marxists, of however eccentric a stamp, and could therefore ground their analysis in the dialectic of a class-divided society. For Foucault, however, the naked, undifferentiated operations of power underlying all discourse appears to present the only option, and the more effectively instrumental the more malign. To cite Dews again, 'For Foucault, the mere fact of becoming an object of knowledge represents a kind of enslavement. Cognition is itself a form of domination.'[37]

Apart from the concept of power-knowledge, Foucault's other main original offering to historical understanding, developed early in his work, is that of the episteme, which might be defined roughly as the collective mental framework which structures the discourses of a particular epoch, the received assumptions about what can and cannot be thought. On Foucault's showing the epistimes (supposedly four of them succeeding each other since the sixteenth century) are hermetically sealed mental boxes, the nature of meaning and understanding in any of them being incommensurable with that in any other. There is indeed a resemblance to Kuhn's paradigms, but Foucault's is a more far-reaching and radical concept. No explanation is offered, however, to account for the transition from one epistime to its successor – they appear as inexplicable and arbitrary breaks in cultural consciousness.[38]

Foucault, whatever his disclaimers, must be regarded as having formulated a version of grand narrative or metanarrative, 'a philosophy of history in the "speculative" manner of Vico, Hegel, and Spengler',[39] and as we have seen it is implicitly, whatever the supposed incommensurability of the epistimes, one of degeneration. This is especially apparent in his last work, the three-volume *History of Sexuality*. The title is somewhat misleading, for the text is really an exploration of sexual attitudes and practices in the ancient world, mostly that of Greece and Rome, compared to those of the contemporary era, to the disadvantage of the latter. The essence of the argument is that the inhabitants of the ancient world were not imprisoned within the discourses of sexuality that torment their descendants nowadays, but rather enjoyed beneficially those of desire and eroticism. A particular standpoint however is discernible in the discussion of classical sexual relations, namely that of the free citizen in relation to his equals and his inferiors. (It could be argued that that only reflects the nature of the available sources, but it would presumably be possible, especially for someone of Foucault's intellectual disposition, to read between the lines.) In the *History of Sexuality* slaves are referred to (very briefly) and women, evidently, at greater length but no sense emerges that those were the people on whom the burdens of classical eroticism and sexual practices fell – which might indeed go some way towards explaining the attraction for them of the sexual renunciatory attitudes associated with ancient Christianity.[40]

Both Foucault's conceptual apparatus and his empirical practice have come under severe criticism from practising historians[41] and even theorists in the poststructuralist camp:

> In fact there is no reason why the acceptance of a discursive approach to history should lead to an acceptance of Foucault's particular conception of discourse. Nor is there any reason to endorse his persistent practice of merging the ambition to improve with the ambition to control,[42] the aspiration to emancipate with the desire to punish. It is upon the basis of such shoddy historiographical procedures that Foucault constructs his tendentious picture of the Enlightenment, in which by covertly continuing to rely upon a Marxist conception of the bourgeoisie and its history, Foucault is able to imply that those who sought to establish civil equality and the representative state also in some way colluded in 'the dark side of these processes'.

(This is written by a critic who accuses Foucault of being too materialistic and insufficiently committed to a metaphysic of discourse.[43])

Sweeping assertions regarding the efficacy of social control or the all-pervasiveness of regimes of truth fall apart upon close inspection. Wider claims in relation to epistemes or the history of sexuality appear to be based upon assertion rather than evidence. Foucault's reputation probably owes more to his stylistic energy than to the intrinsic strength of his concepts or theories – again a very Nietzschean outcome. Foucault's overarching historical claims, which he reinforces with terms such as 'archaeology' and 'genealogy' used in senses quite different from the normal, surely embody a deconstructionist version of grand narrative; but if there is any good reason (apart from Foucault's own assertions) for regarding them as plausible in any sense it is nowhere to be found in either his writings or those of his disciples. At any rate they contain no explanatory principle of development. All the same, as Peter Dews notes – from a critical stance:

> ... the core of his historical argument, that modern societies in a panoply of forms of information, theorization and analysis which are not *simply* ideological – and which he groups together as the 'human sciences' – are central elements in techniques of social management and social control, demand to be taken seriously.[44]

Grand narrative or long-term explanation?

It is seldom, if ever, possible to prove a negative and so it is with the question of whether or not modernity as our culture understands it was in some sense encoded into the trend of historical development and bound sooner or later, in some location or other, to emerge into history and go on to engulf the globe. The irony of history is well demonstrated in the fact that until quite recently the intuitive answer for historians would have appeared to have been 'yes' – the combined weight of population growth, scientific rationality, technological innovation and social rationality, once they had reached a certain critical mass, pressing irresistibly towards a breakthrough of the sort which did in fact occur. At the commencement of the twenty-first century, however, an answer of 'probably no' sounds more intuitively convincing – that only very peculiar, contingent and intrinsically rather unlikely conditions supplied the environment in which the crucial breakthroughs would occur – 'stagnation' after a certain level of development well below that of artificial power sources being by far the more probable outcome, as was the case in ancient Egypt or Mesopotamia, classical Greece or Rome and traditional China. Since the site of the transformation was in fact Britain and began with its agrarian structures it is not impossible that an event as insignificant in the overall scale of world history as the Norman Conquest might have made the crucial difference.

That, however, is not the same thing as saying that the outcome which did prevail and which forms our contemporary reality was accidental, undetermined or inexplicable. Unless the principle of causation is to be denied, then *after the event* the line of development can be understood and explained, although actually doing so may be very difficult and will always be tentative and provisional. To adapt a phrase of R.H.Tawney's: 'All flesh is grass, and historians are more grassy than most.' Nonetheless some explanations will encompass more empirical data than others, more accurately identify and define chains of causation

– will in general terms wear better and will do so despite cultural changes taking place over centuries. For these reasons the great historians of the classical world are esteemed for historical insight as well as literary quality, and likewise the Venerable Bede, precisely because his work succeeds in rising above the conceptual limitations of the early medieval Anglo-Saxon culture which produced it.

Explanation of this kind is always likely to take on the appearance of a grand narrative, or at least to assume one implicitly as a background. To stick with our example above, Bede was writing the history of the English church and people with the assumptions of Christian revelation as his foundation and the conversion of the English to the Roman version of Christianity as a manifestation of divine providence. The situation of most contemporary historians is of course very different. Few concern themselves with themes embracing the long-term progress of human society, but confine their endeavours to much more manageable and restricted fields of vision. Nevertheless, no present-day historian, no matter how localised his or her field of study in time or space, can escape awareness of the unique historical transformation which produced the modern world and at least an outline knowledge of how it happened. Everything they study and write is placed willy-nilly and produced in that context – the grand narrative in that sense at least is inescapable.

E.H. Carr, although he explicitly spurned the Victorian confidence in historical progress, nevertheless undoubtedly shared it and the chapter entitled 'History as Progress' in his famous text now looks as dated as anything coming out of the nineteenth century. On the other hand Francis Fukuyama's assertion that history has come to an end carries the implication that it was indeed progressing somewhere up until the present, although it has now arrived at its terminus. It must be acknowledged that (although Fukuyama is nothing if not superficial and simplistic) it is indeed difficult at present to see a horizon beyond global liberal capitalism with a democratic top-dressing (other than the abyss of environmental catastrophe) that is more probably due to the imperfections of our perception rather than because all other alternatives are genuinely exhausted. Nevertheless the past century has unquestionably been very educative for historians and has subjected all the grand narratives of the modern era to an unforgiving scrutiny. From the vantage point of the current stages reached by both history and historiography a number of cautious and limited postulates may be offered regarding what we now know of the historical process in general. In a sense the modernity of the past two centuries has functioned as a historical laboratory, in that it has enormously accelerated processes which were previously glacial in their rate of change and transformation – population growth and shift, technical innovation, production processes, the interaction of social groups and cultural renovation. The consequences of such developments are observable in a fashion that has been true for no previous historical era.

First, it is unlikely that it will ever be possible to identify a single driving force or motor of historical evolution, such as contradictions between forces and relations of production or the class struggle. Though these may continue to have great explanatory force in particular historical contexts, whatever it is that has pushed history to the point that it has reached is diverse and multifarious. If Marx's insights continue to have validity it is the very considerable gaps and absences within them that have evoked the explorations of writers such as Gellner, Runciman or Mann. Second, contingency almost certainly plays a very significant role, which if one attributes major importance to human agency, is certainly what is to be expected. History could have taken a different course on many past occasions and likewise its future development is not predetermined. If the historical record were available only up to the fifteenth century it would be plausible to conclude that human society was structurally so constituted that only a very limited range of social possibilities was available and that history could be no more than a series of endless repetitions on a few restricted themes. We know in actuality that is not the case. The logic of history has to be evaluated in the light of the reality that modernity actually occurred. Twentieth-century historiography, any more than its nineteenth-century predecessor, has not succeeded in identifying an explanatory frame which satisfactorily comprehends, on a broad scale, the empirical realities of actual historical development. However it has, in conjunction with the realities of the age of extremes, removed a number of illusions. The challenge of the forthcoming century will be to establish whether such a framework can in fact be constructed – or otherwise.

7

Identity and Morality

All historical reconstruction is intrinsically partial and limited – no matter whether it be a survey of world history or an examination of how English origins can be inferred from the surname of an obscure medieval Sicilian bureaucrat.[1] As with these extreme examples, reconstruction is always partial and limited in different ways.

Particular instances may diverge, but the standard convention is that all historians at the beginning of their career select a field in which they will specialise, and this defines the area in which they conduct their own research (whether singly or in collaboration) and comment on that of others. Eric Hobsbawm, for example, does not write on medieval history, nor Natalie Zemon Davies on women in classical Rome. The initial choice may be contingent in the sense that the individual could equally well have selected something else; though not arbitrarily, as there will always be a reason why a particular choices were made – Edward Thompson's for example are well documented.

Once made, the incentives to stick with that particular choice are very great. For one thing life is short, and having invested time, intellectual energy and commitment in one particular branch, to begin all over again and acquire expertise elsewhere is a daunting proposition. Very few people have the facility for languages that enables them to acquire a reading (let alone a speaking) knowledge of a new one in a short time. If the historian has achieved early in life a mastery, let us say of English, French, German and Russian – an impressive enough accomplishment – and has produced creditable work in twentieth-century European history based upon that knowledge, there would have to have very pressing motivations to decide also to acquire the linguistic skills to begin working in Chinese or pre-colonial Indian history.

Linguistic restrictions of this sort, which apply *a fortiori* the further away in time the historian's chosen field, are only the most obvious ones. For work outside the modern era a range of technical skills is necessary, such as palaeography (the interpretation of earlier handwriting styles).[2] Such technical considerations are only the beginning. Practising historians must, as we have seen, become and remain constantly familiar and up-to-date with all the secondary literature in their chosen field, both books and periodicals, and they need to know their way around the published and unpublished primary sources. This does not mean that they must read all the latter (or even all the secondary material), which would be a totally insane ambition, but that they must know what and where the archives are, and have a working knowledge of what they can expect to find in them when they go looking. They must of course be familiar with the principal documentary sources relating to their particular focus of interest.

Expertises which involve opportunity costs for historians would not include cognate disciplines such as geographical, sociological or anthropological skills, since, in principle, knowledge acquired in those could be applied to any historiographical area and is therefore not restrictive in terms of opportunity cost. It is easy to see, however, why nearly all historians' lifetime projects come to focus on a particular restricted area in time and space, and often on a fairly specialised one within that.

Moreover, on every occasion that a historian selects a topic for research or a theme around which to construct an article or book within the area of that historian's specialism, a choice is being made which *ipso facto* excludes other possibilities. Again, such choices are not accidental, they express particular dispositions, interests and above all values on the part of the historian concerned. Overall, what historians choose to write about (or, no less important, *not* write about) is an index of the social and cultural milieux in which they operate, as are the areas of historical reconstruction which are most highly esteemed in the academy and among the general public.

At the time of the Rankean revolution, partly determined by the nature of the records available and partly by the cultural outlook of the times, the themes accepted as most fitting for the historian's attention were the thoughts and deeds of mighty men, and, by extension in the intensifying climate of nationalism, the rise to power and respect of the sovereign nations they governed or guided or could be viewed as ancestral to. Something of this emphasis remained when the field of enquiry came to be broadened to the economy or 'the people'. It tended inevitably, for the most part, to fall within a national framework and focus upon institutional development and the same remained true when the labour movement in its turn was accepted as a legitimate object of historical enquiry – great men and institutions once again appeared as the central focus. The *Annales* approach indeed represented something very different; its emphasis, however, tended to be towards the denigration of *histoire évenementelle* and effectively the suppression of existential personalities in favour of constructs of geographical determinism or mass mentalities.[3]

The historiographical revolution of the 1960s and the emergence of 'history from below' in its various shapes marked an explicitly different approach, closely connected to the social and cultural radicalisation of that era, demonstrating the possibility of different historiographical forms which emphasised the particular agency of individuals or groups among the anonymous masses, for which no shortage of evidence was available if the trouble was taken to look for it. It also put into question the position of historians' relation to their material and the social, cultural and ideological standpoints from which they were writing. It questioned and repudiated the notion of historiographical objectivity, commonly accepted up to that point, and demanded that hitherto unstated intentions and projects should be explicitly formulated. Carr had recommended in an aside that before studying history one should first study the historian. This was now reformulated as a central issue and the demand raised for it to be known on whose behalf the historian was speaking.[4]

Rescuing the hitherto voiceless from historical oblivion and allowing them to speak to contemporary audiences came in many respects to be regarded by radical historians as a moral imperative, to expose the manner in which these categories of persons had been hidden from history, to chronicle – so far as possible from the inside – what they had endured during their suppression and the forms of resistance that they had developed. In the event the focus came to be upon several broad and very different, though sometimes overlapping, groupings – women, unorthodox sexualities, ethnic and cultural minorities in the West and the populations from which these ethnic minorities has been derived, whether by force or otherwise.

As a consequence of these developments historiography has been transformed. Whole new branches have come into existence and the force of the process has profoundly affected pre-existing areas. It would be impossible now to write, say, a general history of Britain in the style which would have been regarded as appropriate 40 years ago – it would now be viewed as intolerably outdated. The historiographical scope has been enormously expanded, and this must be welcomed unreservedly by all serious historians. One of the boasts of poststructuralist theory as applied to history is that by radically challenging the credibility and epistemological status of official discourse it empowers and encourages previously silenced voices to be heard and acknowledged.

Whose history?

Nevertheless these benefits are not gained without difficulties, for if a historian is claiming to speak on someone's behalf, even if the subjects are many years dead, the claim and the act carries with it responsibilities and is open to the challenge as to by what right the claim is being advanced. The resulting product, the historical reconstruction, is also liable to be subject to more intense scrutiny than in less contentious areas – and not always on historiographical grounds. There is an additional feature involved in giving a voice to the historically voiceless, one which is brought out by a comparison with *The Making*. When Thompson wrote, the British labour movement was a powerful social and political force, near the peak of its historic achievement; the story he told was one of triumph over adversity, and yet its readers knew that the greater triumphs were to come after the period with which the book concluded. The subordinated class which formed the subject of the book had come to have its interests and aspirations embodied in mighty political and industrial institutions. None of the subordinated groups, whether sexual, ethnic or whatever, who emerged into the historiographic light in the 1960s and 1970s, had anything comparable. Their institutions, if they existed, were far weaker and much more marginalised. Retrieving the history of women, or gays, or African-Americans therefore implied a still heavier responsibility, for it was intrinsic to the process of establishing a group identity and sense of self-recognition, and might well be politically controversial.

It has been well remarked that every act of writing history refers to a political agenda, conscious or implied, and that this is true not least for historians who imagine themselves to be exempt from any such considerations. Writing within the framework of established traditions only appears to be uncontroversial because they *are* established – and that can mean established oppositional forces as much as conservative ones. The difficulties are, however, not only more apparent when it is a question of historiographically establishing new insurgent identities, but there exist also genuine additional problems, starting with the question of whether any historian outside the oppressed group itself is entitled to discuss its history.

In brief, the temptation is very strong intellectually, and there may well be powerful political pressures in addition, to confine participation to select insiders and to present a sanitised version, to refrain from a public washing of the oppressed group's dirty linen. From the point of view of any scientific approach this constitutes distortion. Distortion may go further and descend into outright mythologising, carried out with various degrees of conscious intention. As Eric Hobsbawm has noted,[5] such mythologised histories are seldom total fabrications (though these do occur), rather they are founded upon historical realities treated in a manner illegitimate in the light of scientific protocols.

We have in fact been here before, and notoriously so. In the past, as once more in contemporary politics, national identities have been founded upon mythologised histories. Examples abound. In Europe subordinated groups have found identities and established political projects on the basis of the glorious past enjoyed by their linguistic group, religious sect, cultural tradition or geographical area, cut short by an oppressor from a different linguistic group etc., who can be identified as the absolute Other. They come to learn about the glorious past and national identity emphatically *not* on the basis of oral tradition and folk memory, for all that such traditions may provide some of the raw material, but founded on the purportedly scientific historiography produced by their intelligentsias. In the nineteenth and early twentieth centuries the process affected Greeks, Serbians, Hungarians, Romanians, Czechs, Poles and Irish, to cite only a limited number of examples. In the late twentieth century it was applied to Serbians (again), Croatians, Albanians and other identity-groups in the rubble of the Yugoslav federation. The reader will readily envisage others elsewhere and to take one specific example, especially pertinent for both Britain and the US, out of a compound of pre-literate myths and specific interpretations of historic events which were certainly real enough – invasion, displacement (what would now be termed ethnic cleansing), religious and linguistic persecution, famine, repeated revolt in various forms – an Irish national identity was forged, in both senses of the term. Some of the implications of this are considered below.

A process which was, until the historiographic revolution, largely confined to national identities has since found a much wider remit as identity politics have assumed a position of growing importance in both Western and more generally global culture. A particularly notable example, which embraces disciplines wider than history, but which has supposed history at its centre, is what has come to be known as Afrocentrism. The history of the sub-Saharan African peoples in their contact with Europeans (and Arabs) has indeed been a terrible one, with the Atlantic slave trade and its consequences as only the most infamous episode. On the face of things, African history has been one of invariable subjugation, enslavement, humiliation and denigration. It is therefore not to be wondered at that there should have developed an intellectual and an academic programme aimed at reasserting the dignity of Africans both in the continent and among the descendants of their diasporas.

It is the direction, in historiographical terms, which this programme has taken that is contentious. Systematic distortion of a record for ideological purposes, by omission and unwarranted emphases, has been the standard procedure in the manufacture of nationalist histories, while pure invention, though not neglected, has in the main played a secondary role. Afrocentrist writers have, at the more cautious end of the spectrum, argued in the former manner, most eminently Martin Bernal, whose *Black Athena*[6] enormously exaggerates the undoubtedly real debt of classical Greek culture to Egyptian civilisation,[7] the members of which are dubiously portrayed as being black. Certainly Bernal makes an effective case in exposing the systematic, if unconscious, racist assumptions with which scholars in the past have approached their study of the field, but his own argument is more influenced by the condition of ethnic relations at the end of the twentieth century than by the (systematically distorted) evidence of the classical era.[8]

Far more extensive in this particular field though has been the production of wholly invented mythologies which are supported by no evidence whatsoever and comprise more a form of poetic mysticism than historiography in any recognisable sense, with African communities prior to and since the European classical era portrayed as engaged in bizarre exploits which are in fact wholly fabricated by their authors and for which no evidential basis exists.

> The central tenet of Afrocentrism is that every important feature of 'civilisation', everywhere in the world, is of African origin. In ancient Egypt came the fullest flowering of the African cultural system: a system distinct from and superior to that of Eurasian societies in its matriarchal, spiritual, peaceful and humanistic character. Ancient Greece and, hence, all European civilisation took everything of value usually claimed to be theirs from African-Egyptian culture.
>
> Most Afrocentrists also believe that this superior culture has been passed down, undiluted, to diasporic peoples of African descent. Thus, African-Americans are a distinct nationality – with their own

> civilisation, values, belief system, social practices and language ('Ebonics'). These are superior to those of other groups and especially to those of European-descended peoples.
>
> On the wilder fringes of Afrocentrism, stranger ideas circulate. Not only the ancient Greeks, but also the biblical Jews, were black Africans: modern Jews and Greeks are impostors on a grand scale. The civilisations of India, China, Japan, Europe and the precolonial Americas were created by African voyagers. Ancient Africans had scientific and technological knowledge equal to or far in advance of the modern world. A striking range of figures not usually thought of as 'black' – from Socrates or the prophet Mohammed to Beethoven, Karl Marx and Abraham Lincoln – were actually Africans ... The controversies have also reflected a sadly typical kind of US parochialism. Argument has rarely been about what schoolchildren and students should know of the world, but about rival visions of Americanism.[9]

Afrocentrism is exceptional in that it has been able to establish a strong organisational base in the academy, in departments of African Studies in the United States, which have little relation to any other academic discipline, but are to a great extent insulated from criticism or questioning by the reluctance of outsiders to risk accusations of racism or cultural intolerance. On one occasion a planned television series on the slave trade had to be abandoned because of objections to the fact that it would have shown the historical reality of African chiefs' participation in slave trading activities.

In achieving these outcomes Afrocentrists have had a very different degree of success from that of the neo-fascist Holocaust-deniers, who have, under the innocent-sounding name of 'historical revisionists', also tried to establish academic credentials for their particular version of the past, but in their case have failed.[10] The reasons for this are political rather than scientific. Fascism's record has made it so obnoxious that no respectable academic institution will touch organisations or discourses in that tradition, although in the light of historiographical protocols the revisionist lies, sadly, are more plausible than Afrocentrist fantasies.

Although the extent of Afrocentrism's institutional success and cultural reach is new, there are some analogies with past practice. In the days when Christianity possessed a higher cultural profile than it does now, it was not uncommon for groups of one sort or another to equip themselves with a spurious biblical ancestry, whether organisational or biological. The Freemasons, for instance, base their ritual around entirely mythical, self-invented events associated with King Solomon's temple. More sinisterly, a racist sect which called themselves the British Israelites (now probably extinct) purported to demonstrate the descent of Germanic and Celtic peoples from the alleged (and wholly spurious) 'lost tribes of Israel', which, being also virulently antisemitic, they were at pains to imagine as being distinct from Jews. Neither of these two could be plausibly suggested as oppressed communities, but (albeit less harmfully) some contemporary women's neo-pagan cults have adopted the notion advanced by the archaeologist Margaret Murray in the 1920s that the victims of early modern witch-hunts were practitioners of a pre-Christian fertility religion.[11] Murray was a serious scholar and the idea was an interesting speculation, but there proved to be not a shred of evidence to support that hypothesis and plenty to refute it. Coming back to contemporary politics, it is possible to envisage plausible narratives of the Soviet bloc's downfall which attribute everything that went wrong to malign outside agencies and nothing to inherent flaws – and there are in fact a few scattered fragments of the former communist movement which indulge themselves in that manner – but it would be a pretty disastrous manoeuvre for serious historians whatever their political persuasion.

But if written history is not a reconstruction of past actualities and relationships, but rather the outcome of a 'poetic act',[12] a story that we tell ourselves and for our own purposes, the relationship of which to the surviving documentary evidence is problematic at best, what can there be amiss and what business is it of anybody else if oppressed and marginalised groups – women, Africans, African-Americans, African-Caribbeans, Irish republicans, nature-worshippers, stalinists – construct histories that validate their identities and their dignity? In what sense can they be condemned as fictive? And in any case, do not all cultures do the same kind of thing to a greater or lesser extent – noting the successful national movements which have been built in this fashion?

The quotation which springs to mind when confronted with such an argument is 'ye shall know the truth and the truth shall make you free'. There are several interlinked intellectual and pragmatic reasons why basing social and political outlooks upon consolatory myths represents a cultural dead end.

In the first place it centres the consciousness of its adherents upon a bogus past, sometimes, at worst, with the implicit promise that this might be reinstated once more in the present, but in any event diverting the subordinated group from the more difficult but more valid enterprise of tearing its hopes and projects away from an anguished past and creating its identity in the here and now. Second, such fictive constructions are always open to devastating critique based upon deployment of the empirical evidence. Norman Cohn's exposure of the origins and historical emergence of the *Protocols of the Elders of Zion*[13] destroyed forever the credibility of that forgery, which all good people would applaud, but the same process can as readily be applied to more innocent identity-myths. To coin another phrase, your historiographical sins are always likely to find you out.

And to stay with the cliches, what is sauce for the goose is equally sauce for the gander. It is not only oppressed groups who validate themselves by historical myth, oppressing ones do it with, if anything, even greater force and energy. The defenders of historical mythologising are aware of this – their argument is that the multiplication and circulation of such historical narratives, the very consciousness of their plurality, letting everyone invent and formulate their own histories, will undermine and serve to discredit the dominant one.[14] Unfortunately there is no reason for believing this to be true. More likely either the ruling power is in a position to make its version prevail or the clash of rival mythologies takes on murderous and pathological forms. Moreover if the oppressed group should succeed in reversing its status the probability is that its historical mythology will continue to haunt it to its severe disadvantage.

The deadly and sanguinary struggles of competing historical mythlogies in Northern Ireland or in the Balkans are in the forefront of current political concerns. The Israeli regime justifies its repression of its Palestinian subjects by historical fabrications drawn from over two millennia, as well as distorted interpretations of twentieth-century history; Muslim 'fundamentalist' regimes derive their inspiration from an imagined return to imagined medieval practices.

Even comparatively benign examples illustrate the point and impose oppressive burdens on the individuals subject to them. The fate of independent Ireland during most of the twentieth century is a classic example. Central to the national consciousness as it had evolved by the early twentieth century was an intense perception of historic wrong – as well it might be, considering the wrongs that had been indeed inflicted. During the long era of colonial subjection the central focus of Irish identity in opposition to and defiance of the oppressor was the Catholic church and the adherence to it of ordinary folk, so much so that the church came to be regarded as all but synonymous with the national identity, and indeed as having created it. The heroes of the 1916 rising underlined the authenticity of their national consciousness and their claim to represent the nation by the fervour of their Catholic sentiment prior to their executions – even the Marxist James Connolly – and despite the fact that the Fenian movement and its successors, from which the other leaders had emerged, had in the past been denounced by the church hierarchy. Historical, national and religious consciousness were so tightly intertwined that when practical independence was at last achieved, there could be no question in the Irish Free State of the church being treated as simply one ideological and material interest among others in a modern secular state. The result was the imposition upon the citizens of the state of a culture of stifling clericalism, censorship, superstition and ignorance from which the most intellectually able tended to flee as fast as they could.[15] Only in the later years of the century did the church's hold begin to weaken and the cultural oppression to lift. The historical mythology of the national struggle itself has, it scarcely needs to be said, provided a source of extreme tension in Irish politics and still underlies the main lines of political division in the Republic (not to speak of the North).

It would of course be misleading to suggest that mythologised historical consciousness bears the sole responsibility for the social fate of the Irish Free State/Republic, Kosovo, or any other part of the globe where internecine strife has been particularly virulent – much also depends on contemporary realities, but the two cannot really be dissociated; it is the historical mythology through which the contemporary realities are interpreted and given their murderous meaning. The argument for a politics or a history of 'difference' or 'pluralism' is not necessarily a 'progressive' one in any sense of the term. All historians are the bearers of a grave responsibility, but particularly those who deal in the area of collective identities – as Eric Hobsbawm has put it, 'the sentences typed on innocent keyboards may be sentences of death'.[16]

The argument I am advancing is that it is both intellectually impermissible and ethically irresponsible to advocate a free-for-all in the historic construction of identities. That identities may properly be constructed by connecting up the past with the present is not at issue – that process is both necessary and legitimate. If however the outcome is to avoid falsehood and illusion, possibly of a deadly sort, then the construction must be made on valid historiographical principles. No favours are done to anybody, least of all the left, by issuing intellectual licences endorsing deliberately spurious historical constructs.

In my own view history is indeed an intrinsically left-wing enterprise, despite the fact that there have been and are many conservative historians (and able ones at that) and paradoxically despite the fact that conservatives so frequently appeal to the past for justification. This proceeds from the reality that conservatism is in its deepest principles a static philosophy designed to justify the permanence of particular exploiting classes, while history exhibits the transience and mutability of all social formations along with never-ending aspirations on the part of degraded and subjugated people to alter their situation. It is my conviction, though, that history is capable of serving as a theoretical resource for left wing positions only so long as it continues to pursue that impossible but necessary goal, elusive but not illusory – the truth.

Evaluation in history

'The past is a foreign country, they do things differently there.' The implications of this statement (which is the opening sentence of Hartley's *The Go-Between*) are both true and profound. There is no fixed human nature, or if there is it is so malleable that any common elements are either wholly banal (we all eat, we all sleep, we all die) or buried so deep (generative grammar structures) as to be invisible to common observation. Differing cultures (and even subcultures) in space and time do not imply simply different forms and norms of behaviour, but different modes of perception, alien ways of thinking, wholly divergent structures of mentality. This, incidentally, is why twentieth-century novels, plays and films set in the past almost always fail however painstakingly accurate their recreations of dress, landscape, buildings, etc., may be – the characters represented are not true to their own time but are simply present-day individuals in costume. The problem is not absolutely insuperable, but it is very difficult to accommodate.

It is also difficult for historians, although this is their professional responsibility. A bald narrative of events (setting aside the questions of narrativity and emplotment) tends to be thin and unsatisfying in the absence of any consideration of the motives or sentiments of those involved. There are, it is true, areas of historical research where the question of motivation on the part of the agents has no bearing – much of demographic analysis and certain themes in economic history for example – generally speaking where the question of agency is abstracted from the picture. Mostly, however, the question of why such and such a course of events was entered into, of the reasons behind particular decisions or the reactions to them, is an implicit even if not explicit feature of the analysis. A presumption of motivation on the part of historical actors is generally present in the reconstruction, whether we are discussing, say, the system of government in ancient Assyria or that in the Soviet bloc. Even archaeologists, working with non-written evidence, cannot escape such questions; they have to try to interpret, for example, the meaning of particular funerary customs.

Such presumptions though are made in the face of the disturbing question of whether it really is possible on the basis of its documentary, or other, remains to enter the foreign country of the past, or whether historians do not deceive themselves, by ignoring the reality that the consciousness of past individuals must be so radically different from that of our own age that their motives and sentiments are forever closed to us and that neither historians nor their readers can ever grasp the mentality of these strangers in time. On this argument Pepys's diaries, for instance, seemingly so clear and elegant, intimate and informative about their subject's deepest feelings, are literally incomprehensible to a sensibility of the twenty-first century, their apparent transparence no more than an illusion because the mental universe of the seventeenth century out of which they were created is forever out of reach. If you believe in addition that reality is constituted by language, and since language unquestionably changes over time, the argument is reinforced. Certainly Keith Jenkins argues for the impossibility of ever understanding the thought-processes of past cultures but then his argument as he presents it would apply no less, even in the context of common discourse, to the thought processes of one's closest friends; he is indeed presenting a philosophical defence of solipsism.

There is no reason however to give credence to the view sketched above. It in fact represents a logical slippage, a non-sequitur, to argue that because the past is a very strange country it is therefore impossible to understand what is going on there. The past may be a foreign country, but it is not a different planet. Every one of its inhabitants had a life that was just as valuable to its owner as yours or mine is to us – a point amply demonstrated by the universal reluctance to lose it.[17] In Simone de Beauvoir's novel *The Mandarins*, one of the characters, a naive communist convert defending the Gulag, argues that, 'we tend to forget that a Soviet man's way of thinking is different from ours; he finds it natural, for example, to be relocated according to the needs of production', to which the opponent answers, 'Whatever his way of thinking no man finds it natural to be exploited, undernourished, deprived of all his rights, imprisoned, brutalised by work, condemned to die of cold, scurvy, or exhaustion.'[18] This is undoubtedly true, although it is important to be aware of what cultural pressure is capable of; centuries of Chinese women once accepted the crippling of their daughters' feet, having themselves suffered the same tortures, centuries of African ones have similarly accepted and enforced the genital mutilation of their daughters, centuries of Hindus approved the burning to death of their mothers, sisters and daughters. The attitudes behind such realities are certainly alien, and less than totally comprehensible to a different culture, but they are by no means impenetrable once the 'logic' behind them is grasped. Although outsiders might never *fully* understand, this doesn't mean that they can understand nothing.

Equivalent principles apply in relation to the comprehension of any past social or cultural practices, and, to repeat what has been the theme of this volume, reconstruction and explanation of the past is both difficult and problematic, but it is not impossible. The instances cited above, however, raise a second and even more contentious issue, and that is the question of judgement or evaluation, not of the skill of the reconstruction or the depth of understanding of the relationships involved, but of the ethical or normative implications of what is being historically examined.

The matter in its essence is a simple one – can historians, assuming that they are able to interpret and understand what has been going on in the past, legitimately make any moral comment or judgement about the object of their study, appreciating of course that to do so is to invite their reader (or listener or viewer) to share that evaluation? And can the historian claim any better qualification to advance such judgements than the persons to whom the argument is being addressed? In short should the historian act as a retrospective judge, or even as a prosecuting or defence counsel?

Whichever way the question is answered serious difficulties emerge. Lord Acton, the great English nineteenth-century historian, was particularly insistent that the historian's duty was to adopt a position of moral censure And this view has also been advanced by leading twentieth-century intellectuals. Isaiah Berlin insists 'with great vehemence'[19] on the need to arraign the great criminals of the past – Nero, Charlemagne, Genghis Khan, Pizarro, etc., as well as their twentieth-century counterparts – before the bar of history, though leaving the question open as to whether the indictment was best emplotted in a subtle and and nuanced mode or a strident and raucous one.[20] Certainly the reaction of most readers to accounts of massacre, enslavement, torture and all the other kinds of horror which feature so prominently in the historical record is likely to be one of moral reprobation – it is a standard human reaction and evoked by the very words normally used to recount these sorts of practices.

Such a straightforward response is both attractive and tempting, but runs up against the circumstance that evidently the perpetrators of the said horrors did not find them morally repugnant and who are we to judge between the accused and the victims? After all, the classical cultures of Greece and Rome continue (for different reasons) to be admired, though both were founded upon slavery, and in the Roman case, torture. The Spanish Inquisition and the early modern witch-hunt can both be demonstrated to have been conformable with the values of their time and place, and neither the inquisitors nor the witch-finders were sadists as a rule. In short, can the values of the present century (and generally speaking, of the West) be legitimately imported into past situations where values and perceptions took a radically different form?

One possible answer, more frequently applied in the past than nowadays, was to deem as meritorious practices which contributed to human progress and condemn those which retarded it. This shifts the basis of the argument somewhat, for something might be deemed progressive, and therefore to be applauded, even though morally objectionable by the standards of the commentator. Engels for example endorsed ancient slavery as a progressive development in human history, a 'good thing', since it enhanced productive powers, but equally of course endorsed its disappearance once it had become a fetter on productive advance as well as being morally repugnant.[21] Marx is known to have had a sentimental preference for the Jacobites, though he would have deplored their victory in the British state.[22] In Marx's central work the contradictions are very explicit and are not theoretically resolved. The first volume of *Capital* famously contains a burning moral indictment of the human costs, in Britain and on a world scale, through which the capitalist mode of production, 'dripping with blood and filth', was brought into existence; yet Marx was never in any doubt that socialism and all the possibilities of human emancipation in the future depended upon the establishment of capitalism in the first instance as a precondition.

E.H. Carr's historiographical disposition is rather similar and though no Marxist (despite accusations to the contrary) he never concealed the fact that (like the Webbs) he regarded the USSR as representing in essence a more advanced social order than capitalism did, neither did he attempt, in his multi-volume history of Soviet Russia or elsewhere, to conceal the human costs and shortcomings of the regime. His attitude, expressed in *What is History?*, was that it is the historian's task not to be ruled by sentiment but to concentrate upon the historical winners rather than the losers, and he (mistakenly) regarded the USSR as having received Clio's unequivocally favourable verdict. Consequently he mocked writers who could not resist asking 'what if?' the Bolshevik Revolution had not taken place. It is readily appreciated though that such a robust form of evaluation, apart from any other problems involved in separating moral reaction from cost/benefit analysis, depends on firmly held conviction in the reality of a grand narrative of (social) progress, which is, to say the least, not adhered to with any great confidence on the part of historians following the age of extremes. To be sure, Carr tends to self-contradiction in places in the section of *What is History?* where he discusses the relationship of moral values to history. He states that it is not the historian's business to condemn, excuse or commend particular individuals, but notes nevertheless that historians may properly deliver judgements on institutions such as slavery or democracy. A couple of pages later however he is suggesting 'supposedly absolute and extra historical values are rooted to history', that values vary in different historical epochs and 'every group has its own values which are rooted in history', and that: 'It is that the attempt to erect such a standard is unhistorical and contradicts the very essence of history. It provides a dogmatic answer to questions which the historian is bound by his vocation incessantly to ask.'[23]

The trouble with all approaches which advocate the relativisation of moral judgment in history or abstention from it, is illuminated in the history of our own age and takes the form of the question 'are then such standards to be applied to the Third Reich and what took place in Europe between 1933 and 1945, especially during the last six of those years'? The question contains its own answer. No serious historian can write about the Third Reich and the Second World War without expressing moral abhorrence whether explicitly or implicitly. The historian does not have to say in so many words 'this was an unspeakable abomination' – the narrative, however emplotted, and the language, no matter how measured it may be, will contain the judgement. The Third Reich however cannot be bracketed off from all other historical episodes, and a comparable horror (even if in lesser degree) occurring simultaneously was the Gulag. It is difficult to suggest any reason why the same criteria should not apply in principle to all the appalling episodes, tracing backwards from the extermination of the Amerindians through the holocausts of Timur the Lame to the ethnic cleansings of the Babylonian monarchs.

A strategy sometimes suggested to reconcile this difficulty is to argue that a sharply different attitude is justifiably adopted towards those grisly historical episodes whose resonance still continues into the present, compared with those which are simply known from the record and have no longer any contemporary relevance. Among the former the Holocaust evidently stands out, but the category would also include what happened in the nineteenth century to the Native Americans or the Australian Aborigines, for those remain relevant to contemporary policy. It is difficult however to see on what basis it is possible to justify such a drastic ontological separation between the two categories.

The relationship in the moral dimension between historians, their audience and their material is further complicated by the fact that, if they live in any of the world's developed and currently political peaceful economies, they are the legatees and beneficiaries of previous eras of massacre, enslavement and pitiless exploitation. Without the extermination of indigenous peoples, the Atlantic slave trade, child labour in factory and mine, our high-tech, affluent culture (or more accurately subculture) of material comfort conjoined with personal choice and potential would never have come into existence. As Carr puts it, 'Those who [in history] pay the cost are rarely those who reap the benefits.'[24] Although we cannot be held responsible for what our ancestors did (and historical apologies by US presidents or Australian prime ministers or anybody else are beside the point) it should nevertheless make us feel uncomfortable.

Carr declares that serious historians will assume, without having to formulate it explicitly, that the atrocities cited above were part of the unavoidable cost of industrialisation (making the point that his forthcoming discussion of Soviet collectivisation will adopt the same perspective) and that he has never heard of a historian who argued that in view of the cost it would have been better to 'stay the hand of progress'. In the aftermath of the influence of Foucault and his disciples and the general climate of postmodernism, that could no longer be assumed with confidence and progress is no longer an unproblematic concept.

Carr, in view of his position that specific moral categories are inappropriate to historical analysis, concludes that historians tend to express their moral judgements in words of a comparative nature, like 'progressive' and 'reactionary', rather than in uncompromising absolutes, like 'good' and 'bad'; these are attempts to define different societies or historical phenomena not in relation to some absolute standard, but in their relation to one another.[25]

If we adopt this perspective, however, we encounter a double dilemma. In the first place the very concept of historical progress is now regarded as questionable for the reasons noted above. Even if one remains convinced of its validity, it is impossible not to acknowledge the reasons why it has been put in question. Second, Carr's standpoint here would require us to attach the epithet 'progressive' to developments like the slave trade and various episodes of mass murder – not an easy position to adopt. 'Progressive' and 'reactionary' are by no means neutral terms, they carry scarcely less moral connotation than 'good' and 'bad'. He does have a point though in insisting that we live in the world that we do and the historian's responsibility is to examine how it came into being regardless of anybody's personal feelings about the nature of the process. Nostalgia for a dead world is futile. Wishing that industrialisation, or globalisation, or the Russian Revolution or the Soviet regime's collapse had never happened is no substitute for understanding these events.

It is certainly the case that historians commit themselves to three broad remits. In the first place they have an obligation to provide a narrative account when investigating areas where narrative accounts are appropriate, either because one does not yet exist or because the currently accepted one requires revision. Second, which can be separated from the first conceptually though not in reality, they must interpret and explain the relationships and mutual interactions between individuals, institutions and processes. The third is more problematic but for the most part inescapable, and that is an obligation to try to enter to a greater or lesser degree the consciousness of the objects of their historical study. The commitment is clearly of central significance if the historian is writing from the standpoint that human agency is important, but is nevertheless also relevant if it is assumed that history is a process without a subject, for this approach is needed to underline the otherness, the alien quality, of historical actors even if it should be the case that they act under structural determination.

This last point relates to the question of empathy between the historian and the people of the past who are being examined. Major discussion focused upon this issue as far back as the late nineteenth century when Wilhelm Dilthey counterposed it to deductive procedures as a mode of historical analysis; some of his successors aimed to combine the approach with Rankean source-criticism.[26] Are such sentiments legitimate ones for a historian to hold? My own view on this aspect is that 'empathy' is largely a red herring, being separate in essence from questions of exploring past mentalities. A historian may indeed empathise with the subjects of the research, as E.P. Thompson famously does with the emergent working class, but it is imaginable in principle, if scarcely in practice, that a conservative-minded historian could have written a similar kind of book from a position of hostility to the radical and labour movement of the period but nevertheless with insight into its modes of perception and consciousness. Historians continue in large numbers to explore in detail the character of fascist and Nazi mentalities, and in particular that of their most infamous representative, Adolf Hitler, but very few if any possess any empathy with those movements or that individual.

It appears unlikely that there can be any final or definitive solution to the dilemmas associated with moral evaluation in historiography. On the one hand it is inescapable, on the other there clearly *is* an equally inescapable difference in response to the atrocities of the distant past as compared with those of the modern era. Judgement of this kind, even if and when it may be appropriate, is certainly not the historian's *primary* responsibility. What is important is that historians should be honest with the evidence as far as it is in their power to do so, and also be clear about where they themselves are coming from in ethical terms, in order that readers and audiences may make their own judgements.

Conclusion

Although this volume has engaged with a number of general epistemological concerns regarding the relationship of representation and discourse to whatever it is that is represented and discoursed about, the central thread of its argument has been that the situation of historiography in the present has itself to be explained historically if it is to be meaningfully understood.

In this respect it has been part of a broader cultural current running throughout the twentieth century, affecting social theory and its associated disciplines, literary creation and the fine arts generally. The current has been driven both by its own weight and force and by the nature of the terrain over which it has flowed. To speak less metaphorically, it has been directed on the one hand both by the evolution of its own internal conceptual logic and on the other by the pressures of political and social change.

Culture, however that is defined, is invariably a response to and a reflection of the society which produces it, sometimes very directly, often at several removes, as we may note by comparing, say, the art of the European Middle Ages with that of subsequent centuries. At the same time it may be in tension and contradiction with its sociopolitical surroundings (assuming there exists a measure of freedom of expression). Such tension, T.S. Eliot's 'dissociation of sensibility', has tended not to be manifest in the cultures of past eras; on the whole it is a feature of modernity and has been particularly marked in the last hundred or so years.

By the closing years of the nineteenth century, once industrial society was well established in Western Europe and the Unites States and the remainder of the globe had been drawn into the orbit of the industrial powers, the contrast between the material and personal promise opened up by technological civilisation on the one hand and the human costs of capitalist society on the other, were pressing issues both politically and in the sphere of cultural creativity. Wealth generated on a prodigious and ever-expanding scale, unprecedented levels of consumer innovation, choice and comfort are intertwined with abysses of poverty, social dislocation and cultural-moral panics over the direction of events.

In the twenty years prior to 1914 modernism as a cultural trend in the arts and social sciences became fully established as the wave of the future in terms of a critique of contemporary reality (its penetration assisted by the apparently bizarre discoveries and theories then occurring and being developed in the physical sciences). Among philosophers the legacy of Nietzsche, the work of Husserl, Bergson, the early Wittgenstein; among social scientists Weber, Simmel, among purported social scientists Freud contributed to the trend. In the arts the legacy of Baudelaire and Rimbaud, Symbolism, Rilke, Yeats, Futurism, Art Nouveau and its developments, Cubism, Expressionism – and other stylistic innovations did likewise. In one important dimension the tendency can be understood as a critique and rejection of all 'realist' forms of representation, which were held to be inadequate to expressing the essence of the new age. The political universe, if placid compared with what was to come after, was nevertheless also already heaving with the irresolvable tensions which would explode in 1914. Apart from the steadily intensifying diplomatic conflict and arms race, Perry Anderson notes that there also existed a widespread expectation of imminent social revolution,[1] regarded variously with hope or fear depending on the social and political outlook of the observer.

Not surprisingly, in the wake of the calamity, the new forms of modernism were developed to provide a yet more insistent critique of the existing reality of what Eric Hobsbawm has termed the 'age of catastrophe' between 1914 and 1945, when the political universe was radically shifted by the emergence out of revolutionary upheaval of the Soviet Union and all that it represented, accompanied by economic paralysis and slump in the West – together with the ferociously violent reaction against all these things on the part of social classes and groups threatened materially and culturally. Revolution failed in the West, the hopes and expectations of the prewar era were aborted, as it turned out forever. The new regime on the territory of the old Russian Empire became the focus of the hopes and aspirations of millions, yet it was clear to others of a radical disposition that it could only do so because these millions wilfully blinded themselves to what was taking place within its borders.

The resulting critique of bourgeois and/or Soviet reality took on a variety of forms. Georg Lukács and Antonio Gramsci who remained committed to orthodox communism, upheld in principle the perspective of proletarian revolution, but their work nevertheless reflected its defeat.[2] The Trotskyists, few in numbers in any case, suffered total political defeat, but were to have a significant cultural influence (in the broadest sense) particularly after the Second World War. The Hegelian Marxists of the Frankfurt School differed in their formal politics, some being close to the German Communist Party (KPD) and others actively hostile to it, but their common project was the analysis of Western culture in all of its dimensions as the alienated and profoundly inhuman product of developed capitalism. In the arts, proper 'high modernism' flourished with movements like the Bauhaus, writers such as Kafka, Joyce, Pound or Eliot and painters like Picasso, Matisse or Monet. In all their variety these movements and individuals were products and reflections of blocked revolutionary hopes, or categorical rejection (which might equally well take reactionary as well as radical forms) of the social and cultural reality of the interwar era.

The trend however which concerns us in particular, because of the influence that developed out of it towards the end of the century and consequently the bearing it ultimately has on the fate of historiography (among much else), is that of Dada – a reaction to the unintelligible monstrosity of the First World War and the society which had precipitated it – followed by its offspring, Surrealism. Although now viewed primarily in terms of an artistic movement, it is important to recognise that these represented a forceful political intention as well, albeit a somewhat abstract one. Founded in Switzerland during the midst of the European military holocaust, Dada's name was chosen so as to be deliberately meaningless. Its political orientation drew more upon anarchist traditions than anything else, in reaction against the parties and politics responsible for the disaster, and it represented essentially a violent rejection of the entire European cultural tradition, though Switzerland constituted a somewhat narrow stage upon which to launch such a far-reaching project. Its artistic/political practice consisted of the creation of scandals, 'The polemical attacks were directed at everything and everybody.'[3] 'Dada makes anticultural propaganda out of honesty, out of disgust, out of a profound distaste for the high-flown pretensions of the certified intellectuals of the bourgeoisie.'[4]

Not unremarkably the antiwar activists, artists and intellectuals who had founded the movement left Switzerland once the war was over and worked to disseminate its outlook in Western and Central Europe, for they took themselves and their project very seriously. According to one of its central figures, Max Ernst,

> For us in Cologne in 1919, Dada was first of all a mental attitude ... our aim was total subversion. A ghastly and senseless war had cheated us out of five years of our lives. We had seen all that had been held up to us as good, beautiful and true topple into an abyss of ridicule and shame. The work I produced in those days was not meant to please but to make people scream.[5]

The development of Dada into Surrealism occurred in Paris, as an artistic movement with curious and contradictory borrowings from anarchism, Freudianism and the Third International. It was a movement with a leader, and one who showed distinctly Stalinist tendencies in his leadership style, André Breton. Although now best remembered for its impact on the visual arts, Surrealism was in its time as much (indeed more so) a literary and political project – Breton was a writer, not a painter. Although of its two most celebrated painters the Belgian René Magritte was from time to time a CP member and the Spaniard Salvador Dali a political conservative, the ostensible politics of the movement as such tended towards Trotskyism and Breton ran it – or rather tried to – with the forms of the communist movement, including a would-be authoritarian Central Committee.

The distinctive quality of Surrealism, from which the name is derived and which the paintings of the school embody very effectively, is the representation of objects or parts of objects, rendered with photographic realism but juxtaposed in wholly irrational fashion, usually so as to produce an eerie or sinister effect, though occasionally a humorous one. Even more than abstract painting, Surrealist products, because of the incongruity created between the parts and the whole, are designed (possibly unconsciously because the Surrealists laid great stress upon the unconscious) to lead the viewer into a questioning of the categories of reality, rationality and representation. Surrealism, I would argue, should be seen as the direct ancestor of deconstruction,[6] and the actual filation of ideas and groups reinforces this conclusion.

In the aftermath of the Second World War – again following the analysis of Perry Anderson – the great age of high cultural experimentation was over, and its demise was directly related to the hardening of world politics between two opposed blocs; superpowers holding their respective satellites in thrall, threatening each other with nuclear annihilation and in their different ways insisting upon cultural conformity. In the Soviet bloc modernism was outlawed, as it had been since the 1920s, in the West, by contrast, with economic and social prosperity reaching undreamt of heights in the 'long boom' it was integrated as effectively the official style of high culture, with far-reaching impact upon popular culture as well, especially in the visual arts. That represented 'freedom' and left plenty of room for experimentation and novelty, but only on condition that the products were non-threatening to the official definition of reality, otherwise, while not of course suppressed by force, they would be denied acceptance and acclaim.[7] It was no accident that the favoured style of painting in the 1950s US was 'abstract expressionism', with the emphasis on abstract, for that, whatever its aesthetic merits, embodied nothing oppositional. An expressionism which commented upon contemporary reality in the style of Munch would surely have been perceived as un-American.

It was against such a politics and culture, seen as hypocritical, stagnant, infinitely threatening and in relations with the Third World bloodthirsty in the extreme, that the New Left opposition erupted in the late 1950s and early 1960s. The blockages were already being explored, from different angles, by dissident Marxists such as Isaac Deutscher and Jean Paul Sartre, the latter attempting indeed (though not very successfully) to achieve a reformulation of the modes of historical determination in his *Critique of Dialectical Reason*. There also existed some groupings working along similar lines, such as the French Socialisme ou Barbarie – 'new left' was in fact initially a French term. The New Left was an amorphous, chaotic, contradictory phenomenon, both in Europe and even more so in the United States, mingling Marxism (which underwent a theoretical renaissance), anarchism and hedonism, but hostile alike to the capitalism of the West and the frozen republic east of the Elbe. However, a wholly fanciful understanding of the events in China during the late 1960s, the 'Cultural Revolution' led some part of it to look to the Chinese regime and Mao Zedong as a source of inspiration – an echo in some respects of what had occurred among the left in Western Europe following the Bolshevik Revolution.

Even the postures of the Dadist/Surrealist pranksters were re-embodied at the time in the self-designated Situationist International, which seems to have exercised a not inconsiderable influence on the poststructuralist consciousness. The group was initiated by Guy Debord, who aspired to combine theoretical critique with revolutionary action, which meant, until the opportunity of May 1968 presented itself, action which mostly took the form of orchestrating cultural scandals. As with the Surrealists the contents of its politics were anarchistic in essence; it presented itself as in total opposition to modern reality in every single one of its aspects (it would be naive to enquire what sort of alternative was envisaged) and well exemplified its outlook in one of its slogans during the May Days of 1968 – 'Abolish Everything!' Small, secretive and authoritarian (a not uncommon anarchistic combination)[8] its notions were to provide nonetheless a significant part of the cultural driving force of subsequent years once the Maoist froth, which formed the initially most prominent manifestation of the far left during that time, had dissipated.

During the late 1960s and early 1970s an intense but unfocused radicalism infused very large sections of the youthful intelligentsia of Western Europe and the US, the very people who were in subsequent decades to staff the academic institutions of those countries, or at least their humanities faculties. The political aspirations remained wholly unrealised – the wound in Western political culture closed and Thatcher, Reagan, Mitterrand and their like inherited the future. The radicalism of the period, while certainly more than the psychodrama that some of its critics alleged, was unquestionably as much a cultural as a political phenomenon, and driven from the political arena it redeployed upon a cultural terrain, particularly in the milieu of the academy and especially and essentially that of literary culture, picking up on the writings of certain authors whose writings reflected a cultural critique anchoring itself in Nietzsche. Postmodernism, poststructuralism, deconstruction – whichever name is attached – this current is above all a literary phenomenon in the broadest sense of the term, its prime concerns are with works of the imagination. Its reach and penetration derive from its aspiration to accomplish in the imagination the revolution which proved so elusive in reality and the more that the values of the global free market have entrenched themselves apparently immovably[9] (not least in the academy itself), the more the projects of its proponents, when not engaged in 'desperate, sterile iconoclasm',[10] have busied themselves with deconstructing representation and denouncing the mirages of totalisation by which they were once deceived – what else, after all, is there to be done?

Such currents, whether for good or ill, are by nature imperialistic (their Nietzschean heritage alone would see to that) and seek extension beyond the central and original site of their application. Since there is always value in novelty, even while being resisted they will never fail to achieve some measure of success. This has tended, because of the institutional inertia (using that term non-pejoratively) discussed in Chapter 4, to be less in historiography than in other social science/humanities disciplines, but it has not been absent. They have generated a considerable (and significant) historiography, principally in the exploration of identities and representations, and in addition a parallel discipline of their own in historiographical theory. Above all it has been the confluence of deconstructionist theory with the new social history of the 1960s, springing especially from E.P. Thompson's work, but taking a wholly different direction, which has given strength to the current. Sympathetically probing the outlooks, aspirations and mentalities of the rejected and outcast, and enabling them to speak in their own voices, can be a powerful corrective to teleological complacency whether on the right or the left, but it can also be an invitation to relativism, rejection of interpretative truth and a perspective on the historical past which denies it any coherence or evolutionary direction whatever, let alone one of improvement. It can be especially tempting if in addition one adopts the viewpoint that all knowledge and all human projects of any sort express first and foremost the will to power. Homer remarks upon the irony that at a time when the political right embraces the primacy of economic determination in social and politcal matters, sections of the cultural left 'abandon this terrain of critique altogether'.[11]

It remains, however, to consider how novel the new currents really are. The idea has been suggested by more than one writer that post-modernism, far from representing a break with modernism, is in fact its continuation by other means. Ignacio Olábarri has applied it to historiography.[12] He argues for contunity between the *Annales*, Marxist historiography, the US social science school, *Past & Present*, the Bielefeld School[13] and *their* continuity with the nineteenth century German approach. He suggests that postmodern histories are likewise in the same line of continuity, the continuity being provided by the fact that all of these schools, not excluding poststructuralism, whatever its proponents might say to the contrary, have progress and emancipation as their basic postulate – which certainly accords with the anarchist-surrealist underlay of poststructuralism, particularly evident in Barthes writings, or in a more degenerate form, those of Baudrillard. The basic principles of modern philosophy are said to be subjectivism, criticism and emancipation and 'the postmodern critique of modernity has a clear emancipatory tendency'.[14] Olábarri quotes Sean Burke to the effect that 'it being only as a particularly vigorous form of anti-phenomologism that French structuralism and post-structuralism can be properly understood'.[15] He goes on to argue that the postmodern historians are converging towards a neo-Rankeanism with new insights – accepting moral relativism while rejecting of the cognitive relativism of deconstruction or 'disintegrative textualism'.

Olábarri may well exaggerate the extent of continuity or the degree of likely convergence, but there is undoubtedly substance in what he says. It is perfectly posible to agree that the impact of postmodernism/poststucturalism/deconstruction has certainly been to expand the field of historical consciousness, mostly in three directions. The first of these is the rescue from oblivion of ignored or historically despised groups, not previously regarded as worthy of historiographical attention, linked to, though not identical with the second, the examination of how identities – social, cultural, personal or otherwise – are constructed and constituted, both intrinsically and in oppositon to outsiders (what postmodernists like to designate as 'the Other'). The third is the exploration not of how situations and events develop or are structured, but how they are understood and represented – to take at random the titles of two (juxtaposed) articles, 'Imagining Vermin in Early Modern England'[16] and, 'The Besotted King and his Adonis: Representations of Edward II and Gaveston in Late Nineteenth-Century England'. None of these approaches – the latter two reflecting the deconstructionist suspicion of the possibility of knowing anything outside the contents of consciousness – is in any way less valid or legitimate than the more traditional ones (which were themselves controversial in their time). It would after all be possible to write the first three chapters of this volume in a different register – in terms of the support systems, mostly female, which enabled the great names that appear in those pages to perform their intellectual labours, and the way in which their wives and/or servants constructed their own identities in relation to *their* subordinate situation. That would form no less legitimate an enterprise than the one I've undertaken, and it would certainly extend the corpus of knowledge and understanding, but it would be no *more* historiographically legitimate either, constituting simply a *different* form of historical investigation.[17] The lesson of historiography from the nineteenth century onward is that new methodologies have constantly emerged and all have gone on to make significant contributions to the understanding of the past. The further lesson is that such methodologies should refrain from advancing imperialistic claims, for the effect of such arrogance – even though the methodology should be as vigorous and strong as the *Annales* paradigm – is always only to narrow the scope of the historiographical enterprise. The same remains true, *a fortiori*, for poststructuralist deconstruction.

Raphael Samuel's remark that 'What does seem new is the self-conscious drive to make representation the only legitimate field of study',[18] though made ten years ago, therefore fairly accurately sums up what the current dispute is still about. The grand theoretical claims based on the specifics of language, the protean character of texts, the intrinsic incompleteness of all answers – are still with us. And while it is never possible to disprove the claims embodied in the notion that it is impossible to achieve concrete knowledge about actual events and situations – any more than it is possible to disprove the claim that human destinies are controlled through sub-space vibrations by little green persons located on a galaxy far away[19] – there are no valid grounds for taking them seriously; they are both conceptually flawed and empirically vacuous. They are also the product of a particular historical conjuncture which will not last (in spite of Fukuyama) and whose passing will put the nature of the phenomenon into perspective. This consideration does not in itself invalidate their claims to expose the truth of historical and historiographical reality – abstractly it might be the case that the times have at last enabled the veil of illusion to be penetrated – but there is no better way to *underline* the defects of dubious ideologies than to place them in their historical context. Sometimes the two are so intertwined as to be inseparable. Exposing and refuting the allegations in the *Protocols of the Elders of Zion* requires at the same time historical reconstruction of the manner in which the forgery came to be composed and disseminated.

Before any deconstructionist accuses me of drawing an intellectual comparison between deconstructionist historiography and the *Protocols*, let me issue an emphatic denial (not that it will make any difference). I am using an extreme example to point out the separation and the conjunction between intellectual refutation and historical interpretation of erroneous beliefs. I hold that certainly poststructuralism/deconstruction is invalid in its basic premises (for all that its proponents have produced some interesting and useful historiography) and on the whole culturally detrimental, but it is not in any sense vicious.

There is moreover the traditional Marxist contention that every ideology which achieves significance contains its kernel of truth and is in fact a distorted perception of the real. It would indeed be difficult to imagine that the big deconstructionist claims, even restricting them to the field of historiography, are no more than a creation of fantasy and contain nothing worthy of consideration – if that were the case they would never have succeeded in getting a hearing of any sort.[20] Conceptual error, empirical vacuity and a distorted perception of reality does not mean that there is no reality being perceived. The current has provided insights which, purged of their fantastical aspects, can and certainly will be used by and integrated into mainstream historiography; it has drawn attention to the importance of language and the relation of the form to the content – matters which tended to be taken for granted by historians prior to the irruption of the linguistic turn. Closely related is the question of emplotment, appreciation of which can remove a great deal of careless assumption in historiographical practice. Furthermore, though the attack on 'grand narrative' has many questionable aspects, it is certainly valuable in pointing out the degree to which historians have unthinkingly internalised a model of progress based exclusively upon the experience of Western Europe and North America. None of those perceptions however necessitates the insubstantial theoretical structure in which the postmodern sensibility has embedded them. The writings of theorists in this tradition, for such it has now become, give the impression of people who, in developing a number of valuable insights, imagine that they have discovered the key to unlock the secrets of the historiographical universe. This emperor is not quite naked, but he is wearing no more than fancifully embroidered underpants.

Notes

Preface

1. E.H. Carr, *What is History?*, Macmillan, 1961.
2. In the British context, at the History Workshop of 1980, which featured Stuart Hall as the principal speaker, postmodernism was not an issue; three years later it was starting to make an impact.
3. Excellent brief surveys can be found in Michael Bentley (ed.), *Companion to Historiography*, Routledge, 1997, and entries in the *Encyclopaedia of History and Historians*, edited by Kelly Boyd, Fitzroy Dearborn, Chicago, 1999.

Chapter 1

1. J.H. Plumb, *The Death of the Past*, Macmillan, 1969.
2. Marshall Berman, *All That Is Solid Melts Into Air*, Verso, 1983, p. 15.
3. Sean Homer, *Frederic Jameson: Marxism, Hermenuetics, Postmodernism*, Polity, 1998, p. 57.
4. Which did not prevent him from being an observant member of the Lutheran church, any more than Newton's theological heresies stopped him doing the same in the Anglican one.
5. Guido de Ruggerio, quoted in Geoffrey Barraclough, *History in a Changing World*, Blackwell, Oxford, 1955, p. 2.
6. Alex Callinicos, *Against Postmodernism*, Polity, 1989, p. 63.
7. For an analysis of Hegel's conception in this regard see Herbert Marcuse, *Reason and Revolution: Hegel and the Rise of Social Theory*, Routledge & Kegan Paul, 1968.
8. For instance the obsession of the French revolutionary politicians with the imagined political culture of classical Greece or Rome.
9. Charles Beard, quoted in Peter Novick, *That Noble Dream: The 'Objectivity Question' and the American Historical Profession*, Cambridge University Press, 1992, p. 254.
10. Novick, ibid., p. 28, quoting Georg Iggers.
11. Ibid., p. 27.
12. Except possibly the Gospel according to John – see Robin Lane Fox, *The Unauthorised Version: Truth and Fiction in the Bible*, Viking, 1991.
13. Novick suggests that Ranke's late nineteenth-century American disciples seriously misunderstood him by focusing solely on the methodology and ignoring the German philosophical context.
14. Michael Bentley, 'Approaches to Modernity: Western Historiography since the Enlightenment' in M. Bentley (ed.), Companion to Historiography, Routledge, 1997, p. 437. Similar considerations applied to historians such as J.R. Green who proposed to write the history of English civilisation or society rather than its political or constitutional development.
15. Charles Victor Langlois, and Charles Seignobos, *Introduction to the Study of History*, Cass, 1966.
16. Novick, *That Noble Dream*, pp. 55–6. See also Bentley, *Companion*, p. 429.
17. Bentley, 'Approaches', p. 449. and ff.

18. Which did not preclude fierce and sometimes embittered disputes among English historians over interpretations of the national past. See for example, Michael Kenyon, *The History Men, the Historical Profession in England since the Renaissance*, Weidenfeld & Nicolson, 1984, and J.W. Burrow, *A Liberal Descent: Victorian Historians and the English Past*, Cambridge University Press, 1983.
19. Marx and Engels had notoriously referred to some of them as 'nations without a history'.
20. Though not without challenge: 'a systematic understanding of source materials helped generate new questions about their use and limitations'. Michael Bentley, 'Approaches', p. 449.
21. 'Contributors will understand ... that our Waterloo must be one that satisfies French and English, Germans and Dutch alike; that nobody can tell, without examining the list of authors, where the Bishop of Oxford laid down the pen, and whether Fairbairn or Gasquet, Liebermann or Harrison took it up.' Lord Acton, circular letter to contributors, 1898.
22. '... a thorough understanding of historical development is first achieved when the course of history is relived in imagination at the deepest points at which the movement forward takes place.' Dilthey, quoted in Bentley, 'Approaches', p. 454.
23. For Bloch's life see Elizabeth Fink, *Marc Bloch: A Life in History*, Cambridge University Press, 1989.
24. Febvre did not exactly cover himself with glory under the Occupation. Making a priority of the journal's continued existence, he insisted that Bloch, who was of Jewish background, resign his editorial position in order to avoid the journal being closed down by the German authorities.
25. Peter Schlötter, 'Lucie Varga: A Central European Refuge in the circle of the French "Annales", 1934–1941', *History Workshop Journal*, No. 33, Spring 1992, p. 100.
26. Michael Bentley, *Companion*, p. 466.
27. Ibid., p. 464.
28. Karen Schönwälder, 'The Fascination of Power: Historical Scholarship in Nazi Germany', *History Workshop Journal* 43, Spring 1997, pp. 134–5.
29. However it has to be noted that Collingwood's text, *The Idea of History*, was not written as a unity but was a posthumous compilation.
30. Novick, *That Noble Dream*, p. 126.
31. 'those of our craft who wrote pontifically ... during the war spent most of their subsequent vacations, sabbatical leaves, and savings going round second-hand bookshops, furtively buying and burning all the copies they could find of their war-time utterances.' Ibid., p. 127, citing Herbert Heaton.
32. Richard J. Evans, *In Defence of History*, Granta Books, 1997, p. 29.
33. Ibid., p. 240.
34. The titles encapsulate the argument: Becker in 1931, under the title 'Everyman His Own Historian' and Beard in 1934, 'Written History as an Act of Faith'.
35. There are parallels, in principle, with the police in democratic states framing a suspect in a case for which they have no proof but whom they 'know' must be guilty.
36. So termed because, in contrast to the intransigent Marxists, they agitated for social reforms (far-reaching ones all the same) which would be 'possible' within the framework of the Third Republic.

37. Konstantin F. Shteppa, *Russian Historians and the Soviet State*, Rutgers University Press, Brunswick, New Jersey, 1962, p. 14.
38. According to Shteppa nothing comparable was seen until Stalin's seventieth birthday in 1949, but this must surely be an exaggeration.
39. See John Barber, *Soviet Historians in Crisis 1928–32*, Macmillan, 1981.
40. One intriguing puzzle, which certainly contradicts the practices of *Nineteen Eighty-Four* however, is that the regime, when it could have easily destroyed them, did nevertheless preserve the archives which demonstrated its terroristically-enforced interpretations of Soviet history to be a tissue of lies.
41. After 1933 it emigrated to New York. See Peter Gay, *The Dialectical Imagination*, Heinemann 1973, for an account.
42. Novick mentions a very few – it is clear that they were very isolated. He also quotes hair-raising racist comments from established members of the profession. Novick, *That Noble Dream*, pp. 225–7.
43. Harvey J. Kaye, 'Capitalism and Democracy: A Retrospective on Leo Huberman's *"We the People"*', *Our History Journal*, No. 15, April 1990.
44. Both were also published in the UK as Left Book Club editions.
45. Tawney was instrumental in the establishment of the Economic History Society, somewhat ironically in view of the apologetic function which appeared to dominate the discipline.
46. Raphael Samuel, 'People's History' in *People's History and Socialist Theory*, History Workshop Series, RKP, 1981, pp. xviii–xix.
47. Though not altogether. Tom Johnson, a Scottish labour activist and MP wrote a famous exposé of the history of the Scottish aristocracy under the title *Our Noble Families*, copies of which he tried to buy up and destroy once he'd joined the establishment.
48. 'Historians who for a century and a half have followed Ranke's precept to the letter have been guilty of a sorry failure of imagination which did much to bring history into disrepute.' Arthur Marwick, *The Nature of History*, Macmillan, 1970, p. 35. This sentence disappears in later editions.

Chapter 2

1. Peter Novick, *That Noble Dream: The 'Objectivity Question' and the American Historical Profession*, Cambridge University Press, 1988, p. 281. The relevant chapter is entitled 'The defense of the West'.
2. Ibid., p. 327.
3. An entertaining sketch of Namier is to be found in Michael Kenyon, *The History Men: The Historical Profession in England since the Renaissance*, Weidenfeld & Nicolson, 1984; for a fuller account see Linda Colley, *Lewis Namier*, Weidenfeld & Nicolson, 1998.
4. Perry Anderson, 'Components of the National Culture' in Alexander Cockburn and Robin Blackburn (eds), *Student Power*, Penguin, 1969, p. 245.
5. He also planned a large-scale biography of Lenin, and no one would have been better equipped to undertake it, but died before he was able to proceed very far.
6. His *Stalin* was an exemplary demonstration of what could be achieved using nothing but secondary sources in the public domain, the Soviet archives being of course totally closed; for his *Trotsky* he had access to the Trotsky archive.

7. A particularly vituperative review of *Stalin*, composed by Andrew Rothstein, a devoted Stalinist, appeared in the Communist Party's *Modern Quarterly*, Spring 1950, all but accusing Deutscher of writing on behalf of the Western secret services.
8. See Harvey J. Kaye, *The British Marxist Historians*, Polity, Cambridge, 1984, for an examination.
9. It initially appeared in the series of the Left Book Club, a body much influenced, though not entirely controlled, by the CP.
10. He taught at Cambridge University.
11. For a more recent application of Dobb's approach on a smaller canvas see John Foster's *Class Struggle and the Industrial Revolution: Early industrial capitalism in three English towns*, Methuen, 1974.
12. See T.H. Aston and C.H.E. Philpin (eds), *The Brenner Debate*, Cambridge University Press, 1985, also Ellen Meiksins Wood, 'The non-history of capitalism', *Historical Materialism*, No. 1, Autumn 1997.
13. See Kaye, *British Marxist Historians*.
14. The initiative in this came from Stalin's spokesperson on cultural matters, Andrei Zhdanov.
15. For the writers, see Andy Croft, 'Authors Take Sides: Writers and the Communist Party 1920–56', in Geoff Andrews, Nina Fishman and Kevin Morgan (eds), *Opening the Books: Essays on the Social and Cultural History of the British Communist Party*, Pluto Press, 1995.
16. Editorial in *Socialist History* 8, Autumn 1995, p. 9.
17. See above. In this connection the archaeologist and prehistorian Gordon Childe should also be mentioned.
18. R. Samuel, *People's History and Socialist Theory*, RKP, 1981, p. xxx.
19. Eric Hobsbawn, George Rudé and Victor Kiernan were also among the critics. Hobsbawm however, remained a party member; the latter two resigned at a somewhat later date. Dona Torr, who had been a particular inspiration for and organiser of the Group, had died earlier.
20. George Huppert, 'The Annales Experiment', in Michael Bentley (ed.), *Companion to Historiography*, Routledge, 1997, p. 882.
21. Recorded by E. Le Roy Ladurie in his memoir, *Paris-Montpellier: PC-PSU 1945–63*.
22. 'Here academics are dealing with their own past, the past of their institutions and of their teachers. It has taken a third generation to overcome the scruples arising from personal involvement and personal links to those involved.' Karen Schönwälder, 'The Fascination of Power: Historical Scholarship in Nazi Germany', *History Workshop Journal* 43, Spring 1997, p. 134.
23. Konstantin F. Shteppa, *Russian Historians and the Soviet State*, Rutgers University Press, 1962, pp. vii–ix.
24. Ibid., p. 407.
25. Elizabeth Waters, 'View from the Lenin Library: The Changing Shape of Soviet History', *History Workshop Journal* 32, Autumn 1991, p. 78.
26. Roy Medvedev, *Let History Judge*, Macmillan, 1972.
27. Similar ideas had been advanced beforehand, but significantly it was Carr's text which had the far-reaching impact.
28. In an interview in the *Scotsman*, 4 November 1998.
29. See Andy Croft, 'Walthamstow, Little Gidding and Middlesborough: Edward Thompson. Adult Education and Literature', *Socialist History* 8, Autumn 1995.

30. Though during this period he was also engaged in editing first the *New Reasoner* and then *New Left Review*. Altogether these were exacting commitments.
31. Anna Davin, quoted in Bryan D. Palmer, *E.P. Thompson, Objections and Oppositions*, Verso, 1994, p. 1.
32. Mark Poster, *Foucault, Marxism and History: Mode of Production versus Mode of Information*, Polity Press, 1984, pp. 2–7. A volume published in 1968, the *Tel Quel Théorie d'Ensemble*, with contributions from Barthes, Foucault and Derrida, argued that writing and revolution are a common cause. Raphael Samuel, 'Reading the Signs', *History Workshop* 32, Autumn 1991, p. 109.
33. Unrealised expectations generated by the consumer society; the Vietnam war; growing suspicion towards established elites and power centres; rejection of traditional social mores by the 1960s youth – might figure among the more likely explanations.
34. See Miles Taylor, 'The Beginnings of Modern British Social History?', *History Workshop Journal* 43, Spring 1997, for a different angle on the origins of the movement.
35. It had less well-known equivalents in Scotland (Newbattle Abbey, near Edinburgh) and the north of England (Northern College, Barnsley).
36. R. Samuel, 'Afterword' in Samuel, *People's History*, p. 410.
37. Peter Burke, 'People's History or Total History' in R. Samuel, ibid., p. 8.
38. This approach is even more emphatically present in the imitative volume by James D. Young, *The Rousing of the Scottish Working Class*, Croom Helm, 1979.
39. Peter Novick, *That Noble Dream*, p. 440. The summary of US developments which follows is largely based on Novick's admirable volume.
40. The received interpretation which laid responsibility at the Soviet door was supposedly guaranteed by objectively established evidence. 'Objectivity was prized and if objectivity in no way conformed to reality, then all the worse for reality.' David Halberstam, quoted ibid., p. 416.
41. The forms of campus protest were ultimately modelled on the civil disobedience and sit-ins used by the anti-segregation activists.
42. Novick, *That Noble Dream*, p. 416.
43. Ibid., p. 425.
44. Ibid., p. 439.
45. Ibid., p. 432.
46. Ibid., p. 429.
47. Staughton Lynd, interview, 1977, in Henry Abelove, Betsy Blackmar, Peter Dimock and Jonathan Scheer, *Visions of History*, Manchester University Press, 1983, p. 151.
48. Novick, *That Noble Dream*, pp. 432, 434; Abelove, *Visions*, p. 10.
49. Novick, *That Noble Dream*, p. 440.
50. Ibid., p. 443.
51. Ibid. p. 481.
52. See Richard Evans, 'Women's History: the limits of reclamation', Review article, *Social History*, Vol. 5, No. 2, May 1980.
53. Novick, *That Noble Dream*, p. 494.
54. The *Annales* had always stressed the importance of quantification as far as possible: 'il faut compter', Bloch had insisted. Quantitative method, especially in the form of family reconstitution, a variety of historical demographic analysis, was also developed during the 1960s in Britain.

55. R. Fogel, quoted in Michael Bentley, *Companion*, p. 485.
56. The text was *Time on the Cross*, by Robert Fogel and Stanley Engerman, Wildwood House, 1974, which in spite of its title purported to show that slavery in the American South was not only a profitable system, but relatively advantageous to the slaves. It was taken apart by Herbert Gutman, a leftist historian with some resemblance to E.P. Thompson, both in personality and historiographical approach.

Chapter 3

1. Peter Novick, *That Noble Dream: The 'Objectivity Question' and the American Historical Profession*, Cambridge University Press, 1992, p. 574ff.
2. Ludmilla Jordanova in *History in Practice*, Arnold, 2000, pp. 142–3, defines 'public history' in a somewhat different sense, in terms of activities that diffuse historical consciousness among a wide public: 'Museums and heritage sites are prime examples of the complexities of public history. Indeed, when the phrase "public history" is used this is what many people have in mind ... Also relevant are cathedrals and churches that attract visitors.'
3. George Huppert, 'The Annales Experiment', in Michael Bentley (ed.), *Companion to Historiography*, Routledge, 1997, p. 883.
4. François Furet, *Interpreting the French Revolution*, Cambridge University Press, 1981. The most popular and widely read of these denunciations however was that by the British/American historian, Simon Schama, *Citizens*, Viking, 1989.
5. R.W. Davies, 'Soviet History in the Gorbachev Revolution: The First Phase', *Socialist Register*, 1988, p. 38.
6. Ibid., p. 39.
7. Elizabeth Waters, 'View from the Lenin Library: The Changing Shape of Soviet History', *History Workshop Journal* 32, Autumn 1991, p. 78.
8. Traditionalism died hard. In the permanent photographic display of the Russian Revolution in the Lenin Museum beside the Kremlin, as late as 1987 no reference could be found to any of Lenin's colleagues who were later purged.
9. Davies, 'Soviet History', p. 59.
10. Waters, 'View', p. 82.
11. Ibid., p. 83.
12. Judt, 'A Clown in Regal Purple: Social History and the Historians' *History Workshop Journal* No. 7 Spring 1979, pp. 66, 76, 82, 86.
13. Ibid., p. 86.
14. Ibid., pp. 71, 72–3.
15. Harold Mah, 'Suppressing the Text: The Metaphysics of Ethnographic History in Darnton's Great Cat Massacre', *History Workshop Journal* 31, Spring 1991, p. 2.
16. Robert Darnton, *The Great Cat Massacre and Other Episodes in French Cultural History*, Vintage Books, New York, 1985.
17. Mah, 'Suppressing the Text'.
18. '... multiple but loosely convergent assaults on received notions of objectivity which swept across the academic world from the 1980s onwards. The most common designation is "postmodern".' Novick, *That Noble Dream*, p. 523.

19. See for example Arthur Hirsch, *The French New Left: An Intellectual History from Sartre to Gorz*, South End Press, Boston, 1981; David Archard, *Marxism and Existentialism: the Political Philosophy of Sartre and Merleau-Ponty*, Blackstaff Press, Belfast, 1980.
20. A fragment examines the role of Stalin in the 1920s. Sartre also worked at length on a massive biography of Flaubert (though his techniques were certainly not those of academic historians), intending to situate a particular individual fully in his historical time and explore the dialectical relationship between an author, his neuroses and society. Neither was this ever completed.
21. Interestingly Sartre, opposed though his philosophical outlook was to Althusser's, also adopted Maoist stances during and in the wake of the 1968 events.
22. Hundreds of his Maoist followers were nonetheless expelled, an issue on which Althusser remained silent.
23. Quoted in Hirsch, *French New Left*, p. 168.
24. Ibid., p. 166.
25. A structuralist interpretation fits much better however with a society like dynastic Egypt, virtually unchanging over millennia.
26. Peter Dews, *Logics of Disintegration: Post-Structuralist Thought and the Claims of Critical Theory*, Verso, 1987, p. 2. Dews's volume is a discussion of the principal different strands of poststructuralist thinking.
27. Important in this respect was Frederic Jameson's *The Political Unconscious*, published by Methuen, London, 1981.
28. Roland Barthes, *The Pleasure of the Text*, p. 22, quoted in Sean Homer, *Frederic Jameson: Marxism, Hermeneutics, Postmodernism*, Polity Press, 1998, p. 73:

    With the writer of bliss (and his reader) begins the untenable text, the impossible text. This text is outside pleasure, outside criticism, *unless it is reached through another text of bliss*: you cannot speak 'on' such a text, you can only speak 'in' it, in its fashion, enter into a desperate plagiarism, hysterically affirm the void of bliss (and no longer obsessively repeat the letter of pleasure).
29. Novick, *That Noble Dream*, p. 589.
30. Homer, *Frederic Jameson*, p. 76, quoting Terry Eagleton.
31. Cited in Novick, *That Noble Dream*, p. 544.
32. Ibid., p. 605.
33. Alun Munslow, *Deconstructing History*, Routledge, 1997, p. 138.
34. Adrian Wilson, 'A Critical Portrait of Social History' in Adrian Wilson (ed.), *Rethinking Social History: English Society 1570–1920 and its Interpretation*, Manchester University Press, 1993, p. 33.
35. The key text is 'Postmodernism, or the Cultural Logic of Late Capitalism', first appearing in *New Left Review* 146, July/August 1984, later expanded under the same title, 1991.
36. Aijaz Ahmad, 'Postcolonial Theory and the "Post"-Condition', *Socialist Register*, 1997.
37. Eileen Yeo, 'History Today: Round-table Dialogue', *Socialist History* No. 14, 1999, p. 34.
38. It is only fair to note however that some postmodernists or post-modernistically inclined individuals have also been political activists in the

ordinary sense. Foucault for a time after 1968 was active in campaigning against grisly prison conditions in France; Edward Said was a member of the Palestinian National Council and suffered severe denigration for it.

39. Joyce Appelby, Lynn Hunt and Margaret Jacob, *Telling the Truth about History*, W.W. Norton, New York, 1994, p. 219.
40. Elizabeth Fox-Genovese, 'Placing Women's History in History', *New Left Review* 133, May/June 1982, p. 7.
41. See Joan Wallach Scott, *Gender and the Politics of History*, Columbia University Press, New York, 1988. See also the symposium 'History and Feminist Theory' constituting the Beiheft 31 of *History and Theory* (Vol. 31, No. 4, 1992).
42. Ibid., p. 29.
43. Novick, *That Noble Dream*, p. 501, quoting Carroll Smith-Rosenberg.
44. F.R. Ankersmit, 'Historiography and Postmodernism', *History and Theory*, Vol. XXVIII, No. 2, 1989, p. 144.
45. See his contributions in the *Past & Present* and *Social History* debates, and 'The Return of History: Postmodernism and the Politics of Academic History in Britain', *Past & Present* No. 158, February 1998.
46. Peter Novick comments that the establishment of the journal also meant that theory was pushed into a separate and isolated sector, like the history of some marginal industry or South Dakota.
47. Raphael Samuel, 'History and Theory', in *People's History and Socialist Theory*, RKP, 1981, pp. xlix.
48. Bryan Palmer, *Descent into Discourse: The Reification of Language and the Writing of Social History*, Temple University Press, Philadelphia, 1990.
49. Raphael Samuel, 'Reading the Signs', *History Workshop* 32, Autumn 1991.
50. Ibid., p. 97.
51. Ibid., p. 94.
52. See, most conveniently, the volumes of *History and Theory* cited above. A useful collection of extracts is provided in Keith Jenkins (ed.), *The Postmodern History Reader*, Routledge, 1997.
53. 'The Return of History: Postmodernism and the Politics of Academic History in Britain', *Past & Present* 158, February 1998, p. 221.

Chapter 4

1. See Ludmilla Jordanova, *History in Practice*, Arnold, 2000, pp. 5–8, for a brief reference.
2. Peter Novick, *That Noble Dream: The 'Objectivity Question' and the American Historical Profession*, Cambridge University Press, 1988, p. 577.
3. There are however a few 'notable exceptions': Isaac Deutscher was one, and at the present time and for most of his career, Tom Nairn is another.
4. Which is unfair. Standards of teaching on the undergraduate degrees of the British new universities are generally *better* than those of the old because of the greater amount of planning and organisation that is put into them.
5. Russell Jacoby, *The Last Intellectuals: American Culture in the Age of Academe*, Noonday Press, New York, 1987, p. 145.
6. In UK universities (outside Oxbridge) the body charged with the allocation and supervision of resources, the Court, mainly constituted from relevant

outside interests, is less likely than its US counterparts to interest itself in academic content.

7. The controllers of the system are aware of this and have instituted yet further bureaucratic procedures to try to ensure that historical consciousness is developed among students, but there is no likelihood that these will succeed in their objective.
8. In the British system of classification of three classes of BA (in the old Scottish universities the equivalent is confusingly known as an MA) a first-class degree, though not an absolute requirement was in reality generally regarded as a prerequisite for funded further study or permanent appointment. Nowadays the tendency is to require not merely a first but a *good* first.
9. It has been argued, notably by Elizabeth Ermath, that the notion of historical progression (even as distinct from progress and even in the form of 'one damned thing after another') is fallacious and should be abandoned; but though her writing has evoked admiration from deconstructionists, practice according to her prescriptions has found few takers.
10. This can work in the same manner in the opposite direction, where the academic disciplines have been colonised by the new epistemological and stylistic fashions – such as cultural studies.
11. Since the 1960s politically motivated academic dismissals or failure to grant tenure are rare, but they do happen. Russell Jacoby cites a number of grisly examples in *The Last Intellectuals*.
12. It seems unclear whether this will continue beyond 2001.
13. Archivists constitute a major academic profession, with associations and journals. For a survey of the international state of affairs see George MacKenzie, 'Archives: The Global Picture', in the journal of the British Records Association, *Archives*, Vol. XXIV, No. 101, October 1999.
14. See for example Perry Anderson's *Passages from Antiquity to Feudalism* and *Lineages of the Absolutist State*, NLB (New Left Books), London, 1974.
15. MacKenzie, 'Archives', p. 3.
16. Medieval documents ironically wear far better, being written on vellum – calfskin or sheepskin. The physical condition of the Domesday Book is nearly as good as when it was written over nine centuries ago. However in the end even documents of this kind will deteriorate. Documents preserved only on computer disks face a particularly alarming fate, for even if the disks are adequately preserved the machines capable of reading them are likely to become shortly obsolete and disappear. See the appendix, 'The End of Ranke's History?', in Gerhard L. Weinberg, *Germany, Hitler and World War II*, Cambridge University Press, 1995.
17. Documentation released by government departments to the PRO at the beginning of every year occupy about a mile of new shelving. They represent around 5 per cent of what is generated, the remainder, apart from those files retained in secrecy, having been weeded and destroyed.
18. For their origins and circumstnaces of establishment see Arthur Marwick, *The Nature of History*, Macmillan, 1989.
19. Self-publishing always remains a possibility for historians who are unable to find regular publishers, the more so in present circumstances with the possibility of using the web.
20. Its career can be compared with that of the philosophically-orientated alternative journal *Telos*, highly respected and successful, but which could

make no impact upon its discipline in the US. See Jacoby, *The Last Intellectuals*, pp. 151–2.

21. However it is fair to note that this form of ranking is less pronounced in historiography than in most other social sciences.
22. It has a counterpart in the *Social Sciences Citation Index*.
23. Jacoby, *The Last Intellectuals*, p. 146.
24. Funding bodies for research in quite other areas, for example the Wellcome Trust in medicine, will fund historical research which has a medical dimension.
25. There are other significant historical associations in the US, such as the Mississippi Valley Historical Association, later renamed the Organization of American Historians, but none can compare in centrality and importance with the AHA.
26. In the 1990s the HA was thought to be so stagnant and in such dangerous decline that its small central organisation was drastically restructured with a number of compulsory redundancies.
27. Peter Novick, *That Noble Dream*, p. 580.
28. This remains the case in spite of the intellectual peculiarities and bizarre metaphysical beliefs of the seventeenth century pioneers – for example, the fact that Isaac Newton was addicted to preposterous religious fancies and seems to have regarded them as no less important than his scientific work.

Chapter 5

1. The argument that if we abolish the concept of truth it would be necessary to invent another word for what has been hitherto meant by that concept is a strong one and not to be easily dismissed.
2. The distinction is sometimes raised between a truth and a fact, but I think this is spurious and depends on context – for example it could be said that it is a fact but not a truth that I flew between Glasgow and New York on a particular day. However if my conviction or acquittal on a serious charge depended on whether I had actually made the flight, it would be a truth as well as a fact.
3. Without exception. Every 'primitive' culture (it is hard to come up with a better term) posits a spirit world both separate from and permeating through the material one.
4. Thomas Kuhn, *The Structure of Scientific Revolutions*, University of Chicago Press, 1970.
5. Paul Feyerabend, *Against Method*, Verso, 1993.
6. Someone has suggested that by using methodology of this sort *Mein Kampf* could be rendered as a critique of antisemitism.
7. David Harlan, 'Intellectual History and the Return of Literature', *American Historical Review*, Vol. 94, No. 3, June 1989, p. 589.
8. '... scholars are having to recognise that there are severe limits to what we can really know about witchcraft. The sources tell us not what happened but what witnesses and commentators believed.' Ludmilla Jordanova, *History in Practice*, Arnold, 2000, pp. 85–6.
9. Alex Callinicos, *Against Postmodernism*, Polity Press, 1988, p. 70; or Raphael Samuel:

This line of attack was launched, with characteristic panache, by Roland Barthes, in an essay in 1968. He argued that history was a plaything or creature of narrative which depended for credence on the practice of multiple duplicities ... a parade of signifiers masquerading as a collection of facts ... The past was not something out there waiting to be discovered but a void which historians filled with their own imaginings. Raphael Samuel, 'Reading the Signs', *History Workshop* 32, Autumn 1991, p. 93.

10. If non-written evidence is being used exclusively the investigator is an archaeologist rather than a historian. There is of course no barrier in principle between the two disciplines and particular investigations (Anglo-Saxon England for example) may equally involve both.
11. Hayden White, 'Foucault Decoded: Notes from the Underground', *History and Theory*, Vol. XII, 1973, p. 24.
12. The question of forgery is a different (though related) issue.
13. The number of people, including historians, with personal acquaintance of events like that must be legion. The keeping of minutes is a field which deserves a historical study of its own.
14. Richard Fletcher's *The Conversion of Europe* gives actual examples of similar types of records. The historian may of course be concerned to inquire why such beliefs were prevalent, but that is a different matter.
15. Raphael Samuel, 'History and Theory', in *People's History and Socialist Theory*, RKP, 1981, p. xlvi.
16. It is an interesting question as to whether an author deliberately setting out to falsify history would be capable of writing so effectively, or whether a mastery of style is dependent on the sincerity of the author's intentions (not of course the validity of the interpretation).
17. Samuel, 'History and Theory', p. xlix.
18. As Mark Poster writes with reference to Sartre:

    The theorist's totalisation was not the perfect, certain, objective knowledge of God or Descartes, because the theorist was situated in a specific historical field and had a specific history. The theorist's totalisation was profoundly his own, but it was also available to others who could choose to adopt it. In this way dialectical reason was both subjective, limited by the situation of the theorist, and objective, a possible project for everyone. *Foucault, Marxism and History*, Polity Press, 1984, p. 22.
19. Hayden White, *Metahistory: The Historical Imagination in Nineteenth Century Europe*, Johns Hopkins, Baltimore and London, 1973, p. 7.
20. Peter Novick, *That Noble Dream: The 'Objectivity Question' and the American Historical Profession*, Cambridge University Press, 1992, p. 542.
21. White, *Metahistory*, p. ix.
22. Ibid.
23. Ibid.
24. Ibid., p. x.
25. Ibid.
26. Ibid., p. xi.
27. Northrop Frye, *The Anatomy of Criticism: Four Essays*, Princeton University Press, 1957. Kenneth A. Burke, *A Grammar of Motives*, University of California Press, 1969. White also concedes that he has profited from Barthes, Foucault and Derrida, but regards them as 'captives' of tropologiccal strategies in much

the same way as the nineteenth figures he is examining. White, *Metahistory*, p. 3.
28. White, *Metahistory*, p. 6.
29. Ibid., p. 283.
30. See Alun Munslow, *Deconstructing History*, Routledge, 1997, pp. 142–3.
31. For example: 'When Nietzsche reflected on history therefore, he was always concerned to determine how history itself ... could be transmuted into a kind of Tragic art', White, *Metahistory*, p. 333; or on Ranke, 'But [Ranke's] "empiricism" stems less from a rigorous observation of particulars than from a decision to treat certain kinds of processes as inherently resistant to analysis – and certain kinds of comprehension as inherently limited'. Ibid., p. 189.
32. Ibid., p. 303–4.
33. Ibid., p. 285.
34. Maurice Mandelbaum states:

    The four forms of emplotment, as White has characterised them, can be accepted independently of any relations they may bear to his theory of tropes ... it is difficult to see how an historian's acceptance of one or another ideological stance can be clarified by relating it to one of the four linguistic tropes. 'The Presuppositions of Metahistory', *History and Theory*, Vol. XIX, Beiheft 19, 1980 ('Metahistory': Six Critiques), pp. 47–8.
35. White, *Metahistory*, p. xii.
36. Munslow, *Deconstructing History*, quoted, p. 161 (source not indicated).
37. Louis Mink, quoted in ibid., p. 61.
38. William Dray, 'Philosophy and Historiography', in M. Bentley (ed.), *Companion to Historiography*, Routledge, 1997, p. 778.
39. Peter Munz, 'The Historical Narrative', in M. Bentley, ibid., p. 852.
40. Patrick Joyce, 'The Return of History: Postmodernism and the Politics of Academic History in Britain', *Past & Present* 158, February 1998.
41. Hans Kellner, 'A Bedrock of Order: Hayden White's Linguistic Humanism', *History and Theory*, Vol. XIX, Beiheft 19, 1980 ('Metahistory': Six Critiques), p. 27.
42. Hans Kellner, 'Narrativity in History: Poststructuralism and Since', *History and Theory*, Vol. XXVI, Beiheft 26, 1987, p. 4.
43. Ibid., p. 8.
44. F.R. Ankersmit, 'Historiography and Postmodernism', *History and Theory*, Vol. XXVIII, No. 2, 1989, pp. 141–2.
45. Ankersmit, 'Historical Representation', *History and Theory*, Vol. XXVII, No. 3, 1988, p. 228.
46. Ankersmit, 'Historiography and Postmodernism', p. 139.
47. Ibid.
48. Ibid.
49. Ibid., pp. 149–50.
50. Samuel, 'History and Theory', p. li.
51. Munslow, *Deconstructing History*, p. 148.
52. Ibid.
53. Ibid., p. 149.
54. To be fair to White he is aware of this, unlike his disciple.
55. Munslow, *Deconstructing History*, pp. 146–7.
56. Ibid., p. 12.

57. I prefer the term to 'empiricism' with its negative connotations and suggestion that no conceptual problems exists in relation to 'facts'.
58. I won't say 'distorted', for to use such a term would imply that there could in principle exist evidence which was not distorted, i.e., free from the subjective input of its producers – something impossible to imagine.
59. What must surely be the ultimate in such experiments was Martin Amis's novel *Time's Arrow*, which is actually written backwards.
60. H. White, 'Response to Arthur Marwick', *Journal of Contemporary History*, Vol. 30, No. 2, April 1995, p. 240.
61. A. Callinicos, *Against Postmodernism*, Polity Press, 1989, pp. 68–70.
62. Adrian Kuzminski refers to it as 'a more condensed verisimilitude', 'Defending Historical Realism', *History and Theory*, Vol. XVII, No. 3, 1979, p. 346.
63. *I, Rigoberta Menchú : An Indian Woman in Guatemala*; edited and introduced by Elisabeth Burgos-Debray; translated by Ann Wright, Verso, 1984.
64. Truman Capote, *In Cold Blood*, Random House, New York, 1965.
65. For instance Simon Schama, whose *Dead Certainties* introduces imaginary individuals and events whose imaginary status is only revealed at the end of the book, though paradoxically Schama does not believe that a true past is irrecoverable – on this occasion he was playing games.
66. Munslow, *Deconstructing History*, p. 140.
67. Ibid., p. 147.
68. Ibid., p. 149.
69. For example, 'The choice of a farcical style for the representation of some kinds of historical events would constitute not only a lapse in taste, but also a distortion of the truth about them.' White, 'Figuring the nature of the times deceased', in Ralph Cohen (ed.), *The Future of Literary Theory*, New York, 1989, p. 30.
70. H. White, 'Historical Emplotment and the Problem of Truth', in S. Friedlander (ed.), *Probing the Limits of Representation*, Harvard University Press, 1992.

Chapter 6

1. Sean Homer, *Frederic Jameson: Marxism, Hermeneutics, Postmodernism*, Polity Press, 1998, pp. 153–4.
2. A counter-argument is contained in Hans Blomberg, *The Legitimacy of the Modern Age*, Cambridge, Massachusetts, 1983.
3. See A.L. Morton, *The English Utopia*, Lawrence & Wishart, 1969, and *The World of the Ranters*, Lawrence & Wishart, 1979, for an extended discussion.
4. He did proclaim the Paris Commune of 1871 to have constituted the dictatorship of the proletariat. That definition was however made after the fact.
5. Francis Williams, *Fifty Years' March: the Rise of the Labour Party*, Odhams, 1949.
6. G.D.H. Cole and Raymond Postgate, *The Common People 1746–1946*, Methuen, 1961 (3rd edition).
7. Winston Churchill, *A History of the English-speaking Peoples*, Cassell, 1956–58.
8. Jean-Antoine-Nicolas de Caritat, Marquis de Condorcet, *Sketch for a historical*

picture of the progress of the human mind, Noonday Press, 1955.

9. According to Raphael Samuel, in the liberal version of people's history, 'Modernisation is synonymous with the march of mind, the progress of civil liberty, and the extension of religious toleration.' Raphael Samuel, 'People's history', in *People's History and Socialist Theory*, RKP, 1981, p. xxii.
10. Francis Fukuyama, *The End of History and the Last Man*, Penguin, Harmondsworth, 1992, pp. 110–11.
11. See Stephen Jay Gould, *Wonderful Life*, Penguin, Harmondsworth, 1991.
12. Biologically speaking, the human body is a rather inefficient organism, having to support a brain that absorbs 20 per cent of the creature's metabolic resources.
13. It has been refined since Darwin's time, particularly through the location of the hereditary mechanism, and may be refined further in the future, for example via the concept of 'punctuated equilibrium', but none of that diminishes the essential power of the concept.
14. Mark Poster, *Foucault, Marxism and History*, Polity, Cambridge, 1984, p. 16.
15. See Detlev J.K. Peukert, *The Weimar Republic: The Crisis of Classical Modernity*, trans. R. Deveson, Lane, 1991; and David F. Crew, 'The Pathologies of Modernity: Detlev Peukert on Germany's Twentieth Century', *Social History*, Vol. 17, No. 2, May, 1992.
16. Though it is worth noting that a non-metallurgical neolithic civilisation is possible – witness Mayan and Aztec Central America and Inca Peru.
17. To be sure, the water mill has potentialities for power generation which were never fully exploited, but that does not affect the overall argument.
18. The developing sub-discipline of world history – i.e., the examination through time of the separate world regions *in relation to each other* implicitly has this focus, it is, in the words of R.I. Moore, 'the set of all sets'. R.I. Moore, 'World History', in M. Bentley (ed.), *Companion to Historiography*, Routledge, 1997, p. 949.
19. Ernest Gellner, *Plough, Sword and Book: The Structure of Human History*, Paladin, 1991. W.G. Runciman, *A Treatise on Social Theory* (3 vols), Cambridge University Press, 1983–97. Michael Mann, *The Sources of Social Power* (2 vols), Cambridge University Press, 1986–93.
20. Sean Homer, *Frederic Jameson, Marxism, Hermeneutics, Postmodernism*, Polity Press, Cambridge, 1998, p. 124.
21. See Gary P. Steenson, *After Marx, Before Lenin: Marxism and Working-Class Parties in Europe, 1884–1914*, University of Pittsburgh Press, 1991, for an acute analysis of tensions between theory and practice in the Marxist labour movements of this period.
22. Ralph Miliband in *Marxism and Politics*, Oxford University Press, 1977, made an interesting and troubled effort to grapple with this reality.
23. Leaving on one side in this definition the question of gender considerations.
24. However G.E.M. de Ste Croix in *The Class Struggle in the Ancient Greek World*, Duckworth, 1983, advances a detailed argument that slave production did nevertheless define the character of ancient society.
25. Roger Chickering, *We Men who Feel most German: A Cultural Study of the Pan-German League 1886–1914*, Allen & Unwin, 1984.
26. For the latter see Ishay Landa, 'Nietzsche, the Chinese Worker's Friend?', *New*

Left Review, 236, July/August 1999.
27. For Junger and his intellectual progeny see Lutz Niethammer, *Posthistoire: has history come to an end?*, Verso, 1992.
28. From 'Ecce Homo', tr. by Walter Kaufmann, in Walter Kaufmann, *Existentialism from Dostoevsky to Sartre*, Meridian Books, Cleveland and New York, 1956, p. 112.
29. F. Nietzsche, *The Gay Science*, (1882), aphorism 121, trans. Walter Kaufmann, Random House, New York, 1974.
30. Hayden White, 'Foucault Decoded: Notes from the Underground', *History and Theory*, Vol. XII, No 1.
31. Ibid., p. 26.
32. Ibid., p. 54.
33. Ibid., p. 53.
34. He was at pains to draw a distinction with the physical sciences, but never elaborated it theoretically.
35. Setting aside the 'pathological modernity' of the Third Reich, particularly horrific examples are the forced sterilisations of the 'mentally incapacitated' carried out in the US during the early twentieth century and in Sweden as late as the 1960s.
36. Most popularly expressed in Herbert Marcuse's *One Dimensional Man: Studies in the Ideology of Advanced Industrial Society*, Routledge and Kegan Paul, 1964.
37. Peter Dews, *Logics of Disintegration: Poststructuralist Thought and the Claims of Critical Theory*, Verso, 1990, p. 176.
38. Dews points out that since Foucault rejects any criterion for judging between the validity of different discourses, truth as against ideology, he has difficulty in formulating any justification for his left-leaning political positions. Dews, *Logics*, pp. 190–2.
39. White, 'Foucault Decoded', p. 49.
40. See, for example, Elaine Pagels, *Adam, Eve and the Serpent*, Penguin, 1990.
41. For example, 'It is not that Foucault was a historian himself or, if he were, he was a very bad one.' Michael Bentley, 'Approaches to Modernity: Western Historiography since the Enlightenment', in *Companion to Historiography*, Routledge, 1997, p. 490.
42. Unless of course one recalls the intellectual climate of *Mai '68*!
43. Gareth Stedman Jones, 'The Determinist Fix: Some Obstacles to the Further Development of the Linguistic approach to History in the 1990s', *History Workshop Journal*, 42, Autumn 1996, p. 26.
44. Dews, *Logics*, p. 192.

Chapter 7

1. This is an actual example from the *English Historical Review* of the 1970s.
2. Christopher Hill has worked entirely from printed sources, but this is unusual.
3. Though that could scarcely be said to be the case for Le Roy Ladurie's *Montaillou: Cathars and Catholics in a French village*, Scolar Press, 1978, which combines social analysis with individual portraiture.
4. A parallel debate was taking place in anthropology, a questioning of the

relationships and exercise of control between Western anthropologists and their Third World subjects of study; likewise regarding middle-class sociologists and their working-class subjects.

5. Eric Hobsbawm, 'The New Threat to History', in Brian Brivati et al. (eds), *The Contemporary History Handbook*, Manchester University Press, 1966.
6. Martin Bernal, *Black Athena*, Vol. 1, *The Fabrication of Ancient Greece*, Rutgers University Press, Brunswick, New Jersey, 1987; *Black Athena*, Vol. 2, *The Afroasiatic Roots of Classical Civilisation*, Rutgers University Press, 1991.
7. Bernal '[denies] any qualitative transformation of the Near Eastern heritage by the Greeks of historical times ... he posits the existence of the Greeks, and yet, in effect, he would deny that existence'. R.A. McNeal, review of *Black Athena*, Vol. 1, *The Fabrication of Ancient Greece*, in *History and Theory*, Vol. 31, No. 1, 1992, pp. 52–3.
8. Paradoxically, as one commentator points out, the superiority of Greek culture is taken for granted, the issue becomes one of its derivation, while 'Africa, including Egypt, is taken as a timeless representative of black culture', and 'inspiring fictions' are disseminated. David Konstan, review of Mary Lefkowitz, *Not Out of Africa: How Afrocentrism Became an Excuse to Teach Myth as History*, and Mary R. Lefkowitz and Guy MacLean Rogers (eds), *Black Athena Revisited*, in *History and Theory*, Vol. 36, No. 2, 1997, p. 261.
9. Stephen Howe, 'Blinded by Blackness', *Times Higher Education Supplement*, 27 February, 1998.
10. The recent David Irving libel case in the British courts was emblematic. The judgment stigmatised Irving as a liar and his 'history' as a fraud. Nonetheless he achieved enormous publicity, not only in the extent of reporting the case received but in that the broadcast media hastened to interview him on numerous subsequent occasions.
11. *History Today*, August 1999.
12. See the discussion of Hayden White, above.
13. Norman Cohn, *Warrant for Genocide*, Penguin, Harmondsworth, 1970.
14. A theme which runs through the writings of Munslow and Jenkins.
15. See, for example, Charles Townshend, *Ireland: The 20th Century*, Arnold, 1999.
16. Sean Homer remarks ironically that 'It is worth recalling at the outset, however, that ... the rejection of totalizing theory in favour of concepts of heterogeneity and difference is itself a peculiarly Eurocentric ideology.' Sean Homer, *Frederic Jameson: Marxism, Hermeneutics, Postmodernism*, Polity Press, 1998, p. 3.
17. This observation is not invalidated by the reality of voluntary martyrdom. The point is that martyrs are always viewed as making a supreme sacrifice, not acting, in Shakespeare's words, so as 'to throw away the dearest thing he owned/As t'were the merest trifle'.
18. Simone de Beauvoir, *The Mandarins*, Collins, 1957, p. 466.
19. E.H. Carr, *What is History?*, Macmillan, 1961, p. 71.
20. 'If the historian litters his account of the past with explicit, stentorian moral judgments, then the result is likely to be a piece of very ugly writing indeed.' Adrian Oldfield, 'Moral judgments in History, *History and Theory*, Vol. XX, No. 3, 1981, p. 273.
21. See, for example, C. Wickham, 'The Other Transition: From the Ancient

World to Feudalism', *Past & Present*, No. 103.
22. See Perry Anderson's critique in *Arguments Within English Marxism*, Verso, 1980, pp. 88–93, of Thompson's moral-historical judgements.
23. Carr, *What is History?*, pp. 77–8.
24. Ibid., p. 75.
25. Ibid., p. 78.
26. Michael Bentley, 'Approaches to Modernity: Western Historiography since the Enlightenment', in M. Bentley (ed.), *Companion to Historiography*, Routledge, 1997, pp. 446–54.

Conclusion

1. It is also worth noting that the UK was on the verge of civil war in 1914.
2. For an excellent summary discussion see Alex Callinicos, *Social Theory*, Polity Press, 1999.
3. Uwe M. Schneede, *Surrealism*, Harry N. Abrams, Inc, New York, 1973, p.12.
4. Richard Huelsenbeck, quoted ibid, p.11.
5. Ibid., p.11.
6. A relationship also suggested by Raphael Samuel, 'It is a curious fact that "reading the signs" [i.e. postmodernism] though dedicated to evaporating the notion of the social, and exposing the artifices of the real, should be associated with a kind of hyper-realism which grounds itself in the study of minutiae.' 'Reading the Signs', *History Workshop* 32, Autumn 1991, p. 103.
7. As happened to the murals of the Mexican revolutionary painter Diego Rivera commissioned in the US.
8. In 1972 Debord announced on his own authority the dissolution of the Situationist International – possibility in imitation or intertextual mockery of Marx's effective dissolution of the First International a hundred years earlier.
9. The reciprocity between globalisation and postmodernism is suggested by Sean Homer with the comment that postmodernism in architecture can be seen as deriving form the need to distinguish one skyscraper form another. Sean Homer, *Frederic Jameson: Marxism, Hermeneutics, Postmodernism*, Polity Press, 1998, p. 176.
10. Alex Callinicos, *Against Postmodernism*, Polity Press, 1998, p. 161.
11. Homer, *Frederic Jameson*, pp. 3–4.
12. Ignacio Olábarri, '"New" History: A *Longue Durée* Structure', *History and Theory*, Vol. 34, No. 1, 1995.
13. The Bielefeld historians, Olábarri writes, were influenced by the Frankfurt School, particularly Habermas. Ibid., p. 11.
14. Ibid., p. 13. The general attachment of postmodernists to a left-wing agenda of some sort, however contradictory, is indicative.
15. Ibid., p. 20.
16. Containing the following claim, established by assertion in place of evidence, that 'vermin's taste for fancy human food, gobbled without human manners, hints that the social bonds established around a dinner table by means of manners may not be suficient to restrain appetites so that there will be food for all'. Mary Fissell, 'Imagining Vermin in Early Modern England', *History*

Workshop Journal 47, Spring 1999, p. 23.

17. Something of this sort has in fact been undertaken by Natalie Zemon Davis in relation to the disregarded work of women concerned with the *Annales* project. Natalie Zemon Davis, 'Women and the World of the *Annales*', *History Workshop* 33, Spring 1992.
18. Samuel, 'Reading the Signs', p. 96.
19. Readers will appreciate that this trope has been deliberately chosen for its absurdity, but postmodernist historians who take astrology (as distinct from the belief in astrology) seriously are not too far removed from it.
20. It could be objected that racism and antisemitism are fantasies which have nonetheless found wide audiences. However, while certainly fantasies, they are nonetheless the product of real social contradictions which create the opening for scapegoating ideologies.

Brief Bibliography

As pointed out at the beginning of this volume, the historiographical literature in English, much of it related in one aspect or another to the question of postmodernist/poststructuralist theory, has expanded prodigiously during the past four decades, and the references in this text cover only a diminutive fraction of the field. Inevitably any bibliographical selection is bound to be even more arbitrary. Very full annotated bibliographies are provided, from their strongly differing standpoints, by Richard Evans and Alun Munslow, and readers are referred to those. In relation to the themes pursued in this volume, the following will be found particularly useful. (Place of publication London unless otherwise stated.)

General surveys, reference works and selections

The *Blackwell Dictionary of Historians*, edited by John Cannon et al., Blackwell, Oxford, 1988, and the larger and more recent two-volume *Encyclopaedia of Historians and Historical Writing*, edited by Kelly Boyd, Fitzroy Dearborn, Chicago, 1999 (though it has some surprising gaps), are extremely valuable works of reference and sources of basic information. For a major multi-author survey of the field, containing chapters of analytical penetration and depth, *Companion to Historiography*, edited by Michael Bentley, Routledge, 1997, is invaluable. A useful selection of pieces related to postmodernism is to be found in *The Postmodern History Reader*, edited by Keith Jenkins, Routledge, 1997, in which Jenkins, to his credit, includes items attacking the positions he defends as well as ones advocating them.

Single- or joint-author surveys of a general nature include Jacques Barzun and Henry Graff's entertainingly written *The Modern Researcher*, Harcourt Brace Jovanovitch, New York, 1970; Arthur Marwick's useful and comprehensive – though opinionated – *The Nature of History*, Macmillan, 1989 (3rd edition) and John Tosh's esteemed *The Pursuit of History*, Longman, 1999 (3rd edition). More recently published is Ludmilla Jordanova's *History in Practice*, Arnold, 2000. For the American historical profession Peter Novick's classic *That Noble Dream: The 'Objectivity Question' and the American Historical Profession*, Cambridge

University Press, 1988 is indispensable, as Richard Evans observes, 'far wider in scope than its title implies'.

Journals

By far the dominant journal in this field is *History and Theory*, (http://www.historyandtheory.org/histjrnl/search.html) published in the US. American journals not specifically devoted to theory but with a marked theoretical orientation are *Gender and History* ('committed to examining gender relations and the symbolic representations of gender in a variety of national contexts', http://www.umich.edu/~irwg/gandh.html) and *Radical History Review* (http://chnm.gmu.edu/rhr/rhr.htm). The leading US historical journal, the *American History Review* (http://www.indiana.edu/~ahr/) takes note of theoretical issues on occasion (especially the symposium of 1989) as do *The Journal of Modern History* (http://www.journals.uchicago.edu/JMH/home.html), *The Journal of Social History* (http://muse.jhu.edu/journals journal_of_social_history/) and *Social Science History* (http://www.pitt.edu/~sshist/index.html) The US-published *Central European History* has included debates on the implications of postmodernism for German historians. The British historical journal in which historiographical theory is most frequently discussed and where the concepts at issue most regularly permeate its articles is *History Workshop Journal* (http://www.library.nwu.edu/journal/hisworjou/). Others which include such discussion from time are *Past and Present, Social History, Labour History Review* (http://facstaff.uww.edu/sslh/labourhist.html), *Socialist History* and the *Journal of Contemporary History* (http://www.swetsnet.nl/link/).

Schools and individuals

The *Annales* has, not surprisingly, been the subject of serious attention in English-language historiography. Traian Stoianovitch's *French Historical Method: The Annales Paradigm*, Cornell University Press, Ithica, 1976, the earliest full monograph, was greatly approved of by Braudel himself. More recent is Peter Burke, *The French Historical Revolution the 'Annales' School 1921–1989*, Polity, Cambridge, 1990; and extensive reference is to be found in all general surveys of modern historiographical development. Some *Annalistes* of the different 'generations', such as Bloch, Febvre, Braudel, Le Roy Ladurie or Marc Ferro have been widely translated into English, both in full text and selection.

Harvey J. Kaye has been the pioneer of the study of the British Marxist historians, initially with the volume of that title, Polity, Cambridge, 1984, followed by *The Education of Desire: Marxists and the Writing of*

History, Routledge, 1992. The Communist Party Historians' Group, out of which this school emerged is discussed in Eric Hobsbawm's 'The Historians' Group of the Communist Party', in Maurice Cornforth (ed.), *Rebels and their Causes*, Lawrence & Wishart, 1978; and Bill Schwartz, '"The People" in History: the Communist Party Historians' Group 1946–56' in Richard Johnson et al. (eds), *Making Histories: Studies in History-writing and Politics*, Hutchinson, 1982. A set of interviews of radical historians of various persuasions (including Thompson and Hobsbawm) was brought together by the Mid Atlantic Radical Historians' Organisation (MARHO) under the title *Visions of History*, Manchester University Press, 1983.

An enormous bibliography now exists on women's and feminist history. Sheila Rowbotham's *Hidden from History: 300 years of Women's Oppression and the Fight against it,* Pluto Press, 1973, can justifiably be regarded as the foundation text for women's history. The development of feminist historiography has been most prominently exemplified by Joan Wallach Scott, particularly in *Gender and the Politics of History*, Columbia University Press, New York, 1988.

Twentieth-century historians have, with exceptions, not been all that well served by biographers, at least until recently. However both Becker and Beard have had biographies as well as several studies devoted to them. In Becker's case these include Burleigh Taylor Wilkins, *Carl Becker, A Biographical Study in American Intellectual History*, MIT Press, 1961; and in Beard's, Ellen Nore, *Charles A. Beard: An Intellectual Biography*, Southern Illinois University Press, 1983. For two figures who were both, whatever their other great differences, mainstream Rankeans, see Linda Colley, *Lewis Namier*, Weidenfeld and Nicolson, 1998, and Robert Cole *A.J.P. Taylor: The Traitor within the Gates*, Macmillan, 1993. Marc Bloch's career, both historiographical and personal, has been covered by Elizabeth Fink, in *Marc Bloch: A Life in History*, Cambridge University Press, 1989; and the same has been done for E.H. Carr by Jonathan Haslam in *The Vices of Integrity: E.H. Carr 1892–1982*, Verso 1999.

There is unhappily no biography of E.P. Thompson, but there do exist two full-length studies of his work. The earlier of these is a collection edited by Harvey Kaye and Keith McClelland, *E.P. Thompson: Critical Perspectives*, Polity, Cambridge, 1990; and Bryan D Palmer's *E.P. Thompson: Objections and Oppositions*, Verso, 1994.

Historical theory – general

The classic texts appearing before the 1960s revolution are, from the UK, Herbert Butterfield's *The Whig Interpretation of History*, Bell, 1931, and

R.G. Collingwood's *The Idea of History*, Oxford University Press, 1948; from France, Marc Bloch, *The Historian's Craft*, Macmillan, 1994; and from the US, Carl Becker, *Everyman His Own Historian: Essays on History and Politics*, Crofts, New York, 1935.

Carr's seminal text, first appearing in 1961, was updated by R.H. Davies with new unpublished material by Carr: E.H. Carr, *What is History?*, Penguin, Harmondsworth, 1987. Carr was pugnaciously challenged in 1967 by G.R. Elton with *The Practice of History*, Fontana, 1969, asserting a narrowly traditionalist Rankean stance. Thompson's centrally important *The Making of the English Working Class*, Gollancz, 1963, is, as has been apparent from from its impact and influence, as much of a theoretical initiative in historiography as a study of the English working-class emergence. From the 1960s also J.H. Plumb, *The Death of the Past*, Macmillan, 1969, is well worth noting. Thompson's *The Poverty of Theory*, Merlin, 1978, as well as being an attack on the then fashionable structuralism, was also an essay in more general historiographical theory. For commentary upon it Perry Anderson, *Arguments Within English Marxism*, Verso, 1980, is useful. From subsequent years Georg G. Iggers, *New Directions in European Historiography*, Methuen, 1985 (2nd edition), is particularly valuable, and Novick's text, cited above, is a theoretical as much as a historical discussion, as is the case with Christopher Parker, *The English Historical Tradition since 1850*, Edinburgh University Press, 1990. From a left-wing perspective Raphael Samuel (ed.), *People's History and Socialist Theory*, Routledge and Kegan Paul, 1981, contains a very comprehensive discussion of the issues as they were seen up to that point.

The postmodern argument

This is probably best followed in the journal literature referred to above and throughout this volume, but certain book-length texts are especially important or illuminating. Though none of the founders of French poststructuralism, with the dubious exception of Foucault, can in any sense be considered a historian, Derrida, Barthes and Foucault can clearly not be neglected. The latter is interpreted by Jan Goldstein in *Foucault and the Writing of History*, Blackwell, Oxford, 1994, and Mark Poster, *Foucault, Marxism and History: Mode of Production versus Mode of Information*, Polity, Cambridge, 1984, is also informative.

Hayden White's *Metahistory: The Historical Imagination in Nineteenth Century Europe*, Johns Hopkins, Baltimore and London, 1973, is of central significance, and even pivotal. His most important other volumes, compilations of articles, are, *Topics of Discourse: Essays in Cultural*

Criticism, Johns Hopkins University Press, Baltimore, 1978, and *The Content of the Form: Narrative Discourse and Historical Representation*, Johns Hopkins University Press, Baltimore, 1987.

A British historian who early embraced the linguistic turn is Gareth Stedman Jones, demonstrating this with his *Languages of Class: Studies in English Working Class History, 1832–1982*, Cambridge University Press, 1983. The most high profile of the British historical postmodernists is undoubtedly Patrick Joyce. His preferred vehicle for historiographical argument is the journal article, most recently with 'The Return of History: Postmodernism and the Politics of Academic History in Britain', *Past & Present* No. 158, February 1998. He has also written full-length texts on British nineteenth-century history in which he has attempted to apply deconstructionist principles, for example *Democratic Subjects: The Self and the Social in Nineteenth-century England*, Cambridge University Press, 1994. Equally the most strident without doubt is Keith Jenkins, his two main titles being, *Re-thinking History*, Routledge, 1991, and *On "What is History?": From Carr and Elton to Rorty and White*, Routledge, 1995. Alun Munslow's *Deconstructing History*, Routledge, 1997, while mistaken in almost every respect, is a useful coverage of the issues from a deconstructionist perspective.

Critical stances of various intensity are expressed by Bryan Palmer in *Descent into Discourse: The Reification of Language and the Writing of Social History*, Temple University Press, Philadelphia, 1990, unquestionably the most ferocious attack so far published on postmodernist historiography. More nuanced are two central texts, Joyce Appelby, Lynn Hunt and Margaret Jacob, *Telling the Truth about History*, W.W. Norton, New York, 1994, and Richard J. Evans, *In Defence of History*, Granta, 1997. Evans also has a website in which he responds to critical reviews of his volume, at http://www.ihrinfo.ac.uk/ihr/reviews/discourse.html. A very balanced critique of the trend is provided by Raphael Samuel in his two-part article 'Reading the Signs' in *History Workshop Journal* nos 32 and 33, and another short and penetrating critique can be found in Richard Price, 'Postmodernism as theory and history', in John Belchem and Neville Kirk (eds), *Languages of Labour*, Ashgate, Aldershot, 1997 – the book's title evidently intended as a riposte to Stedman Jones.

Index